Thank you for purchasing my book, Gangster Redemption.

We have come a long way on our YouTube channel and we wouldn't be where we are today if it were not for you. Your continued love and support will help to get our voice heard to fix the broken prison system.

We hope you enjoy the book! It's an honest recount of my experiences in and out of the system.

Please share it with loved ones as it has helped many avoid the bad choices I made.

Below is a QR code with a link directly to our YouTube channel. Share with friends and family and help us spread the word.

Stay safe and God Bless,

Being from Iowa and reading this book opened my eyes about life in the mob and life in prison. I was mesmerized by Larry's stories from childhood and his experiences in prison. He never gave up!! What a message for our young. You can change, become a better person, and learn from your mistakes and go on to help others learn from your mistakes.

Larry is stronger than any person I have ever known and the fact that he could move on from all the injustices in his past life, is a miracle. Yet he did!!

The book is easy to read, keeps your interest, and reaches your soul in a way that I haven't experi-enced in any books I have ever read.

Theresa Sample Nunez—Teacher, mother of 4, grandmother of 7: Cedar Rapids, IA

You truly amaze me . . . . you "walked the walk" and came out with a positive and up-beat attitude. Your program to help young people avoid the life you clearly and honestly detailed in this riveting book speaks volumes as to the man you are. Your vivid descriptions reflecting what life is really like in prison should be a wake-up call to society, especially to those who are dangerously close to crossing the line. It brings to the forefront, a serious problem in our society that most people are not aware of and leaders tend to shy away from. It's a great book.

Joe Fraumeni—Retired business owner: Melbourne, FL

Larry Lawton is a man of many experiences! Larry Lawton is a man of trial and error! Larry Lawton is success! His book "Gangster Redemption" will have you looking over your shoulder as if he's brought you with him as he describes in detail his life story. "Gangster Redemption" is all things right and wrong with society today. Larry Lawton is not a man who uses his past as an excuse. He doesn't blame any-one for his past except himself. While he certainly has endured immense trauma throughout his life as you will read in "Gangster Redemption", he takes ownership of the life changing decisions and comes out of the fire with an influence for children and adults that is almost incomprehensible. "Gang-ster Redemption" is a compilation of action, history, biography and politics that ends with a feel good story with proven positive results. Larry Lawton doesn't tell you what you want to hear, he tells you what you need to hear and you will listen when Larry speaks!

Justin Wasson—Golf Professional, Father of one: Viera, FL

As the first-ever Chairman of Florida's Children and Youth Cabinet I have worked with hundreds of chil-dren who have made bad choices in life---but have so much good to offer the world. This book is an inspiration to anyone who wants to turn their life around. Mr. Lawton's story is inspirational and au-thentic. He opens his heart and soul to the reader. I highly recommend this "must read" book.

Jeff Kottkamp—Florida's 17th Lt. Governor: Ft. Myers, FL

Your book is amazing....Connor LOVED it so don't forget teens in your marketing plan. It's so honest Larry…scary,...real...and you don't apologize for be-ing a bad guy in a former life. It was your life...and you paid dearly.

Your description of the loneliness (and torture) of prison life is a must read for any kid who might think that prison is what you see in those Discovery Chan-nel TV shows. It's also a must read for the rest of us... the political nature of the system is not something I had ever given thought to…

Billy Cassara—60 Minutes and 20/20 Cameraman and the late Don Hewitt's son-in-law: New York, NY

"There is no more important asset to the state of Florida than our children, and their paths through life are defined by the choices they make, and the guid-ance they receive along the way. Experience is often the best guide, and we should all look to learn from those who have traveled the path before us. Larry's story is genuine and stirring, and this book can be a fantastic tool for anyone looking to change his or her life for the better."

Dominic M. Calabro—President & CEO of Florida Tax Watch: Tallahassee, FL

Your book was very inspiring. Though the abuses you withstood were very difficult to read, I couldn't put it down. I was especially impressed with how you turned your life around and your dedication to helping teens do the same with their lives. The book is well written and awe inspiring. A must read for anyone, especially anyone with teens.

Carol Kalet - Teacher with 30 years experience working with children: Atlanta, GA

GANGSTER REDEMPTION

How Ex-Con Larry Lawton's Life
Has Inspired Thousands of Kids To
Stay Out of Prison

GANGSTER REDEMPTION

HOW AMERICA'S MOST NOTORIOUS
JEWEL ROBBER GOT RICH, GOT CAUGHT,
AND GOT HIS LIFE BACK ON TRACK

LARRY LAWTON

Gangster Redemption - Copyright © 2012 by Lawrence Lawton. All rights reserved

Published by Reality Check Program, Inc. Palm Bay, Florida

No part of this publication may be reproduced, stored in a retrieval system, or transmitted in any form or by any means, electronic, mechanical, photocopying, recording, scanning, or otherwise, except as permitted under Section 107 or 108 of the 1976 United States Copy right Act, without either the prior written permission of the Publisher. Requests to the Publisher for permission should be addressed to Reality Check Program, Inc. Palm Bay, Florida (844) 922-4800, email: info@RealityCheckProgram.com

Limit of Liability/Disclaimer of Warranty: While the publisher and the authors have used their best efforts in preparing this book, some names, characters, places, and incidents have been changed or are used fictitiously. Any resemblance to actual events or locales or persons living or dead is entirely coincidental. The advice and strategies contained herein may not be suitable for your situation. You should consult with a professional where appropriate. Neither the publisher nor the author shall be liable for any harm, loss of life, profit or any other commercial damages, including but not limited to special, incidental, consequential, or other damages.

For information about other products by the Reality Check Program and for special discounts for bulk purchases, please contact Reality Check Program, Inc. at (844) 922-4800, or info@RealityCheckProgram.com.

Larry Lawton is available for speaking engagements, consulting, expert witnessing, and other services. For more information or to book an event contact (844) 922-4800, email: info@RealityCheckProgram.com or visit our website at www.RealityCheckProgram.com.

Library of Congress Cataloging-in-Publication Data – Lawrence Lawton
Printed in the United States of America
10 9 8 7 6 5 4 3 2 1

ISBN 978-0-9854082-0-6
ISBN 978-0-9854082-1-3 (ebook)

This book is dedicated to my son Larry Jr. and daughter Ashley, we were physically apart, but you were always in my heart.

"Gangster Redemption"

How Ex-Con Larry Lawton's Life Has Inspired Thousands of Kids to Stay Out of Prison

A Goodfella Becomes a Good Guy

How America's most notorious jewel robber got rich, got caught, and got his life back on track

By Larry Lawton,
Founder of Lawton911 and the
Reality Check Program

and

Peter Golenbock,
7 Time NY Times Bestselling Author
C2012

Table of Contents

Preface: 1
Chapter 1 Who Wants To F*ck Miss Armellino 3
Chapter 2 Earner For The Mob 27
Chapter 3 Loyalty 51
Chapter 4 The Daytona $800,000 62
Chapter 5 Diamonds Are a Guy's Best Friend 84
Chapter 6 The Single Life 100
Chapter 7 The Last Heist 126
Chapter 8 Journey to Atlanta 140
Chapter 9 The Worst of the Worst 154
Chapter 10 An Atmosphere of Violence 171
Chapter 11 Coleman and Jessup 208
Chapter 12 The Abu Ghraib of America 221
Chapter 13 Yazoo and Forest City 244
Chapter 14 Free At Last 257
Chapter 15 The Beginning of the Reality Check Program 273
Chapter 16 The Reality Check Program Takes Off 285
Chapter 17 Spreading the Word 302
Chapter 18 The Reality Check Program 318
Chapter 19 It Works 341
Afterword: Larry Lawton 361
Biography of Peter Golenbock 363
Acknowledgments: 365

PHOTOS

Larry 12 years old 197
Larry Lawton December 1961 197
Bronx NY - Throgs Neck Little League 1970 197
Larry 7 Years old 197
Lawon Family Picure 1972 198
Grandmother 2003 198
St Frances De Chantel Report Card - Mrs. Armelleno 1972-73 199
Coast Guard Sandy Hook NJ - 1981 199
Larry Coast Guard 1979 199
Angela Cusano childhood date 1979 200
First wife Roselyn 9-11-1987 200
Coast Guard ship running a gambling night 1985 201
Tommy, Louie, Me 1992 201
Joe Fraumeni 1993 201
Lukes Piano Lounge - Queens NY 1987 201
Louie, Cruiser Weight Champ Mark Randazzo, Larry 1992 201
Uncle Louie Constantino 1993 201
Larry with sisters Lynne and Debbie 1993 202
Second marriage to Missy 1994 202
Joe Fraumeni and me golfing 1994 202
Larry Lawton & Tom Ferrara with his wife -
    1996 Larry's Block Party 202
2nd wife Melissa visiting in prison 1999 202
Larry Jr. age 11 203
Daughter Ashley age 4 203
Federal Prison ID's 204
Parents visting 2000 204
Wife & Daughter visit 2003 204
Joe and Louie visiting 2002 204

Me at my sister's pool 2007 205
Huckabee Show 2010 205
John Oliver Daily Show 2009 205
Doing RCP 2010 205
Tommy Chong 2010 205
Governor Huckabee 2010 206
Parenting Program 2011 206
Theresa and Me 2011 206
Fox Anchor Keith Landry, Larry, Judge Babb and
    Lt. Governor Kottkamp Orlando Matters 2011 206
Today 207

PREFACE:

As a man who is not an author by profession, but a man who loves to have his opinion expressed, this book came about after developing the Reality Check Program video. People kept saying I needed to write a book to expose the wrongs with the prison system and also explain how people can change.

I blame no one for the wrongs that happened to me. In fact, I blame myself and myself alone. I also feel for the victims of my crimes. Although I never hurt anyone in a jewelry store robbery or other crime against a civilian (A person not in the criminal world) I do understand that there were emotional harms I caused. I could never change that and work with victim advocates all the time.

Life takes you on an emotional ride and mine was, and is, very emotional. The hurt I caused the victims, my family and society in general is a scar I live with everyday. I ask for no pity or help in dealing with my own emotions.

I also understand that redemption is part of life. You have to forgive yourself before you can move on and help others in anyway. I have moved on and developed the #1 program to help teens and young adults understand that the choices they make will affect the rest of their lives. The Reality Check Program's success rate is well documented.

I met Peter Golenbock through my agent at the time Adam Leibner from N.S. Bienstock. I met Adam in a roundabout way through Michael Kay the sports announcer for the New York Yankees. The stars truly aligned because Peter was able to get things out of me that nobody else could.

After a lot of encouragement from numerous people who I will acknowledge in the next section, and many ups and downs emotionally, financially and personally the book, **Gangster Redemption** was born.

CHAPTER 1

Who Wants To F*ck Miss Armellino

From his jail cell in the hole, he could hear the tier door open. The sound of footsteps was getting louder.

They're coming for me, he thought.

"Cuff up, Lawton," he was ordered.

He knew better.

"What did I do?" Lawton wanted to know.

The four huge guards the size of gorillas opened his cell door and charged at him. They jumped him and beat him. His face bled. His body hurt. They didn't care.

After they beat him they carried him out of the cell, put him in a room, stripped him naked, and strapped him down in a four-point position so he was spread-eagled. They cuffed each leg and arm to a post.

His eyes, half-closed from the beating, saw the hulking figure of one of the guards standing over him. He could see the guard unzip his fly. He took out his penis, and he let loose a stream of urine that splashed against Lawton's face.

As the guard was peeing, he said tauntingly, "Lawton, you keep writing senators. You think you're going anywhere?"

Lawton closed his eyes, and he could taste the salty urine

running down his face. One of the guards then spat out a large gob of spittle on him as he walked past.

"You think you're bad, Lawton," said one of the guards. "Keep writing senators."

Strapped down, immobile, naked, and covered with pee, he was left there alone with his thoughts for more than three and a half hours.

This may well have been the lowest point in Larry Lawton's life.

At one time he had been tight with the Gambino mob. He had been a big earner for the mob, stealing over $15 million in jewels in a string of jewelry store robberies. His take was millions of dollars. He lived like a king.

I was a millionaire, thought Lawton. *I owned a limo, horses, homes, expensive cars.*

Once he had a family, a beautiful wife and two beautiful children. He had lost it all.

Woozy from the beating, strapped naked to a steel bed frame, the smell of urine in his nostrils, he thought to himself, *How did I end up like this?*

*

When Larry Lawton was growing up, he lived at 5565 Hatting Place in the Bronx in the shadow of the Throgs Neck Bridge. From the back of his modest two-story bungalow home he could see the trucks and cars going over the bridge toward Queens, and he could hear the horns and the sounds of the traffic.

His Locust Point neighborhood was Irish, German, and

Italian. It was a neighborhood with its fair share of bookies and gangsters, but it was also a place where if you were a kid the old ladies would watch out for you. If you did something wrong on the block, your mother somehow would find out about it.

It was also a place where strangers weren't tolerated and blacks and Puerto Ricans could get hurt.

"You couldn't come into our neighborhood," said Lawton. "This was the Seventies. If somebody we didn't know came down to the jetties to go fishing under the Throgs Neck bridge, we'd take Molotov cocktails and throw them at their feet. The fire would be on the rocks all around them, and that would make them jump in the water. Nobody was allowed in our neighborhood."

One family that lived near the Lawtons was the wacko O'Reillys.

"It was a big old, Irish family with six kids. They were all crazy. A psycho family. I loved them. They had this old station wagon with the muffler dragging, and the dog chasing the car. They had a rough time of it with money. Billy Joe, who was my brother's age, once went into the local bowling alley, the Fiesta Lanes, and he left wearing the bowling shoes. My buddy Dennis said to him, 'Billy, you have the shoes on.'

"He said, 'These are better than mine.' So he took the shoes.

"One time Billy Joe was playing football with us, and his mother Wilma came out and yelled to Billy, "Come home and put up the Christmas lights."

"Fuck you, Wilma," he said.

"Billy, go home."

"Fuck you."

She said to me, 'Larry, give me that football.'

"Don't give her the football," Billy Joe yelled. He turned to his mother and said, 'I'll break every window in the fucking house.'

"I didn't know what to do. I threw the football up in the air.

"One time Wilma broke a stickball bat over son Eddie's shoulder.

"He said, 'What are you going to do now, Wilma?'

"She came out with a metal pipe, hit him with it, and he was down for the count. Another son broke his arm and didn't even bother to get it fixed. He played sports left handed and became ambidextrous. They were so nuts, but they were tough—and loyal as the day is long."

Another neighbor was Joannie Schmidt. Her father, who had swum in the Olympics, was a heavy drinker. Larry and his friends called him "Have a beer, Bob." "He actually put a beer tap in the sink in his house," said Lawton.

One of Larry's closest friends was Michael Kay, now an announcer for the New York Yankees.

"Michael's father was a bookie back in the old days, a Jewish guy and a real nice guy. He was very old and had emphysema. He'd sit on the stoop and watch us play sports. He liked to tell us stories and loved the tough kids."

One of the neighborhood mobsters, Joey Maccia, would

pull up in front of the Lawtons' home in his fancy Cadillac. In the trunk would be swag – stolen merchandise. Larry's father would buy underwear or steak knives or whatever was the hot item of the day all the time talking gambling and the latest sports line.

Larry, like a lot of the kids in Locust Point, grew up a latch-key child. His mother, a nurse, worked the night shift from eleven at night until seven in the morning. She would come home and sleep, and the kids had to be quiet. Larry, relatively unsupervised, would come home from school and be out playing until he heard his father whistle. The whistle was a call to be home in five minutes.

"You didn't want your father looking for you," said Lawton. "That was *big* trouble."

As a pre-teen Larry and his friends would go to the local candy store on the corner they called "The Wop Shop," and they would wait for an older boy to come along, and they'd have him buy sixty-nine-cents-a-quart beer for them. They would then go to "the field," an acre of patchy grass near the Throgs Neck Bridge toll booths. They drank the beer and played sports all afternoon. On weekend nights they'd use the field to party. All year long, whether it was ten degrees or summertime, when they got older they'd go with their girls and buy a quart of vodka and packets of ice tea mix, and then they'd get water from the spigot near the bridge toll booth and whip up a mixture of vodka and iced tea. They'd play basketball up against the bridge wall, where the maintenance workers had a basketball hoop. Their clothes and sneakers would be black from the grease and soil on the concrete.

There were two places where they all hung out: at the field near the toll booths or the bridge near the jetty.

Larry and his friends would swim in the East River under the Throgs Neck Bridge. On the other side of a long jetty was a sewer, and sometimes raw sewage would float by, but they paid it little attention.

"We thought we lived in a country club," said Lawton. "We felt we were living in high cotton."

Larry's dad was a sheet metal worker from Local 28, part of the civilian army that built the World Trade Center. In charge of two hundred sheet metal workers, his father ran the job, which was to install all the duct work in the hundred-story twin towers.

His boys, David and Larry, would sometimes tag along when he went to the job site. He'd take them to his trailer on the grounds. Even at age ten Larry was captivated by the scantily-clad girls on the calendars on the trailer's walls. Before the World Trade Center job was done, his father took them a hundred stories up to see the top of the world.

As part of his job each week Larry's dad was entrusted by the owner of the Brooks Construction Company to take bribe money and deliver it to the various mob bosses who demanded it. Paying off the mob was what allowed the massive World Trade Center to be built in only four years. The mob controlled the unions, and without the payoffs, there might have been walkouts, scab laborers, or perhaps a truck pouring concrete might be turned away, accused by inspectors of having the wrong density of concrete – and if they couldn't pour the concrete, the entire job would come to a halt. Anything could stop it. Each floor had to be completed before the next floor could be constructed. It was a huge jigsaw puzzle, and every piece had to be placed in order. If the sheet metal work was stopped, then the dry wall specialists couldn't work, and so the most efficient way to make sure everything went smoothly was to pay the mobsters who controlled the unions.

For ten years the city of New York had attempted to build a skating rink in Central Park. The mob-controlled unions kept it from happening. Donald Trump took over the project. The scuttlebutt was he paid off the mob. The rink was built in six months.

The owners of the companies building the World Trade Center knew that paying off the mob was part of doing business, so when they bid for the job, the mob money was included in the bidding. No one stiffed the mob. There was a steep penalty if you did. A construction company owner could find himself wearing cement shoes.

"The Transit Authority built the World Trade Center," said Lawton. "Each company got millions from them. My father used to take the transit authority supervisor to a city-run bookie joint called Off Track Betting and let them bet for free. There was one supervisor who was getting paid to add in phony hours and fake overtime. Everyone was paid off. What a fucking racket it was.

"In the four years it took to build the World Trade Center, there wasn't a single union walk out. The mob goons made sure of it."

Larry was 12 when he accompanied his father making his weekly payoffs. His father would say, "Hey kid, get in the car," and off they'd go to the Triangle Bar in the Bronx or to the Q Lounge on Gun Hill Road.

"The Q Lounge was a pool hall, a gangster hangout where you'd see shady characters. We'd park right in front of the place. No one paid meters back then. My father wore construction clothes, a flannel shirt. He'd always have a pen on him, and he'd always have that envelope in his pocket. The envelope would be folded up, and it contained cash. My father would walk in, pay, and leave."

Larry's father's favorite watering hole was the Triangle Bar, located on the corner of Buerre and Westchester avenues in the Bronx. On some nights his father would take him along for the drops, and on other nights he'd go with him when his dad just sat at the bar and drank Dewars and water. Larry loved the energy of the place.

"We'd go in there," said Larry, "and the guy my father was going to meet would be sitting on a bar stool. I didn't know who he was, but I could always tell if he was a mobster. He had the nice clothes and a pinky ring. My father would drop off the envelope, and the guy would leave. I never knew his name. He'd say, "Hey kid, how ya doin'?" and he'd rub my hair, like I was doing good."

"Listen to your father," he'd tell the kid. "He's a good man."

"Because I went with my dad often, the guys in the bar got to know me. One guy was a steam fitter. They called him Joe

Steam. Another guy was named Dudley, and there was Tony the Butcher, who was of course a butcher. They were friends of my father. They were in the bar all the time.

"The wise guys would give me cokes and coins to go play the pinball machines. These were the real pinball machines, not all this electronic crap."

The Triangle was a bar where patrons came to drink and to gamble. There was a television set behind the long bar that featured whatever New York team was playing at the time. This was before the age of ESPN and up-to-the minute score results. There was no cable, only the basic network fare. The Yankees were on Channel 11 WPIX, the Mets and Knicks on WOR 9, and the football Giants on CBS, channel 2. The local betters had to wait impatiently to hear the scores, and when they were announced you could hear the murmuring of the elated and the distraught.

Vinnie Tramamuno, a large fat man with a cigar and a grunt, was the bar's bookie. He was right out of the Sopranos. He'd grunt, "Wha da ya want?" and wait to hear which team you wanted to bet on and how many times. The basic bet – one time --was five dollars – plus fifty cents vigorish to the bookie for taking the bet. A five-time bet was for twenty-five dollars, plus two-fifty vig. The vig was how the bookie made his money. Vinnie would write the bet on paper that would easily disintegrate – flash paper they call it – a protection against getting caught with evidence by the cops.

When Larry was 12, he made his first bet.

"Making a bet with a bookie was a big deal," he said. "You

were a big shot when you made your bets with your own bookie. We were in the Triangle, and one day the Giants were on TV, and I begged my dad, 'I wanna bet. I wanna bet.'

"He nodded, and I decided to make a one-time bet on the Giants, and I can remember walking into the bathroom with Vinnie, and we closed the door, as though no one knew what we were doing. .

"What da ya want, kid?" He had the cigar hanging from his mouth.

"Give me one time on the Giants."

He gave me the line. "Minus three."

"All right."

And he wrote it down on that flash paper."

It was around this time that Larry began doing some bookmaking of his own. The Bono family lived around the corner from the Lawtons. Louie Bono Sr. was a powerful mobster, and when he got sick, Lawton's mom, a registered nurse, took care of him. Sometimes when Larry stood at the bus stop waiting to go to school, Mr. Bono would come by in his Cadillac, pick him up, and take him to school. Mr. Bono wanted his son Louie to begin hustling, and he set him up selling sports tickets. Louie, who at age 17 was five years older than Larry, would sell them to Larry's father. The idea was for the bettor to choose any three teams on the card. You bet a dollar, and if your three teams won you got five dollars back. If you picked four winners, you'd get ten to one. But picking four winners, it turns out, is very difficult. They do it in Las Vegas today. It's a sucker bet.

One day Louie came over to the house to sell Larry's father the sports tickets, and when Larry found out he could earn a quarter for dollar he sold, Larry begged Louie to let him sell tickets too.

"I can get Mr. Duffy," Larry said. "I can get Mr. Ziel," his next door neighbor. "And Mr. Knapp. I can get them all to bet."

Said Lawton, "Where I lived everyone bet a lot. I was only a kid, but it sounded like a gold mine."

Louie Bono right then and there handed Lawton the neighborhood franchise. He sat down with him, explained which boxes on the cards had to be marked, told him he should make sure to write his own name on the back of the card, and reminded him he'd get twenty five cents for every dollar sold. He also let him know that winners would tip him when he went to pay off.

"My parents were all for it," said Lawton. "Everyone played sports tickets."

Every Monday Louie would come over and deliver his stack of tickets.

"I would take the tickets and go up and down my whole neighborhood," said Lawton. "It didn't take me long to know who the big bettors were. I always made sure to wait for them to come home. My father was one of my biggest customers. Mr. Duffy, a school principal, used to bet twenty bucks every weekend. I'd always get him. Mr. Giordano, who was in the rackets, used to bet thirty, sometimes forty dollars. If he spent a lot of money, I knew he had a good week with the numbers.

"As a young kid I wanted my customers to win, because they'd tip you. I didn't care if I had to pay off a bet. It wasn't coming out of my pocket. If a guy won fifty bucks, he'd throw me five. Almost no one was cheap.

"I was very organized. I'd collect the money and attach it with a paper clip to each slip. I was smart enough to write down all the numbers that everyone bet, so I also could find out if they won without having to wait for Louie to come and tell me."

At age 12, Lawton's take was seventy five to a hundred and fifty dollars a week, a hell of a lot of money for a young kid, but most of it he would fritter away gambling. This would become a pattern in Lawton's life. With Lawton it was always easy come, easy go.

"The smart ones kept their money," said Lawton, "but at that age who was smart with money?"

*

When the World Trade Center job was finished in 1972, his father was laid off, and money became scarce. "Our family had five children and no money. Things were so bad I had to play basketball in my slippers," said Lawton. "It was embarrassing, but you did what you had to do."

At this point Larry's life consisted mainly of going to school, selling sports tickets, and playing whatever sport was in season. Larry was small for his age. At age 12 he was barely five feet tall, but he was an excellent athlete. He would play tackle football with his brother David, who was two years older, and with his brother's friends. The boys would spray paint the concrete and make a football field. They played without helmets or any other gear. Larry was fearless. He felt the need to prove himself, and he would rush in and make the tackle against much larger opponents. He suffered from concussions, and for a while his headaches were so fierce that he would slam his head against the wall of his bedroom in an attempt to make the pain stop. When he finally went to the hospital, x-rays revealed a hairline fracture at the back of his skull.

In the spring Larry played baseball on a team in the Throgs Neck Little League. The field not only had lights, but it had water fountains in the dugouts. The field was right across the street from St. Frances de Chantal, where Larry went to Catholic school.

Since he was ten Larry had been an altar boy at St. Francis de Chantal Roman Catholic Church. Larry attended confession regularly.

"Altar boys had to be good," said Lawton. "You took communion. You were supposed to be good. I guess I was good. I don't know. I was a little kid growing up in the Bronx. You played. You went out and did the little things kids did."

He was a favorite of one of the two priests, a man whose name he can no longer remember.

"It was a nice church. When you walked in there were two confession booths, one on each side of the entrance. The priest sat between them. He'd open the little window. You'd go in and wait while you heard him talking to the person in the other booth. When you knew it was your time, you'd be on your knees, hands folded. 'Bless me Father for I have sinned. It's been....I've done this, this, and this.' There were two priests, and you never knew which one you'd get, but this one priest was always nice to me. He knew me. I was one of his altar boys. And I would want to get him, because I would only have to say two Hail Marys, or two Our Fathers, and he'd forgive me."

One time when Larry was 12, after a funeral had ended he was in the back of the church taking off his robe when the friendly priest walked over to him and said, "You can take everything off if you want."

Larry didn't know exactly what he meant by that, but he became extremely nervous.

"I don't want to take everything off," Larry said, but before he knew what was happening the priest grabbed him, pulled down his shorts, bent down, put the boy's penis in his mouth, and started to give him a blow job.

"I was helpless. I couldn't understand what was going on," said Lawton. "I started getting excited. I started shaking, not knowing what to do. I remember to this day his black, curly hair and his black robe. People might say, *You knew that was wrong*, but I didn't know anything, and there was no way you can say, '*Stop that*' to a priest. He was holy. After he was through, he got up, and I'll never forget what he said to me:

"'Have you been good this week?'

"'Yes father,' I said.

When the priest started taking off his robe Lawton, shaken, made a beeline out the door.

"I didn't tell anybody. You can't say anything. Back then, in the early '70s, no one blew whistles on priests. I hadn't even gone through puberty, and you're wondering what the hell happened, and you don't know if it's normal or what. Now you look back and you want to shoot him. Later when I went to prison I would look up the records to see which inmates were child molesters. We'd beat them half to death, and I loved it. One guy had a floor buffing machine dropped on him from the second floor of prison. He didn't die, but it crushed his head and shoulder. I never felt any remorse."

But as a 12 year old all he did was tell his father the next week that he no longer wanted to be an altar boy.

"I don't want to do it," he said.

"Why?"

"I want to play sports." His father never questioned him again.

"Over the years I read all the stories about priests and young boys, and I can tell you they're all true," said Lawton. "Does it affect your life? You look back, and you had this little weenie with the little mustache hairs on it, and you don't understand. But though I still believe in God, I no longer believe in the Catholic religion. Can you blame me if I have doubts about priests and everything that goes along with them?"

On Sundays thereafter Larry would tell his parents he was going to noon Mass. His mother would give him a dollar for the collection plate. He was supposed to put the money in the basket, but that's not what he did.

Said Lawton, "I would run into the church, grab the weekly

mass pamphlet to show my parents I went to church, and we'd look to see who the priest was in case my mother asked me, 'Who was the father?' It was often the priest with the black, curly hair. Maybe I don't want to remember his name. But we'd take the dollar, go directly to the Whop Shop to buy beer, and go to the field."

What is true is that after being molested by his priest, Larry Lawton changed. He no longer was a nice kid. His edges turned hard, perhaps in an attempt to prove his manhood to himself. The first indication that he had turned bad came when he was kicked out of Catholic school. Though he had one of the highest IQs in the school, he became incorrigible. He became disruptive in class. He cut school. He started fights.

"When I was in the seventh grade we had a young, lay teacher. She was beautiful. In class I wrote a note asking, 'Who wants to fuck Miss Armellino?' I signed it, Scott Gariola signed it, and a third kid signed it. As the note was being passed around, Sister Mary Stanislaus caught us passing the note. We were sent down to the office of the principal, Sister Mary Claire. We waited all day for our parents. The other two kids were crying.

"My father came in, and he said, 'Get in the car.' He didn't say another word. We lived in a bungalow house, and I was sent upstairs to my room. I could hear my parents down below. My father was laughing."

But Lawton's behavior was no laughing matter, and in May of 1973 Larry and his younger sister were kicked out of Saint Frances de Chantal. They now had to go to IS 192 and then

Lehman High School. It was at this point that his life turned. He no longer had any interest in school. He turned to a life in the street.

"I went about half the time," said Lawton. "To get there we had to go by city bus. My friends and I used to go to a music store where they sold bongs and had pinball machines. We bought little pipes. Some kids were into weed back then. I wasn't into it as a kid. It was a place to hang out. We'd go to Westchester Square, where they had a Woolworth's, and that's where Louie Bono, the mob guy in our neighborhood, had a candy store.

"We'd cut school, get on the subway, and go to games at Yankee Stadium. My brother and I made the back cover of *The New York Post*. The stadium had been refurbished, and it had a new Jumbotron scoreboard, and we jumped over the wall and got the first homerun ever hit by a Yankee in the new stadium. Chris Chambliss hit it, and we got the ball, and we were on the big screen and in the papers.

"We would bet on the games. We'd bet on individual batters, whether a batter would strike out. We'd bet the over and under. 'I bet you he grounds out.'

"By this time I was making money hustling. By age 15 my main activity was gambling. I became a big gambler.

"I'd go to OTB. I just didn't care about school. I had zero grades. I never applied myself to school. I applied myself to the streets, and that's what made me smart -- hustling."

Larry and his buddies gambled regularly. In the streets they played the game acey-ducey. Every player put a dollar in the pot. One player was dealt two cards. Say the cards were a three and a queen. The player had to bet whether the next card would fall between the other two. You could bet up to the limit of the pot.

"I was crazy," said Lawton. "Even if I was dealt a three and a seven, I'd still bet the pot. My friend Dennis Broderick was like that too."

They also pitched pennies, throwing coins against the wall to see who could come closest. They would bet on two cockroaches climbing up a wall.

"We were all crazy," said Lawton.

His group had drinkers, druggies, and gamblers. Larry was one of the gamblers. He was constantly in need of money to feed his gambling addiction.

"I stole money in order to be able to play in card games," said Lawton. "We'd go in Woolworth's and other stores, and lift things. I didn't just steal to steal. I stole to convert the items into money. There was a hot dog man on the corner, and I would go into the supermarket and steal mustard, red onions and sauerkraut, and I'd trade them for hot dogs. My friends Dennis and Johnny, who worked at Pathmark, stole all kinds of food – lobsters, steaks – and sold it up and down East Tremont Avenue for money. That was our crew. Everybody was doing stuff like that. It was normal. Everyone I knew was a hustler."

At times Larry and his friends would hail a cab for the ride home. They would pick a random house near where they lived and order the cabbie to take them there.

"We knew what we were going to do — beat the cabbie out of his fare. The guy sitting in the front had to be quick. When the cab stopped, we'd all just fly out of the cab. We'd jump a couple of fences and get the fuck out of there."

Larry and his friends continued to play sports, but now Larry's temper was getting the best of him. One time during a street roller hockey game, Larry and his brother David got tangled in the net. Larry extricated himself, grabbed a two by four, and smashed his brother over the head, splitting David's head wide open. Another time he stabbed his brother with a pair of scissors. For fun Larry and David shot their BB gun out the back window of their home breaking the windows of neighbor's cars. They never got caught.

Larry's first real job was at age 16 working as an usher at the Interboro Movie Theater. Larry had snuck in a six-pack of beer, and during the playing of the movie Americathon, he sat in the back of the theater watching the movie and drinking beer. The theater manager caught him, and he was fired.

At night his father would take him to the Triangle Bar. He got to know the wiseguys there while his dad drank and placed bets. Larry then would drive his father home, even though he wasn't old enough to get a driver's license.

"You have to picture me behind the wheel," said Lawton. "I was 16, but I looked like a baby. I had blond, curly hair. I was a good-looking kid, and my relatives called me 'Loverboy.' The girls loved me. Anyway, my father would drink, and I would drive him home."

One of the characters Larry habitually saw at the Triangle

bar was a man in his forties with salt and pepper hair who was whispered to be a member of the Purple Gang, the notorious gang of Jewish killers from Detroit.

"All the guys would say to me, 'Stay away from him. He's in the Purple Gang.' But he was a nice guy. He'd buy me a drink. In New York everybody buys everyone else a drink. That's how they get to know you. I was a kid, and he knew I was a bounce-around kid. I was hanging out at the bar, selling sports tickets, gambling with a bookie. They all know.

"One time I was sitting at the bar with the guy from the Purple Gang. The guy always carried a brown paper bag, and I asked him what was in it. He showed me a pistol. The only other pistol I had ever seen belonged to John Fenton, a cop who was dating my sister. Back then you didn't see guns. You fought with sticks and knives. I saw the gun, and of course I was impressed with the guy. He didn't show it to be a big shot. He showed it because I asked him. Whenever I saw him, we'd talk. One time he said to me, 'Do you know how to rob cars? Because there's a good chop shop over near the Pelham Split Rock golf course.'

"He was probably involved in a car-stealing ring. I never asked him. You don't say to a guy like that, 'Are you a car thief?' But you knew. Why would he introduce me to a chop shop unless he was involved? So he told me where I could get rid of cars.

"There was good money in that. You got five hundred bucks a car in one hundred dollar bills. You dropped it off, they did everything, and they gave you five hundred in cash."

Stealing cars was becoming a burgeoning industry in the Bronx in the 1970s.

"There were a lot of abandoned cars left alongside the roads in the Bronx. We'd help strip them. If we wanted something off a car, we'd stop on the highway and grab what we wanted. We wanted a radio? We'd take it. Tires? We took them. I knew how to take tires off a car without a jack. Sure thing, you put a cinder block underneath the car, and you'd get two or three guys to lift it up, and when you loosen the nuts, you lift it as much as you could, and you kicked the tire out – you might snap the lug nuts, but you didn't care. You got the tire. It was pretty easy."

Lawton, who badly needed money to feed his gambling habit, was instructed to steal only newer cars. At seventeen years of age he soon became adept at it. His first attempts involved breaking into the car, hot-wiring it, and driving off.

"You use a hanger and pull the little knob that locks the car. You get in there, punch out the ignition switch, put a screw driver in there, turn it on, and go. Then at night I'd take the car to the chop shop in the Bronx over near the Split Rock golf course."

Lawton had to keep an eye on the rear view mirror in case the owner, or the cops, came along, and he had some close calls, where he had to duck down as a patrol car drove past.

A thief had to be quick stealing a car by punching out the ignition. Lawton wasn't, and after stealing a couple cars this way, he looked for an easier MO. It didn't take him long to find one.

"I knew guys who could rob a car in thirty seconds. I wasn't one of them, so I used to wait on the street in front of the candy store in the mornings or at nights, and guys would drive up in front of the store and run in and buy the paper, and they'd leave the car running. I'd jump in the car and go. Or I'd wait and watch for guys who would get up in the mornings during the winter and heat up their car. I'd watch for the exhaust coming out the back of the car. People did that in New York all the time. They'd go down to the street, heat up the car, go back in their house and wait, and while they were waiting, I'd steal the car."

After stealing the car, Lawton would drive it to another part of the neighborhood, drive it around the block two or three times to make sure he wasn't followed, and park it on a side street. He would enlist the aid of a buddy to ride behind him when he took the stolen car to the chop shop.

For Lawton the scariest part of the job was taking the stolen car at night to the chop shop, which was out in a deserted field in the middle of nowhere in the Bronx at the outskirts of the local golf course.

"There's a wooded area over near City Island. It's funny, because the Police Academy is right there. The guy from the Purple Gang told me how to get there. He told me, 'There's a little dirt road on the side, take it, and a guy will step out and wave and point to an area.' I was worried because it was pitch black, and I was always looking over my shoulder. I wondered, *Are they going to kill me?* But they just wanted the car.

The chop shop was open for business seven nights a week.

The shop consisted of a truck with a compressor to strip the car and a lift to pull out the engine. A car would be stripped in less than an hour.

"There were as many as fifty car carcasses in that field. It looked like a field of dead cars. They'd take what they wanted off the car. Back then bumpers were big money. Batteries, radios, seats would come off the car. Tires would come off. They made big money on these items. They took engines. In no time the car was a carcass of metal.

"I didn't hang around. They gave me five one-hundred dollar bills, and I'd take off. You start asking questions, and you're dead."

As much money as Lawton made, he would quickly lose it to his gambling habit.

"I knew eventually I was going to get caught," said Lawton. "We were opportunists. Anything we could steal, we would. But we never robbed from old ladies on our block. We never beat anyone up to rob their money. That comes from the respect you have from your father, or what the guys in the mob taught you. Remember, The Godfather came out in 1972, and we thought that was cool. Now, looking back, you realize what a scumbag everybody was. But as a kid I didn't know that. You think that's the life. So we robbed to gamble."

Toward the end of his junior year at Lehman High School, Larry Lawton started a fight that turned into a riot.

"We were drinking beer at school. They used to sell little nip beers, eight-ounce pony bottles. I'd take an eight-pack of beer to school.

"I was throwing glass beer bottles. Lehman High is built over a highway. What moron would build a high school in the Bronx over a highway? We would throw beer bottles and other things at the passing cars below. We would hang people by their feet over the highway to scare them. We were crazy.

"On this day I was throwing glass beer bottles, and I threw one near a bunch of students, and they said, 'Fuck you,' and we said, 'What are you going to do about it?' They came over, and a fight erupted. There were five of us, but we knew all the football players, all the cool people. Friends came running over, and before it was over we had a mini-riot. The cops came on horseback. We all ran. Everyone took off. Then you go home, and everyone talks about it. No one cared. After it's done, it's done."

When his junior year ended, Lawton decided he was finished with school. He knew he was smart enough. He never took notes, and if he ever went to class, he knew he could pass any course. But school was not his forte. The streets were his forte. Each day at school he took with him one piece of loose-leaf notebook paper, but that was for taking bets.

*

At age seventeen Lawton was aware enough to realize that he needed to get away from this dead-end existence. In August of 1979 he entered the United States Coast Guard.

"I needed to get away from the life," said Lawton. "To get away from the neighborhood and maybe that priest." But, as it turned out, the pull of "the life" would become too strong. Anything else was too boring and much too tame.

CHAPTER 2

Earner For The Mob

As Larry sat on the plane headed for basic training at Petaluma, California, he couldn't believe how free he felt. He was on his own for the first time, though in a very real way he had been on his own pretty much his whole life. He may have entered the Coast Guard as a 132-pound, baby-faced kid, but looks are deceiving. He was strong and tough. He could do a hundred push-ups without breaking a sweat, and it wasn't long after arriving in California that he started growing and putting on muscle.

Boot camp lasted ten weeks. During that time he turned eighteen on October 3, 1979. Lawton loved the regimen. An early bird, he enjoyed getting up at five thirty in the morning and doing calisthenics as the sun was coming up.

The only part of military life he didn't enjoy was the bad vibes he and other New Yorkers got from the Southerners and Midwesterners. Lawton never got into a fight, but he enjoyed taking on some of his detractors in push up challenges. The two would go face to face to see who could do the most. Lawton almost always won as the loser sank ingloriously into the dirt.

After the ten weeks, he returned to the Bronx on leave. When he arrived home on a fourteen-day leave he was thinking he had returned a man.

His first duty station was Cortez, Florida, near Bradenton. He was a seaman apprentice, and he was assigned to a 41-foot, three-man, search and rescue boat. Most of his duties revolved around towing disabled boats back to shore and putting out boat fires. Not long after he began duty, his crew discovered several bales of marijuana floating in the ocean toward shore. The skipper hid two of the bales under a bridge on a catwalk and turned in the rest. Not long afterward the boat captain handed Larry a stack of hundred dollar bills.

Said Lawton, "The other two guys did it. I was a go-along guy. I was loving it. With that money I ended up buying my first car, a big, maroon Mercury Marquis. They gave me three grand. That was big money."

During his time with the Coast Guard Lawton was witness to three historic tragedies in Florida maritime history. The first came on January 28, 1980, when the 180-foot long *Blackthorn*, a Coast Guard buoy tender, collided head-on with a large tanker. The anchor of the tanker ship was embedded into the hull of the Coast Guard ship, and as the tanker sailed on, the *Blackthorn* turned over and sank in ninety seconds, killing all twenty-three men on board. It took thirty days to raise the *Blackthorn*, and Lawton's Coast Guard station was part of the salvage operation. Lawton helped carry the body bags from a barge to a ship that took them ashore.

The second event, which began in April of 1980 and lasted for several months, was the desperate rescue of the Freedom Flotilla from Cuba. Ten thousand Cubans had stormed the

Peruvian embassy asking for asylum, and when the Peruvian ambassador refused to force them to leave, Fidel Castro announced that anyone who wished to leave Cuba could. Cuban Americans then flooded the Port of Mariel with small pleasure boats, commercial shrimp and fishing boats, unsteady rafts, and even inner tubes tied to pieces of wood to bring their relatives and anyone else who wanted to leave Cuba to Southern Florida. President Jimmy Carter announced that America would welcome them all. Before it was over, 125,000 Cubans fled to the United States.

Hundreds of small crafts made their way toward Key West, but not all of them made it. Lawton, who was part of the largest Coast Guard operation in peacetime in American history, was part of an armada of ships that struggled mightily to save as many of the refugees as they could.

"I was sent to the Coast Guard station down in Key West called the Navy Mole. We were among the first people sent there. We were rescuing those Cuban people coming in, and we got a lot of joy and satisfaction from helping them, but at the same time it was very sad."

The official count of those who drowned was forty, but Lawton knows for a fact the casualties were in the hundreds.

"If not thousands. And you can ask anyone who was there. There were dozens of boats that left Cuba that never were seen again. I saw many dead people floating on inner tubes. Many times I saw boats on fire with the people on board dead."

For the Coast Guard men who had to dispose of the bodies of those unfortunate not to survive, the scene was gruesome and unsettling.

"We saw dead bodies. We stacked bodies at the back of some boats. One boat had thirty people on it, and it caught on fire, and many of them died. Some of the Coast Guardsmen had to go to psychologists for counseling. I was okay. I had a tough stomach."

The third tragic event occurred in the early morning of May 9, 1980, when the 600-foot-long freighter *Summit Venture*, riding in a violent rain squall with near-zero visibility and fighting wind gusts up to eighty miles an hour, struck a piling of the southbound span of the Sunshine Skyway Bridge, knocking down 1,200 feet of the roadway. Six cars and a Greyhound bus traveling from Chicago to Miami fell a hundred and fifty feet into the water below. Thirty-five people, including twenty-three passengers on the bus, died.

Lawton's boat patrolled the waters during the thirty-day rescue operation and assisted the salvage crew. They recovered debris, victim's belongings – baby shoes, kids' toys, suitcases, and purses and handbags -- and bodies.

Lawton, not content to be a seaman, applied and was accepted to boatswain's mate school in Yorktown, Virginia. He graduated with the rank of petty officer third class.

His next assignment was at Sandy Hook, New Jersey. A boat captain, he was assigned to a small search and rescue ship. He rescued a lot of people and earned medals. But because Sandy Hook was a short car ride to his old haunts in the Bronx and Brooklyn, he had easy access to his mob friends.

Being in the military didn't curb his excesses. One time on

a bet he drove naked from Sandy Hook, New Jersey, to the Bronx, New York, on his motorcycle at speeds of a hundred miles an hour.

"I flew through the toll booths," said Lawton. "I won my bet. It was a hundred bucks. In 1981 that was a lot of money."

His next stop was Hawaii, and from his base in Honolulu he was assigned to the 378-foot Coast Guard cutter *Jarvis*, which patrolled the waters of Alaska. The *Jarvis* was sent to enforce the two-hundred mile Fisheries Conservation Act, protecting America's seas from Japanese and Russian boats fishing illegally.

One of Lawton's jobs on the ship was ordering supplies, and he would divert some of those goods all the way to his mob friends in the Bronx and in Brooklyn.

"I had fifty guys on that ship working for me, and I used to order all the supplies, the rope, the paint, and paint brushes, and I could send it anywhere I wanted. I sent it back to Brooklyn. I didn't get paid a dime. I was getting on the 'in'. I did it because I could, and because I knew down the line the favors would come back in spades."

Lawton's plan was to stay in the Coast Guard twenty years, but during one of the cutter's stops of a Russian factory ship, made during stormy weather, he fell and was badly injured.

Lawton was standing on the deck of the Russian ship, when it was struck by a powerful wave. Lawton lost his footing and fell twenty feet into one of the ship's fish holds, landing on his back.

"I was lucky I fell on the fish and not steel, but it still hurt.

They pulled me out of there, but right away I could tell I was hurt. My back was all messed up. I couldn't walk, and I had numbness in my legs."

The Coast Guard doctors discovered he also had scoliosis, curvature of the spine, and he was sent to the Coast Guard base on Governor's Island. Lawton would then travel back and forth to the Bethesda Naval Hospital in Maryland.

He was assigned to Fort Totten, on the Long Island side of the Throgs Neck Bridge, not far from his Bronx home, but because of his medical condition he didn't have to live there. Lawton remained based there for eight months while the Coast Guard decided what to do with him.

"I was on the payroll of the Coast Guard, but I had no one to report to, nowhere to go, nothing to do. I was living in Brooklyn with my brother David in an apartment."

While still a member of the Coast Guard, Lawton took advantage of his mob connections and became an associate of the Gambino crime family. The Gambino clan was run by Paul Castallano until December of 1985, when he was gunned down while eating at Sparks Steakhouse by men hired by John Gotti. Lawton became a bartender at one of the mob-owned lounges with the blessing of made man Dominick Gangi, who was close to Castillano.. While there Lawton began his education in the bookmaking business.

"While I was still in the Coast Guard I was told by Dominick Gangi, 'Go to Luke's Piano Lounge on Union Turnpike in Queens, and you'll be taken care of. They are expecting you.' I then started bartending and really learning the bookmaking business.

His teacher was one of the best, Mac the Bookie, the biggest bookmaker in all of New York.

"Mac set up shop at Luke's Piano Lounge," said Lawton, "and all the bookies from around New York City would lay their money off with him. A bookie doesn't gamble. A bookie takes bets on any game in any sport and doesn't care who wins. He takes money on both sides and he makes his ten percent from the vig. But if the betting is running $50,000 on one team and $20,000 on the other, he better lay that difference off, otherwise he ends up becoming a gambler. Who do you lay it off to? Vegas won't take that big of a bet. You negotiate the line and lay the difference off with Mac.

"Mac was a Jew who had a lot of juice because all the big bosses respected him for his brains and his ability to make money. He was an older guy with white hair. Whenever I was here I'd run next door to the deli to get him a toasted English Muffin with cream cheese and jelly.

"Mac was highly respected, but he was tough. The guys who used to take bets from John Gotti, who was a big gambler, would call him, and he'd say to them, 'I don't give a fuck if John is betting. *You* better pay me.' Because who's going to call up Gotti and tell him he has to pay? What if John Gotti didn't pay? What are you going to do? So Mac would say, 'I don't care who it is. I'm coming to collect from *you*.'

Lawton's bookmaking operation was small. Most of the bets he took were for a thousand dollars or less. He learned how to take bets and how to get the line. A customer would call and say, "Give me a nickel on the Giants." That meant he wanted to bet five hundred dollars. "I want to bet a dime." A dime is a thousand dollar bet. "Give me a twenty-time parlay." That's two teams. One time is five dollars, so a twenty time bet is one hundred dollars. Plus the vig, of course. "Give me a round robin." That's a bet on three teams. Lawton would take the action from twenty-five to a thousand dollar bets.

After his apprenticeship at Luke's Piano Lounge, Larry moved his bookie operation from Queens to Brooklyn, where he set up shop at another mob-controlled bar called The Homestretch, an old-time bar on Kings Highway and West 10th Street. The bar was one long room. On the left was a juke box, and there were a couple of tables where the boys would play cards. On the wall a big painting of horses racing was known to all who went there. In the back of the bar was a Skittle game and a Joker Poker slot machine that paid off.

The Homestretch was home base for Dominick Gangi and the bar owner, Willie Ventura, whose nickname was Willie the Weeper. He was called that because Willie was always bitching about something or other.

"Willie was my mentor," said Lawton. "I looked up to him. He had a loan sharking operation, ran the numbers, bookmaking, broads – he ran the place. He owned the whole building, including two apartments above the Homestretch bar. He worked directly for Dominick Gangi."

Larry needed the protection of the Gambinos to do business.

"You had to be connected to one mob or another, because

if you weren't, and if you were making good money, other mobsters in New York would know about you, know you were a big-time earner, and they would kidnap or torture you for your money. One way or another they'd find out where you hid the money. But if you were connected with one of the mob families, then you were protected because you were kicking upstairs, and everybody wants to protect their own interests.

"Some guys were associated with the mob just because they liked to be involved. A mob boss might say to him, 'Go do this.' These are flunkies or hangers-on, and there were a lot of them. I was an associate of the Gambino crime family. I wasn't a made man, but I was protected. I was what you called an earner. For every dollar I made, I kicked something up to my boss, Dominick Gangi. I always paid him something. Greedy guys might have tried to get away with less, but I didn't want to risk Dominick finding out I was shorting him. If he thought I was screwing with him, I'd have bad vibes, and bad vibes can shorten your life."

The Homestretch bar, like all mob-owned bars, was a world unto its own. Almost every day someone would walk into the place with hot merchandise.

"Guys who used to rob tractor trailers full of stuff always had a way to get rid of the merchandise. Some of them had outs up and down the avenue, selling to stores. They might have ten guys selling the stuff out of their trunks on consignment. Those guys would then come into the mob bars.

"If a guy walked in and said, 'Johnny from 18th Avenue sent me,' okay. He wouldn't lie about Johnny, because if I go back and say, 'Johnny, thanks for the hit,' and Johnny says, 'Send what fucking guy down?' then the guy's in big trouble, because then Johnny didn't get his kickback. Everybody involved gets a kickback.

"A couple of times a guy came into the bar who wasn't connected, and we'd rob him. He'd come in and say, 'Hey, I have something to show you,' and we'd say okay and take the guy inside, and while they were talking, we had another guy emptying his trunk. Because he wasn't connected.

"I was violent, and I was smart. A lot of guys were just stupid violent, and these were the guys who never made it. They ended up going to jail or getting whacked. Eventually everyone in the mob either goes to prison or gets killed, but the smart ones last a while.

"I grew up with no money. I learned how to hustle to make money. John Gotti had nothing, and he learned and he was smart. But today the sons of the fathers who made millions are spoiled. They didn't learn how to hustle from the street like their fathers. They don't have a con game, and they aren't smart criminals. That's why the mob today is not what it used to be. The younger generation isn't hungry, and therefore they never learned how to be a *real* gangster."

*

In addition to bookmaking, Lawton became a loan shark, lending money at an exorbitant interest to those who desperately needed it.

"Let me explain loan sharking," said Lawton. "It's exactly like what credit card companies do today. When you borrow money, you have to pay back three points a week. It doesn't sound like that much, but it is. Say I lend a guy $10,000. He would have to pay me $300 a week. Every week he has to give me $300, and that doesn't come off the principal. That's three percent *weekly*."

Lawton's customers were those who couldn't get a loan from a bank. Often they were customers with cash businesses.

"It might be a candy store owner or a bar owner or a business where they get a lot of cash and they don't pay their sales tax. They need money to pay the sales tax, but they can't go to a bank and get a loan, because they're making a lot of that money under the table, and they aren't showing much of a profit. So they come to me.

"Or my customers might be drug dealers, who are the best, because eventually I know I'll get my money even if they don't pay me right away. The only way I get beat is if they go to jail or get killed.

"A lot of them are also gamblers, and gamblers lose, and too often at some point they no longer can pay. I'd loan shark $20,000 to a business owner because his sales tax was due. He'd tell me, 'I'll give it back in a month.'

"I'd say, 'Here's $20,000. I want $600 a week every Friday. You know what happens in six months, right?' 'Oh yeah. You got it.'

"Some guys pay on time, and if they pay in a month I've made $2,400 on my money and get my $20,000 back. Where can you make interest like that in a month? But what if he couldn't pay? After six months I would increase his points to five percent, and this guy who owes me $20,000 now is paying me $1,000 a week.

"I'd say, 'I'll give you six more months, and then I want my fucking twenty grand.'

"He's paying me $1,000 a week. In 26 weeks I make $26,000, and he still owes me twenty grand. Then I'd say, 'Now we have a problem. I want your business. Or I want something. I once took a guy's boat. I had a guy hook it up to a trailer and drive it off. 'You'll get your boat when I get my money.' He found the money. They all do, or I sell their stuff."

Lawton was very effective at collecting from his own debtors. As an associate he also had the job of collecting from those who owed his mob bosses. He provided muscle for the card games, the dice games, and the rest of the gambling operation at Luke's Piano Lounge. When someone owed money and didn't pay, Larry got the call.

Lawton had entered the Coast Guard at five foot six and 132 pounds, but after seven years of service to his country he had grown to almost six feet and 200 pounds of solid muscle. He was a force to be reckoned with. His first gambit was to send a message to pay up by throwing a cinder block through the windshield of the debtor's car. That usually worked, but if it didn't, the next step was blowing up the car.

"One guy didn't pay for a while, and I wanted to show him what was going to happen," said Lawton. "His car was parked in the neighborhood. At night, when no one was around, I took a cinder block and put it under the car's gas tank. I put a can of Sterno on the cinder block and lit it. After a while, depending on how much gas is in the tank – less gas, more fumes, quicker explosion."

Another time a bettor who owed Lawton five hundred dollars made every excuse imaginable in addition to making the mistake of trying to duck him.

"You didn't want to owe me money," he said. "I caught the guy outside the Homestretch, and I beat him down and laid his arm on the curb. I snapped it like a twig. His bone was sticking out of his arm. He was screaming, and the guys in the bar took him to the hospital. He didn't say anything. He knew better.

"I got in trouble with Dominick for doing that. Not because I broke his arm. Because I did it in front of the bar.

"Dominick said, 'You fucking idiot, what are you doing? You're going to bring heat around here. What the fuck are you doing? I don't give a fuck, shoot the motherfucker. I don't give a shit. But don't do it in front of the bar."

*

In September of 1986, while technically still in the Coast Guard, Lawton was sitting at the Turquoise Bar on Third Avenue in Brooklyn when in walked a "hot-looking" girl by the name of Roselyn Giordano. He was 26. She was 19.

"She was a good-looking girl, had the Italian look, and was well respected. She came from a good family."

Lawton also liked her because she worked in a bank.

"She was a teller at the York Savings and Loan on Third Avenue. At night I would dream about how I was going to rob it."

A year later, on September 11, 1987, they were married at Regina Pace Church, a beautiful edifice on 65th Street between 13th and 14th Avenue in Brooklyn in an old Italian neighborhood. The priest informed Lawton the church was booked on the Friday he chose to get married.

"You want to talk about corrupt Catholic priests. I gave the priest two thousand dollars, and he switched the date for the other couple."

They had a typical extravagant mob wedding, which was attended by members of both the Gambino and Columbo crime families. The bride's father, who worked as a foreign exchange broker for Noonan, Ashley, and Pierce, arranged to rent the limousine owned by Carmine Persico, head of the Columbo family.

Lenny, Lawton's future father-in-law, knew the people at Romanique, a mob-owned limo business in Brooklyn on 11th Avenue and 67th Street."

After everyone sang "Ave Maria," the bride and groom took off in Carmine Persico's limousine. On the way Lawton ordered the driver to take him to the Homestretch. While his bride stayed in the car, Larry and his brother David got out and had a few drinks with the guys at the bar. They then got back in the limo and proceeded to the reception at the Oriental Manor, another notorious mob-owned business. Standing guard at the door were two brutes named Bruno and Netti, muscle for the Gambino mob.

Lawton was partying with Lenny, his new brother-in law, doing coke in the bathroom when Lawton's father-in-law walked in on them.

"He never said a word, and I always had a lot of respect for him for that," said Lawton. "He knew I was wrong, and I knew I was wrong, but words didn't have to be said."

During the reception one of Lawton's pals from the Coast Guard became drunk and out of control. Bruno walked over to Lawton and in a heavy Italian accent asked him, "Do you wanna me to take care of him?"

"Bruno, a stone-cold killer, loved me," said Lawton. "He could barely speak English. One time he took me to his house and showed me all his guns taped up with wrapped handles so they didn't leave fingerprints. Another time Bruno was losing at the poker machine at the Homestretch, and he shot it. We got Bruno a job at the Diamond Exchange, and he got mad and shot his boss in the ass. So when Bruno wanted to know if I wanted him to take care of my Coast Guard buddy, I immediately ran to my boss, Willie the Weeper.

"Willie, will you please take care of this fucking nut?"

Bride and groom honeymooned on a cruise to the Bahamas. After they returned, Larry decided he owed it to his new bride to get away from his wise guy life and go straight. He moved to Fort Lauderdale, near Miami on the east coast of Florida, where his aunt got him a job with the phone company as a 411 operator. People called for information, and he gave it to them. He lasted at the job six months. The lack of action drove him crazy.

His father in law had given the newlyweds $30,000, money Lawton spent to buy and open a pizzeria in North Lauderdale.

The pizza business also was too tame.

"I tried to lead a legit life, but I couldn't do it. It was too boring. I needed action."

The action he craved came from the boys at the Homestretch. Though he was living in Florida, anytime Dominick Gangi or Willie the Weeper beckoned him back to New York to perform a service he came running.

"I lived in Florida, and I would often get a phone call from New York," said Lawton. "Often it involved my strong-arming someone who owed Dominick or Willie money. One time I was called to get a kid who robbed one of our bookies to tell us where the money was.

"Willie said, 'Larry, this guy robbed $75,000. We know he did it. He's 21 years old. His friend told on him. He was with another guy. His friend knew somebody, so he definitely did it.'"

Lawton said he'd take care of it.

"Get that fucking money, Larry," Willie said. "I don't give a shit. Get that money."

Lawton and another Gambino flunkie grabbed the kid off the street and brought him back to the Homestretch. They lifted up one of the steel plates on the sidewalk in front of the bar, and walked the kid down the steps leading to the basement under the bar. They dropped the plate. The room was soundproof. Lawton could work his charm without worry that anyone could hear what was going on.

"I tied his hands and legs behind him to a chair," said Lawton. "I unbuckled his pants, and I pulled his pants all the way down to his ankles. I took the tee shirt he wore, and I pulled it up over his head and off. He was sitting there naked with his dick hanging out."

Lawton said to Joe Cap, his accomplice, "Go get an iron and an extension cord."

The kid began screaming, "I didn't do it. "I swear to God."

Listen to me," Lawton said to the kid. "We know you did it. Just tell me where the money is. I'll give you one warning. Trust me. My word is everything."

"No, I swear to God," said the kid. "You have the wrong guy. The guy who told on me doesn't know."

"Listen to me," Lawton said, "I'm telling you we *know* it was you."

The plugged-in iron was getting so hot Lawton could feel its heat. He picked it up and looked into the kid's eyes.

"Where is the fucking money?"

"I swear…." The kid started to say, and before he could say another word Lawton took the iron and pushed it onto the kid's stomach right below his breasts.

His scream was horrific.

Said Lawton, "To this day there's a guy running around with the shape of an iron on his chest."

Lawton could see the fear in the kid's eyes. Lawton stared down at his dick, and he looked back at him, and he said, "I'm going to ask you one more time." Lawton was holding the iron and looking back down at his dick.

Lawton looked at him and said, "Where's the money?"

Frantically the kid said, "Sixty eighth Street and Seventh

Avenue. It's in my apartment behind the bureau in my bedroom."

"You got the keys?"

"I got the keys."

Joe, grab his keys," Lawton said to his accomplice. "I'll wait with him."

Twenty-five minutes later Joe Cap returned with the money. There was $70,000 left. The kid had spent the other five thousand.

"Now let me ask you," Lawton said to the kid, "was it worth you having that nice fucking iron mark on your chest? Here's what I'm going to do. I'm going to let you go, and you tell all your punk friends that anyone who ever fucks with one of our guys around here, they won't come out alive."

"Let him go, Joe," Lawton ordered.

"The kid was crying," said Lawton. "He was really, really scared, and he had every right to be. And we let him go. And we never had another problem."

Another time Lawton was called up to New York because Willie the Weeper had bought a brand new 1991 Cadillac with the fancy chrome bumpers, and while he was visiting his mother down near Prospect Park, someone had stolen the bumpers off the car.

Unfortunately for the thief, a lady on the street saw who did it and left a note on Willie's windshield saying, "I saw this guy taking the bumpers off your car," and she wrote down the thief's license plate number.

Said Lawton "We could find out who belonged to the car

because we had cops on the payroll. This cop ran the plate, and we found the guy who did it lived right around the corner from the Homestretch Bar. He probably knew Willie. He had to be nuts to rob that car. Everybody knew Willie's car.

"We got the guy, and we brought him down to the cellar. We could see he knew he had fucked up bad. This kid almost shit in his pants. We didn't do anything to him. We made him put Willie's bumpers back on, and we made him a deal where whenever he robbed a bumper, he paid us two hundred dollars per. We turned him into a robber for us. Why hurt him? The guy was good at robbing bumpers. He cut them clean as a whistle. He didn't scratch them. He knew never to screw with us, because we knew all the chop shops he was selling the bumpers to. That's where smarts come in."

Wise guys can recognize other wise guys. Not long after Lawton opened his pizzeria in Fort Lauderdale, a man on the fringes of organized crime by the name of Paulie sought him out. Paulie, who drove a Delorean, owned a store that sold cell phones. He was also a small-time jewel robber. They were both New Yorkers, and they got to talking, and Paulie wanted to know if Larry was interested in buying some diamonds. Larry didn't know the first thing about jewelry, but he figured he was smart enough to figure it out. Paulie several times brought him diamond rings which he bought cheap for cash.

"I started running hot diamonds out the back door of the pizzeria," said Lawton. "I'd look at a ring, and look at the Zales jewelry ads. 'Hey, this looks good.' Robbing a diamond or two is what punks do. These guys are smash and grabbers. They go into a jewelry store, bust a display case and run off with a handful of jewels. My guess is that Paulie or one of his guys was breaking into homes and taking private jewelry, and he'd bring it to me.

"Other people were also coming to me with jewelry they stole, and with my connections in New York, I was able to get rid of it. Sometimes the jewels would come from house robberies – three diamond rings. I didn't care where. I wasn't a petty guy. But I would take the jewels to Willie at the bar, and I'd make a little money. I'm talking small, a few dollars."

Seeing that Lawton was involved with jewels, one day while he was at the Homestretch, Willie the Weeper told him, "Hey, we got something going down in Florida for you." Here was a can't-miss scam right in his own back yard. They informed him that a jewelry store owner in Sunrise, Florida, wanted to be robbed so he could collect on the insurance. Willie the Weeper told him, "We want you to rob it. You give us the diamonds, and we'll give you a cut."

"Sounds great," said Lawton, who didn't ask how much of a cut or much of anything else.

Lawton spent a few days casing the store. He saw what time the female employee arrived and when she left. He wasn't as thorough as he would be in subsequent robberies because the owner was in on it. The female worker would be the only employee in the store who didn't know it was a set up.

Willie the Weeper told him, "Do it as a real robbery – in case you get caught. Make sure you clean out the safe and the counters -- make it a real robbery cause it has to look legit."

Lawton went in, looked around, and pulled out a gun. He said, "This is a robbery."

The girl sprinted for the back of the store. She was going for a gun. Lawton jumped over the counter, caught her, put her on the floor, and tied her up. Lawton knew in advance where the jewelry was going to be. There was a counter in the back of the store with shelves of jewelry. Lawton cleaned out the counters and shelves quickly, went to the safe and took everything. It was loaded with jewels.

"I'm sure the owner left everything in the safe," said Lawton.

Lawton walked out the back of the store with two pillowcases full of jewelry. He then went home, put them in a suitcase, drove to the airport, checked the bag, and flew to New York, arriving at his father in law's house in Bay Ridge, Brooklyn. Lawton spread the hundreds of jewels out on a bed. He gave a ring or two to his wife, and a couple of pieces to his mother-in-law.

Larry found the fence with help from his mob buddies. He was told the address, and he drove to Little Italy in Manhattan to meet the men who were going to buy his jewelry. They were members of the Genevese crime family, and they agreed to drive to his father-in-law's home to see the jewelry and evaluate what the jewels were worth.

When they arrived the jewels were laid out on the dining room table. Lawton had no idea what they were worth, but he decided he wanted $225,000 for them. After a fierce negotiation, they haggled him down to $150,000.

The Genovese mobsters said they would bring the cash

to his father in law's house the next day. Lawton didn't know these men, and he was concerned that they might try to rob the jewels *and* the money from him. He had his brother in law behind the bar waiting with a pistol and a shotgun. Larry also had a pistol.

"I was ready to kill people," said Lawton.

It turned out that the fence was as concerned about the transaction as he was. He told Lawton, "I didn't know what was going to happen to me, whether it was a cop set up or whether you were going to kill me."

The transaction went flawlessly, and it was the first of many. One of the fence's men came in, handed Lawton a paper bag full of cash, and walked out with the jewels. In the bag was a hundred and fifty thousand dollars in cash.

"After he walked away, I was pretty damn happy," said Lawton.

With $150,000 in his safe, Lawton had the dough to open his own bookie operation and to start loan sharking. It wasn't long before both businesses were flourishing but Lawton still had the gambling bug.

"Starting businesses like that aren't hard. A guy knows you're in the gangster business, and he comes to you. 'Do you know where I can bet? Do you know where I can borrow some money?'

The loan sharking business would open Lawton up to a number of very lucrative scores. One of his first customers was a man who worked in a large warehouse. He had borrowed $3,000 from one of Lawton's several bookmakers. The bookie told Lawton, "I know he can't pay." Lawton knew what the man did for a living and came up with the next move.

Lawton had a guy named Junior, another man who worked for him, go to the debtor and tell him that he would pay off the $3,000 debt if the man was willing to pay him $90 a week and pay him back in full in six months.

"Is that okay?" Happily, the man agreed.

"Now the guy could bet again," said Lawton. "He's trying for the big score, and for awhile he did win, but then there was a downturn, and he stopped paying.

"He was a typical gambler."

Lawton told Junior to send the debtor to him.

Said Lawton, "He has to come up with the $90, and on Friday he tells me he doesn't have it, can I be a little patient, and when a guy's late a few days, I know he doesn't have the money. When he goes to the bookie to make another bet, the bookie cuts him off. He still wants to gamble, but he has no way out.

"I know what he does for a living. This guy was the warehouse manager for Johnson Enterprises, which had a warehouse the size of a football field. The warehouse was located in Sunrise, Florida.

"I called him up and say to him, 'Listen, you owe $3,000, right. You want to get rid of that debt?'

"What do you mean?" He was all nervous.

"I said, 'Here's what you do. On a Sunday I'll get a truck,

and we'll go to your warehouse, and you help us load up, and that's the end of it. They will never know they were robbed.'

"'Okay, we'll do it.'"

On a Sunday Lawton rented a 32-foot long Ryder truck, drove to the warehouse and helped his crew load the truck. They took gold faucets, urinals, copper wire, three Jacuzzis, one for his house, and a double porcelain sink. Lawton drove the truck to New York and sold the merchandise for $70,000. When he returned he even gave the guy who owed him the money a few thousand dollars,

"And he was happy," said Lawton. "As I predicted, they never knew they had been robbed. I think the guy still works for Johnson. I'm not kidding.

"But that's how you do it. You come up with those kinds of scams and make money. My biggest thing was I liked to win. It was about beating the system. I was smarter than the average gangster. I knew how to hustle and to make money."

CHAPTER 3

Loyalty

After the success of the Sunrise robbery and his other gangsterly pursuits, Larry Lawton was living well for the first time. The mobsters in New York, and Dominick Gangi in particular, wondered whether it had all gone to his head. Now that he had money they wanted to know whether Lawton would be as loyal to them in the future as he had in the past.

One afternoon the phone rang at home. It was Willie the Weeper.

"Larry, Dominick wants you up here in the morning. Nine o'clock."

Larry hung up the phone and caught the first Delta flight out to New York, and when he arrived at LaGuardia he was picked up by a driver from My Way cab service, the Gambino's personal cab company.

"I'd get in the car, and he'd hand me a pistol – because I couldn't carry a pistol on the plane – and I'd be sitting in the passenger seat up front scaring the crap out of the cabbie because I'd be cursing at the traffic on the Belt Parkway going from LaGuardia to the Homestretch Bar in Bensonhurst. Here I had just left beautiful Fort Lauderdale, and you know the way Brooklyn is, dirty and stopped up with traffic.

"I always made sure I got there. At nine in the morning

on a Friday Dominick was there, and we started playing gin. I didn't say a word. That was important. I didn't say, 'Why am I here?' On Friday the mob guys would play cards with the big earners. Joey Grillo, a guy my age who ran drugs while I ran robberies and warehouse hits, was there. Joey and I were very close. We played cards all day. Dominick never once said a word about why he wanted me up there. And I didn't say a word. Later I learned he just wanted to see if I'd drop everything and come up.

"I usually stayed until Sunday. Saturday night I'd go out with the boys. I'd hang out with the guys, and on Sunday I'd go back to Florida.

"One day I asked Willie the Weeper, 'Hey Willie, what was up with my coming up that one time?'

"Listen, you passed a big test," he said.

"What do you mean?"

"We all knew you were making tons of money in Florida." He continued, "Dominick tested to see how big your head was getting. If you'd have said, 'Dom, can it wait?' he might have questioned your loyalty. Because he might need you for something real important. But you passed a really good test. That's what loyalty really is all about."

"If I call up a friend and say, "I need you," you'll know the kind of friend he is if he says, "What do I need to do?" or "What's it about?" Are you going to be there or not? You don't ask questions. You just come. Whatever you had to do, you did."

Lawton had joined with the Gambinos because he knew

he would need their protection, and twice they would come to his rescue. The first time came when a made man from the Gambino family by the name of Mike the Bandit approached Lawton and told him he wanted Lawton to fence his jewels through him.

"He was a short little Italian guy, about 60 years old," said Lawton. "He was a hustler too. He was trying to horn in on my hustle. I was supposed to respect him, but I was making more than he was. A lot of the made men didn't make the money I was making, so I was very well respected as far as being an earner for the family."

To get out from under Mike the Bandit, Lawton appealed directly to Dominick Gangi.

"I said to Dominick, 'Mike wants to move in on my action. I have a great fence. I don't need him, and I don't need his shit. Who needs this crap? I'm making top dollar, and everybody's making money.'

"'Larry, I will take care of it,' said Dominick. 'Don't worry about it.'

"We always went to LaPalina restaurant in Brooklyn on Friday night – mob night.

Eight guys sat around this big round table including Mike the Bandit. There was no menu. They brought us pasta and a table-full of dishes, and at the end of the meal we had the old-time Italian expresso with sambucca.

"Dominick said, 'Nobody in here talks to Larry about anything.' And Mike the Bandit looked right at me. He was glaring. Because he wanted to get in on all my action. He was thinking about some kind of bullshit he could pull. But he couldn't, because Dominick said he couldn't."

After the two and a half hour meal Lawton went back to the Homestretch. Some guys stayed downstairs and others went upstairs to play high-stakes poker including Dominick Gangi. Mike the Bandit never bothered Lawton again.

The next incident Lawton got himself involved in could have resulted in a bad ending for him had Dominick Gangi not intervened. Being connected probably saved Lawton's life.

He was down in Florida living the large life. He visited a nightclub called Flixx, owned by a guy named Ernie (Lawton never did know his last name), a friend of his who had inherited $30 million. His father had owned a company that did most of the asbestos removal in New York City.

Ernie and Larry went to the high-roller area of the nightclub, and they were up there drinking when a guy who Larry had never seen before started mouthing off to a girl Larry knew. Larry slugged him, bam, and the guy went flying backward. The guy quickly got up and came toward Lawton, but Ernie stepped between them.

"We'll take you in the back and put you in a 55-gallon drum, you motherfucker," said Ernie. "Get the fuck out of here." Larry had no idea who the guy was. Six months later Larry was in the Homestretch, when who walks in but the same guy he had decked.

Said Lawton, "He's with another guy, and he recognizes me, and he says, 'He's dead. That guy's dead. I don't give a fuck.'

Who the fuck does he think he is? thought Lawton

"My immediate boss, Willie the Weeper, said, 'What's going on?'

"I'm there with all my guys, Joey, Frankie, Jackie, Mike the Bandit, and Joe Kapp. I hear from Willie that the guy is a made man with the Bonanno family.

"Willie cleared out the bar. Forty people were standing on the sidewalk in front of the bar in Brooklyn. This was a Saturday, and I was at one end of the bar. Joey, my right-hand man, was with me. Joey was my equal. He was an earner who sold drugs. And he was a big guy. He could hit somebody. You don't fuck with us kind of guys.

"I said, 'Willie, I didn't know who the fucking guy was. He was disrespecting a girl down in Florida, and I smacked him. What the fuck you want me to do? It was Florida.'"

Willie knew he had to call Dominick Gangi, his boss, to straighten this out. The man Lawton had hit was equal in rank to Willie the Weeper, powerful, but not as powerful as Dominick. Lawton was pretty sure Dominick would protect him because of all the money he was passing up to him.

"It's all about money," said Lawton. "That's all they really care about. And we had a very strong crew. Even John Gotti knew about our crew. People got a lot of money from us. So Dominick had a lot of juice. If Dominick said something, it got done. Dominick used to meet with Paul Castallano, so Dominick was up there on the mob ladder."

It took Dominick about forty minutes to drive from New Jersey to the bar. He was just in time. The tension at the bar was growing.

"I was always carrying a pistol, and on this day I was carrying two," said Lawton. "I'm saying to Joey, 'I have to kill this motherfucker. I have to kill him. Because he's going to want to kill me. Maybe I should do it now. I ought to shoot the motherfucker.'

"Calm down, Larry, you fucking psycho," Joey says.

"I got two pistols. I can shoot everybody. I don't give a fuck."

"I thought like that. This was the business I was in. The guy was staring down the bar with his gorilla friend, and I was talking to Joey, eyeing that motherfucker, ready to pull pistols. If he made a move, I was going to shoot the fucker."

They were sitting there at the bar exchanging dirty looks when Dominick's car pulled into the spot directly in front of The Homestretch. No one parked there. It was Dominick's spot. If ever someone tried to park there, someone from the bar would come out and say, "Get out of there." They always did.

"When Dominick pulled in, everyone was standing out front," said Lawton. "Dominick knew a little bit about what was going on. You have to picture him: short, slick-back hair, an old timer. He comes walking in with his funny strut. Dominick calls Willie over, and they talk.

"Before he comes over to me, he walks over to the guy and shakes his hand. The guy knew who Dominick was. Then Dominick gives me a nod, and we went into the back. Joey waited at the bar.

"'Come here, kid.' Dominick called me kid. He liked me. Or he called me Larry Florida. I was Crazy Larry, or Larry Florida."

Dominick asked Larry what had happened.

Lawton told him, "Dominick, the guy came into the bar. It was in Ernie's place. The guy was disrespectful to the girl. I smacked him."

"You smacked him?"

"I punched him," Lawton corrected himself. There was a difference: a smack is more disrespectful than a punch.

"I hit the guy."

Dominick told him, "I'm going to have to straighten this out. You have to apologize to this guy." Lawton said he'd do whatever Dominick asked him to do.

At this point Lawton could breathe easy. He feared that maybe he would have had to get out of town, that Dominick would say, "I can't protect you here." But he didn't.

"That's how much juice I had," said Lawton. "Dominick was getting envelopes with thirty thousand, forty thousand from me twice a year. Dominick wanted the money.

"We'd go in the bathroom, and I'd say, "We had a nice score. Here's an envelope, and I took a few diamonds for you." He'd look through them and take one, maybe a nice two carat diamond, for his wife or his daughter. He'd stick it in his pocket.

"Be careful, kid," he'd say. "Shut your mouth. Nobody knows nothing."

After Dominick and Lawton talked in the back, they

emerged into the bar. Dominick called Lawton's antagonist over. The guy was still royally pissed off.

"This fucking punk did this," he was saying. "Who does he think he is?"

"Hold on. Hold on," Dominick said. As instructed, Lawton attempted to apologize.

"I'm sorry," he said. "I didn't know who you were. I do apologize. I was out of line." Lawton wanted to but didn't say, "You were a jerk off motherfucker." Instead he tried to be nice. He said, "I was out of line."

His curt reply: "I don't give a fuck who you know."

Dominick stopped the conversation. He motioned Lawton to sit down, and he made a rare phone call on the pay phone. He only said a few words, because the mob guys knew the phones were tapped by the FBI.

Dominick came back and said to the guy, "I just got off the phone with your boss. Anything happens to this kid, and you won't make six o'clock tonight. I don't give a fuck if he gets hit by a car. Now take your fucking ass and get the fuck out of here."

Sure enough, the guy left.

Said Lawton, "I'm feeling like a million bucks. The guy went out pissed. I was thinking he was going to try something. But I was packing. Dominick said to me, 'You don't tell nobody nothing.'

"Everyone waiting outside came back into the bar. Everyone knew what had happened, that Dominick had my back. My stature went up a notch.

"I said to Joey, 'I thought I was fucking dead, man. Fuck that. I ain't dying for any of these motherfuckers.'"

"You sick bastard," was all Joey could say.

Dominick hung around for a few minutes talking to the guys. He told Willie, "Watch the Kid." He knew he would.

Lawton returned to Florida, and it wasn't long before he decided that with all his other hustles, he didn't have time for the pizzeria.

"I was sitting at the kitchen table with my wife, and I thought, *Fuck this shit. It's too much work. I'm making too much money. This fucking place has got to go. I'll get the insurance money.*"

Lawton decided the way to get rid of it was to burn it down. He didn't know what he was doing, and he had no idea how good the fire marshals were, and they are good. His first attempt was to try to light the ceiling on fire, "just fooling around to see if it would light." Lawton held the lighter up to the asbestos ceiling, but it only made a mark.

Then he told himself, *Okay, on Sunday I'm going to do it.* The pizza parlor had an alarm system. He wondered. *What do I do?*

The pizza parlor closed at seven on Sundays. Lawton had arranged to go to a friend's house with his wife to sit in the Jacuzzi and drink some wine. Lawton's wife didn't know he was going to burn it. She never said a word. Lawton never once questioned her loyalty to even question him.

Before they left the pizzeria Lawton set a garbage can on fire, set the alarm, and walked out. He went to his friend's house and waited for his beeper to go off telling him what number to call so he could learn his place was on fire.

"We went into the Jacuzzi, drank wine, talked. I didn't get a phone call. *What the fuck?*"

Later that evening Lawton returned to the pizzeria. There was no sign of a fire. He walked in. The fire had gone up the wall, but had gone out. Nothing else caught on fire. So he took a lighter, and he lit the pizza boxes piled in the back of the restaurant. He put the alarm back on, walked out, and drove home.

Fifteen minutes later he got a call. "Your pizzeria is on fire."

"I drove down to the pizzeria, and the whole plaza was ablaze," said Lawton. "Fire trucks were everywhere. The smoke from the fire wiped out four other stores. There was a beverage store, an insurance place, and a barbeque restaurant. I wiped them all out of business."

"My God, oh my God. My pizza place…"

The fire adjusters came in, and they talked to Lawton about his insurance. Little did he know that the fire marshals had started an investigation. They discovered three origins of the fire, the one where he hit the ceiling with the lighter just to test it, the one on the side of the wall, and the pizza boxes.

"So holy fuck, they know it's arson."

But that wasn't what he was saying to the fire marshals. He told them, "I don't know who did it. My cook has a code key. The cleaning person has a code key. I have one. My wife has one. A friend has one."

"So now the insurance company won't pay up, and I

take them to court. And I lose. And a detective from North Lauderdale tries to get me for arson. He calls my wife in. He says, 'We know he did it. It'll be okay. Just tell me...'

"She kept saying, 'I don't know anything. I don't know anything. I don't know anything.' I said the same thing, and eventually they dropped the case."

One great irony was that a couple weeks after the fire two of the other store owners approached Lawton.

"I'm sorry you're pizza parlor burned down. The good news is that I'm getting my insurance money."

CHAPTER 4

The Daytona $800,000

After Larry Lawton burned down his pizzeria, he needed to find a legitimate job. How else could he explain his income derived from his bookmaking and loan sharking operations?

"You have to have something on the books," he said. "Someone I ran across, a guy I didn't even know, told me there was a job opening for someone to run a security company."

Lawton had always wanted to carry a concealed weapon, using the excuse of wanting to protect himself from anyone trying to rip him off, so he took and passed the test to become a private detective certified by the state of Florida. The license allowed him to carry a gun. It also enabled him to get the job as the operations manager of the University Security Company.

"University Security was owned by a man by the name of Paul Eidner," Lawton said. "He was a pretty good guy and we became friends, or at least I thought we were. My secretary used to love to give us both blow jobs, and she liked to eat pussy, so then we'd bring in another broad, so it was a wild time. I loved it.

"Paul brought me in to work for him at University Security because he saw he was smart and street smart as well. He wanted to do things on the edge, and even over it, but he didn't have the balls -- things like overbilling, ghost billing, and paying people off.

All the skills Lawton learned in New York City came into play. He immediately began scamming. First he studied his accounts. University Security did security work for condo associations and hotels, and it also had a contract with the school board of Broward County.

"The secret of running a security company is to bill as many hours as possible at eight dollars an hour while paying his employees the minimum of $4.25 an hour," said Lawton. Better yet, Lawton saw, was taking in the eight dollars an hour and *not* paying anyone anything.

Lawton went to the Bahia Mar Hotel, where he paid the hotel manager cash under the table to inflate his hours. As part of the deal Lawton was comped a suite at the hotel any time he pleased.

His most profitable arrangement was with the school board of Broward County. The job of the company was to provide security to the schools, both during the day and also at night.

"I paid a guy by the name of Russ Cochrane five hundred a week, and for that money he signed off hours for guards that were never there," said Lawton. "I was getting eight dollars an hour for every hour a guard was on a building. I paid them minimum wage -- $4.25 an hour. If a school had a broken window, it had to put a guard there. Sometimes I'd hire a kid to break windows at school buildings. Now they had to call me for guards. I made a ton of money."

Lawton was operations manager in charge of a hundred employees. As a result of his organizational ability – and his scamming -- the security company thrived.

It was a decent living, but for Lawton it wasn't good enough, and once Lawton experienced how easy it was to rob the Sunrise, Florida, jewelry store and to dispose of the jewels, he made the decision to make robbing jewelry stores his primary living.

"The big thing I had learned growing up in the mob life was to never rob something if you can't get rid of it," he said. "You always have to have an out. Just like the Johnson Enterprises job. Before we took the merchandise I had met a guy at the Homestretch who had a plumbing company, and he had a contract with the New York Public School System. He was redoing bathrooms, and so he told me he needed pipe, toilets, and urinals. Who else wants to buy a urinal? You have to sell it to someone who wants it. Otherwise the stuff sits in a warehouse and eats up your money."

Before he burned his pizzeria, there was a wedding dress store just a couple of plazas away. Lawton noticed that it was closed Mondays. He was in New York at the Homestretch bar during one of his weekend visits, when he began talking to a man who owned a wedding dress store in Brooklyn. A light went off.

"Do you want some wedding dresses?" asked Lawton.
"You're not kidding, are you?"
"I'm next to a fucking wedding shop."
"I'll give you three hundred a dress."

Lawton rented a truck from Ryder and drove it to the back of the wedding shop near his pizzeria. He had walked into the store during business hours, and he saw no evidence of an alarm system.

"I figured the best way to empty the place would be to go around back and with bolt cutters open up the double doors in the back," he said. "I put a big crowbar between those double doors, busted it open, and me, Junior, and a flunkie who worked for me took the wedding dresses out on racks. A hundred of them. The whole store. I emptied it. Every dress in the store. There were boxes in the back, but most of the dresses were on racks, and we rolled them right into the truck and drove straight to New York."

The Brooklyn store owner owed him $30,000 but only had $25,000 in cash. Lawton didn't sweat the other five grand.

"We're good," he said.

Another time a former employee of his called to say he was the security guard at the Miami Convention Center. There was an art show featuring Michelangelo and Picasso paintings.

"Larry, do you want these pictures? I'm the fucking guard."

Lawton said he first had to make some phone calls. He discovered that hot art is difficult to fence because the publicity is great and the uniqueness of the stolen items makes them virtually impossible to sell.

"I couldn't get seven cents on the dollar," said Lawton. "With all the publicity it wasn't worth doing. Like I said, if you're going to rob, you better have an out for the stuff."

For his jewelry store robberies Lawton had a ready-made outfit to buy the stolen gems. In six years he stole more than fifteen million dollars worth of jewels.

"Two or three times a year for six years I took home a bag of cash with between seventy grand and a three hundred and fifty thousand in it," he said. "We're talking untraceable hundred dollar bills. Who's got it better than that?"

Lawton rarely felt remorse about robbing these establishments. The owners ended up with more money than he did after collecting on the insurance, and he knew from personal experience that most jewelry store employees routinely cheated their customers anyway.

"The diamond business is the biggest crook business in the world – these jewelry store owners rob their customers every day."

The reason for that, says Lawton, is that the quality of a diamond is determined by the four Cs – carat size, color, clarity, and cut. The store salesmen, he says, will talk about the first three, but almost never talk about the fourth, the cut, which is actually the most important factor in determining the value of the stone.

"The cut is the actual geometry of the diamond," said Lawton. "It shows how light will go into a diamond, bounce off the side wall of the stone, go out the other side, and come up. If you take a real good diamond and put it under a table where there is little light, it will still glare back at you. But most jewelers don't do that. They show you a diamond under a light, and it doesn't mean a thing. I can show you a piece of garbage that will glare at you under a light."

Lawton says he knows that jewelers do this because several times while he was casing a store he would ask about a particular expensive stone, and he was almost never told about the cut.

"I'd give my spiel about being a contractor, and tell the guy I wanted to spend about ten grand, and he would sit me down and supposedly teach me about diamonds. Diamonds are all about geometry, but these guys never tell you about the cut. And I would be thinking to myself, *He's robbing me. I want to spend ten thousand, and he's showing me a stone that's worth about four grand.* It happens every day.

"A diamond is the third-largest purchase you will ever make after a house and a car," said Lawton. "Nobody researches how the diamond sellers get them, and few people comparison shop. They go into a store, and they are taken in by the salesman. The customer thinks, *This guy is big in the neighborhood. He's really good.* But he's probably the biggest crook in the neighborhood.

"He's like a guy who sells a used car. He's not going to tell you about the engine that was under water and then fixed. Same principle. It's a big sales game, and a lot of these jewelry store owners are criminals."

*

The Sunrise robbery had been easy because it was a set up. A methodical man, Lawton with each subsequent robbery figured out better and better ways to do it. He pondered every variable.

First he had to determine which stores to hit.

"I would check out fifty stores to find the right location," he said. "I'd get a phone book and look up the address of all the jewelry stores. The first rule: stay away from any store on MLK Boulevard, because the security at the stores in minority neighborhoods would be way too tight. You go to the high-end part of town.

"I would then steal a car or rent a car through a neighbor or somebody I knew. I'd say to my neighbor, 'I'll give you cash. I don't have a credit card.' He'd put me down as the co-driver, and I'd be in business." The neighbor knew Lawton was in the mob, but he never questioned why he wanted the car. Lawton always paid him three or four hundred more than the actual rental cost.

Lawton would drive through the city or town, riding around, looking for the perfect score. He'd pick seven or eight possibilities.

"I was so good that just by riding around I could tell if a robbery could be done," he said. "I always looked for a store in a plaza with a Publix or a Winn Dixie supermarket or a big box store like Home Depot or Loews, because I could stand out front of the anchor store or sit in my car and watch the jewelry store, and nobody would think anything of it. Who knew what I was doing? I could have been waiting for my wife to come out from shopping.

"I also looked for a glass window in front of the jewelry store where the sun would be shining in in the morning, so a passer-by couldn't see in because of the glare. To see what was going on inside, the passer-by would have to put his face up to the glass and cup his eyes. That's why most of my robberies took place in the morning."

Alternatively Lawton wanted the store front window facing east or be obstructed by a jewelry display or maybe even a sale sign. If the window was facing west, he would rob the store as the sun was going down.

"If the store was at a bad angle or if I didn't have a situation where I could make a clean getaway, I'd pass it by. This was even before I went inside to scout out whether the store had a decent stash of jewels to rob."

"Once I went inside I wanted to see if the jewelry store had a lot of high-end diamonds. Wholesalers or high-end jewelers would have a thin box about two feet long, and inside that box would be small, folded envelopes with the diamonds in there, and very rarely would this box be hidden in the safe. It would be in a separate hiding spot."

One reason Lawton wore nice jewelry when he entered a store was to get the owner to bring out that box. Once Lawton saw the jewels in that box, he would calculate the value of that box alone. If the haul was rich enough, a light bulb would go off in his head.

Lawton usually passed on robbing the stores from national chains because they didn't have that box.

"With those stores, if you wanted a diamond, they'd order it for you," said Lawton. "That's why I didn't rob places like Zales or Gordons, though I once did rob a Friedman's Jewelers. Friedman was a factory store – a store I don't usually rob. It had no box in the back with loose diamonds. That's why I only got a crummy hundred and fifty thou from them."

Once Lawton determined that the angle of the sun was

right, he would then watch to see who worked in the jewelry store, what kind of cars they drove, and what time they came and left. He would case the store for up to a week or more, sometimes following employees home to see how long it would take them to get there. He had their name from the business card given to him, and he got their numbers from the phone book, and sometimes he would even call their homes to make sure they were there.

"If the guy went back to a shitty apartment, there probably wasn't much value in robbing that store," said Lawton. "If he went back to a mansion, I knew a nice score was coming."

Lawton chose what he felt was the perfect jewelry store to rob in the city of Daytona, Florida. It was just off the main drag off the circle near the bridge heading toward the beach. There was a park across the street. Sometimes Lawton sat on one of the park benches smoking a cigar and cased the store. The store faced the inter-coastal waterway, but a big sale sign blocked the view into the store from the street. After staking it out, he saw the store had three employees, one of whom left at four in the afternoon.

"So from four to six in the afternoon they only had two employees, one less person for me to have to worry about. And from watching I saw that very few people came into the store in the afternoon."

Days before the actual robbery Lawton would get dressed up in slacks and a nice sports jacket, and would go into the jewelry store and get to know everyone who worked there. Lawton was an expert at deception. Sometimes he would put on a band aid or he would tint his hair – something to throw off identification by the victims.

"For this robbery I wore glasses – fake glasses," he said. "The glasses didn't have a prescription, but they were nice. They looked good. I wore a Rolex. I had on a $13,000 diamond bracelet. I wore diamond pinky rings. When I'd walk in, the owner would think, *This guy has money. I'm going to get a good sale out of this.*"

Lawton walked in, pretending to be browsing.

"Can I help you?" the owner asked.

"Yes," Lawton said, "you can. I'm a contractor building houses in the area. I own a condo. I'll be here approximately six months building three houses."

Lawton tried to pick an area where there was new construction so his story would seem plausible.

Before entering the store, Lawton sometimes would have business cards made up. Of course, the card would have a phony name, but not a fictional one. The name on the card would belong to a real resident of the area. Before the Daytona robbery Lawton drove along the beach looking for unlived in condos boarded up with shutters.

"I went into the lobby, found what the number was, and I would get the name of the owner off the board listing the owners. I'd look up the name and get the phone number, and for several days I'd call. The phone would ring and ring, and I kept doing that until I was certain the place was vacant. I then put that name and address on a business card, and I became that person when I went into the jewelry store."

Later on Lawton would learn that the FBI had gotten his fictitious name and number from the store owner, and when they checked for the whereabouts of the man on the business card, they discovered the condo owner was in prison. For a while the FBI thought this guy had sent an accomplice to rob the jewelry store.

If Lawton was unable to find someone's identity to steal, he would tell the jewelry store owner he was Michael Roberts, his two middle names. Sometimes he was Robert Michaels. In Daytona he was the owner of the vacant condo.

Lawton also had a story prepared that he knew would convince a store owner he was on the up and up.

He said, "I'm looking to buy a diamond ring for my wife. Ten years ago when I got married, I bought her a small ¾ carat diamond. I didn't have money back then. I was just starting out in the construction business. Now I'm looking for a two-carat stone."

"Oh, we'll take care of you."

The jeweler then looked at Lawton's $2,000 pinky ring and said, "This diamond is kind of dirty. It needs cleaning."

"Can you clean it?"

"Oh sure. Can you come back and get it?"

"That's fine."

"Can you fill out a slip?"

Lawton joked, "That's worth money. I don't want you to steal it on me." And the jewelry store owner then wrote down the condo owner's name and his phone number on the slip of paper.

"When it's done, give me a call," said Lawton, knowing the phone call would go unanswered. If he couldn't arrange a phone number to call, he'd tell the owner, "I'll stop by in a couple of days because I'm traveling," or because he was building a house or whatever else he was "doing."

And because Lawton had given him his expensive diamond to clean, the clueless owner felt perfectly comfortable showing him his best pieces.

"The owner sees me as a classy looking guy," said Lawton. "I have tattoos on my body, but I always cover them up. When an owner trusts you, he's no longer afraid of taking his diamonds from the safe or the other hiding spot. He'll bring out the box that contains the loose diamonds for special customers. Getting him to show me that box is an important factor in a robbery."

Lawton already had valued the jewels in the display cases, and he figured there had to be at least $300,000 worth of merchandise including some Rolex watches. The owner brought out the small box with the special cache of diamonds.

"This box is rarely kept in the big safe – that's where the jewelry from the display cases is kept," said Lawton. "That small box is kept in a secret area where it will be safe. The owner figures if he is robbed, the robbers won't take the smaller box with the special diamonds. But of course, by watching the owner very closely, he inadvertently shows me where he keeps it, and it's no longer safe."

The store owner went and got the small box, opened it, and showed him the expensive bling. There was a small fortune inside that box. In his head Lawton added up the value of the diamonds and other jewels stored therein. In his head he said to himself, *There's a half a million here. This is where the money is. This is going to be a big score.* He couldn't wait to tell his crew holed up back in a cheap hotel room under false names.

"Now everything's a go," he said. "I know where all the jewels are, and I know the best time to rob it, late in the afternoon when few people would be entering the store."

Lawton already knew how many people worked there, what kind of cars they drove, and when they arrived and when they left. He knew who opened and who closed the store.

While Lawton was browsing he always looked to see where the security buzzers that summoned the police were located. Some owners had alarm triggers in their pockets on a key chain. They could buzz you in, and they could also alert the police. Often Lawton knew when he announced a robbery he had to make sure the hands of the store owner were visible. He'd put a gun in the owner's face before he could even think to put his hands in his pocket.

Lawton didn't care about the front door buzzer that was rung to admit people into the store. Those were good for Lawton. They kept out customers during robberies. They might stop the smash and grab robbers but not a professional like Lawton. A buzzer doesn't stop a customer wearing a Rolex. Store owners want the Rolex owners *in* their store.

Lawton came back the next day, fully prepared to rob the place. He had bought two large pillow cases, folded them nicely, and put them under his pants in front. He stuffed wire ties like the cops use in his jacket pocket. He hid rubber gloves in another pocket. His bb gun was in his belt in the small of his back. And he brought his unnamed accomplice.

On this day the owner buzzed Lawton in. Lawton opened the door with his knuckles, making sure never to leave fingerprints. He was conscious never to touch anything. In twenty robberies, Lawton never left a single print. The FBI once pulled a palm print after Lawton jumped over a jewelry display case, but the bureau doesn't have palm prints on record.

After Lawton and his accomplice walked into the store, Lawton told the owner, "My partner is also in the construction business." He gave a phony name. He too was dressed well. "He also wants a ring for his wife." The owner had no suspicions at all.

 When they walked in the store owner was talking to his landlord.

"You have a customer," said the landlord. "I'll come back tomorrow." The landlord walked out.

Lawton waited until the owner walked away from the security buzzers that summoned the police. This was the man Lawton had to subdue. He made it a policy to take the guy who might cause trouble down hard.

The owner was standing between the counters. Lawton's partner, meanwhile, walked over to the other employee.

Lawton abruptly pulled his gun and stuck it in the owner's face. His entire demeanor changed from businessman to psychopath. Lawton became an animal. The owner was behind the counter and out of view of anyone who might be walking by.

"Get down on the floor," Lawton screamed. "This is a fucking robbery. Get down or I'll blow your fucking brains out." The owner was petrified. He was on the floor, and Lawton had a gun to his head. Lawton told him, "If you open your eyes, I'll blow your fucking head off, motherfucker. I dare you to open your fucking eyes."

Lawton looked over to make sure his partner had the other employee tied up on the ground behind the counter. He did. Lawton had cased the place perfectly. No one entered the store.

"We were behind the cabinets, and we opened them and started pulling the jewelry off the shelves and out of the safe," said Lawton. "I then went for the hidden box with the loose stones."

Lawton had a third man outside waiting in the car, which carried a fake license plate in case someone noticed. The plan was for Larry to signal, and his driver was to come around to the back door. When Lawton looked out the front window, he could see there was a police cruiser sitting right in front of the store. He would have to wait for the cruiser to leave before he could signal his wheel man. The twenty-minute wait seemed endless.

"I was waiting, waiting, and waiting," he said, "wondering *What are those fucking cops doing*"

Lawton placed two pillowcases stuffed with diamonds and jewelry by the back door. He and his accomplice remained calm while the owner and his employee laid quietly on the floor tied up and out of sight. Lawton kept screaming, "Keep your eyes shut. Don't let me see them open."

Finally the police car left, and Lawton gave the signal. Lawton told the merchants, "You better not fucking move, because I'm going to have someone watching."

Lawton and his partner fled out the back door, threw the two pillowcases filled with jewelry in the trunk, and headed up International Drive.

"The first thing we did was go to a rest stop and change the fake plate back to the legal one," said Lawton. "We got back in the car and from that moment we never stopped driving except for gas and a quick bathroom break. We drove from Florida to Brooklyn, and within twenty-four hours the diamonds were out of our hands and into those of the fence."

Lawton drove to Little Italy, where, he says, the illegal diamond exchange is located. He parked near his fence's place. He always put money in the meter because he didn't ever want to emerge with his bag of cash to find a policeman giving his car a ticket. He left his two accomplices in the car.

There are a lot of jewelry stores in the area of Manhattan surrounded by Chinatown. Fifty vendors sell their goods in a large store, and underground, below that level, is a vault with a man with a shotgun standing guard. Another man sits in a booth behind a cage. These men, who belonged to the Genovese crime family, were the men who fenced Lawton's pillowcases filled with jewels.

"I would go down there with my loot, go in the back room, and dump it out," he said. "If there was any evidence I wanted to get rid of – the pillow cases, the fake license plate, my clothes – I could burn it in their incinerator that they used to melt gold."

Over time Lawton got to know these guys so well that when he went down there, they hardly paid him any attention. In looking around Lawton could see their entire operation. He saw that they kept their money under a false baseboard along the wall. They would move the board and slide out a large suitcase filled with millions in cash in hundred dollar bills. From that suitcase came the money they used to pay Lawton. Before handing it over, they ran the bills through a counting machine which spit out any counterfeit bills. They didn't want Lawton getting caught with wrong money. The Daytona robbery netted $800,000 in jewels. The fences put $300,000 in cash in a plain paper bag and handed it to Lawton, who walked down the street to Positano's to talk with Rocky the owner and have his usual vodka rigatoni.

*

Lawton now knew where the Genoveses kept their money, and he told himself, *Jesus, I'm going to rob these motherfuckers.* His head was spinning. There were millions in untraceable bills down there. There was only one guy with a gun, a man who knew him, and the second unarmed man who sat in the booth behind the cage. *I could tie them up and walk out with millions,* Lawton thought.

After Lawton finished eating, he got into the car where his two accomplices were waiting. Lawton made sure his two accomplices never knew the identity of his fence.

Lawton voiced his plan to them. He said, "Hey guys, there

are millions down there. I'm going to rob them. If I go back down there, they'll let me in."

"No, no, Larry," they chimed in unison. "No no, fuck no. You'll get us all killed. You're fucking crazy, Larry." And they were right.

Said Lawton, "In my head I saw myself walking in, taking all that money in the suitcase, and then taking off, but I also knew if I did that, I'd be dead, because it was the Genoveses. I wouldn't have been able to be protected by anybody. Once I robbed them, the news would hit the streets, and the Genoveses would have a number on my head so large I would have had to leave the country and still worry.

"I had a young son. Everyone knew where I lived. My accomplices knew I was totally crazy, and they were begging me not to do it, because they would have had to go on the lam too.

"After thinking about it, I decided not to do it."

He cleaned out a jewelry store in Sarasota, Florida, instead.

After returning home to Florida Lawton got back on the road in his search for the perfect target, and he drove until he came to Sarasota, on the west coast of Florida. He found a good one right on route 441 next to a dive shop. Stopping in Sarasota gave Lawton and his accomplices an opportunity to take advantage of why tourists came to Florida. During the week Lawton spent casing the jewelry store, they were able to go to the beach and to camp out.

"Sarasota is a great place," he said. "I love Lido Beach, the best beach in the country. The sand never gets hot, and you can drink on the beach. I didn't want to be out in the open, but of course, my two accomplices and I went to the beach. When deciding where we should stay, I thought, *Let's be adventurous. Let's go camping.*

"We were three Brooklyn guys camping. I bought a tent, a lantern, all the camping equipment, and we put it in my Cadillac. We don't know anything about camping, but we went to Myakka State Park, and we set up. We didn't even know how to open the tent."

Every morning at six Lawton drove to case the store, leaving the other two behind. He didn't need anyone with him. He didn't *want* anyone with him. He wanted to be alone.

"This was in 1993, right after Hurricane Andrew," he said. "I got all dressed up, wore my Rolex, and I went into the store. I told the owner I was a director for FEMA.

"'I'm Mike Roberts,' I told him, 'and I'm setting up trailers in case there's another hurricane. I'm looking for something for my wife.' It was a great line of conversation. We got talking, and he could see I was an intelligent guy intending to spend some money for his wife. The idea is to get him to trust you."

At the end of the day Lawton returned to the campsite and put a half dozen hamburgers on the grill. He walked away for a minute, when a raccoon walked over, climbed up, and stole one of the hamburgers. Lawton was furious.

I'm going to catch that motherfucker and kill him, Lawton told himself. *I want to wear that little fucker like a hat, like Daniel Boone.*

Lawton set a sheet on the ground, put food in the middle

of it, attached to the four corners of the sheet, and tied the rope over a tree. Lawton waited for the raccoon to walk into the middle of the sheet so he could yank him up and catch him.

The raccoon did just that, but when Lawton yanked on the ropes, the raccoon was too quick for him. He jumped out of the sheet.

"He was quick, but I was determined to catch him," said Lawton. "I laid down a trail of food leading up to the picnic table, and I got out my nine iron, and I waited for him. The little fucker came walking up, closer and closer, and boom, I whacked him so hard with my club that I killed him. I hung the raccoon from a tree to skin him, but I had nothing but a butter knife. The raccoon was hanging there when some guy walked over and saw these three psycho motherfuckers and said, 'You can get in trouble for that. If the ranger sees that, you'll go to jail.' I had no idea. I also had no intention of getting caught killing a raccoon."

There's a wooden bridge at Myakka State Park, an overpass where huge alligators swim underneath. Lawton took the raccoon carcass and fed it to the gators.

It wasn't the threesome's only bout with nature. On another morning when Lawton was away, his brother went into the IHOP for breakfast, while the third man decided to go hiking. He had sneakers on, and he was walking through swamps, and he came back covered in ticks and bugs. He itched for days.

After casing the jewelry store, Lawton finally went inside. There was only one person inside, and he jumped the counter, got him down, tied him up, and started clearing out the place. It was a little store. The cases were only in the back.

While he was cleaning out the counters, an elderly couple walked in on him. He went up to them and informed them, "You're in on a robbery." He showed them his gun.

"Oh my God," the elderly woman said, and she started to get down on the floor.

"No no no no no, ma'am," Lawton said. "You don't have to do that. Come with me. You two sit in these chairs in the back and don't move." He didn't tie them up.

"Face the wall," he said. "Don't look at me. I'm not going to hurt you. Nothing is going to happen to you. Don't move for two minutes until after I leave the store. I'm going to come back in and check. Don't make me be a bad guy."

Later the woman told the feds, "What a nice man."

Lawton ordered one of his crew to go and get the car. There was a dive shop next to the jewelry store and some traffic. He brought the car around, and Lawton wasn't there, so he came back around the front. All the while Lawton was waiting for him out back.

"The moron is back in front, so I have to go back in the store," he said. "The two old folks were still sitting there facing the wall. I went to the front and again gave him the signal to come around back, and finally he gets there, and we put the jewelry in the trunk, and I drove on Route 27 to I-75 to I-4 all the way to my parents' house in Palm Bay, Florida.

"I emptied the bag of jewelry on a bed. Picture a whole bed full of jewelry. It was cool. I loved it."

Lawton called his father in. He said, "Dad, look at this."

"Oh my God. What is going on, son," he said. "If you get in trouble, give me a call. Be careful."

"No one's getting hurt," Lawton said. "Just the insurance company."

He brought his mother in, and she squealed "Oh my god." She held her hands over her mouth. She picked up a diamond ring.

"Ooooh, this looks nice," she said,

"Keep it," said Lawton.

"Of course, she wouldn't, and she was so worried," said Lawton. "What I put that poor woman through."

"I took the jewels to New York and came home with $200,000 cash. It was a decent score."

CHAPTER 5

Diamonds Are a Guy's Best Friend

Larry Lawton's next robbery took place in Fort Lauderdale, his hometown. After casing the entire area, he picked out a promising store, which was a little different in that the jewelry cases were in the middle of the store and along the walls. He went in to look around and was able to locate the security buzzers. Two women worked in the store.

On this beautiful sunny day Lawton and his accomplice drove to the front of the store. As usual he wasn't scared, but his palms were sweating and his adrenaline was pumping. Lawton liked the feeling of the adrenaline high. Over time it would become addictive.

Lawton entered the store by himself. He announced the robbery and made both women employees lie down on the floor behind the counter. He tied them up with plastic flex cuffs, walked to the front door, and nodded to his accomplice waiting in the car to come in. The accomplice then helped him clean out the place.

During the robbery two customers walked into the store. Larry always looked good, so he walked up to the customers, who had no idea a robbery was taking place, put the gun to them, and said, "This is a robbery. Come with me." He walked them to the back of the store and tied them up. Two more came in, and he tied them up. Then two more, and two more, and two more, until he had ten people tied up lying on the floor of the jewelry store. He was running out of flex cuffs, so when the last two customers came in, he was able to tie their hands, but not their legs. He told them not to move if they knew what was good for them.

Each time customers came in, he would ask them, "Is anyone waiting in the car for you? Do you have to be anywhere?" Each time the answer was no. And then he'd tell them, "Close your eyes, and don't you open them. If I catch you with your eyes open…" Lawton never put a gag in anyone's mouth. He didn't want anyone choking to death.

"I never wanted to hurt anyone, ever," he said.

In all his robberies Lawton took jewelry off a customer only once. If a woman was wearing a wedding ring, he never touched it. But on this day one of the customers became belligerent. He started talking big, and so Lawton, wanting to make sure he wasn't a police officer, pulled the guy's wallet out of his pocket. There was no badge inside.

The customer was wearing a gold bracelet, and Lawton took it off and looked at it to see whether it was really made of gold. It wasn't, and it infuriated him.

"You phony piece of shit coming in here like you're a big shot," said Lawton. "You have fake fucking jewelry, you prick." Lawton threw the bracelet back at him. One of the tied-up girls working in the store from behind the counter began to laugh.

Lawton, concerned that someone might be waiting for one of the tied-up customers, reminded himself to get going.

I have to get out of here, Lawton said to himself. He and his accomplice emptied the place of jewels, went out the back door, and kept driving all the way to New York.

After his third heist it occurred to him that if he didn't learn something about the value of diamonds, he would leave himself open to being cheated. There's a school in Manhattan called the Gemological Institute of America (GIA) that teaches everything you'd ever want to know about diamonds. Lawton couldn't risk enrolling officially, but he was told that one of the teachers at the school taught a class for anyone who didn't want it known he was taking his classes. The instructor taught in his apartment three nights a week for two weeks. There were six other "students" in Larry's class where Larry earned his master's degree in diamonds.

It was in this class that Larry learned about the importance of the cut of a diamond.

"He'd pull the felt out, and he'd show you how different diamonds are cut," said Lawton. "He demonstrated a round diamond, an oval diamond, and a princess cut. He explained why a round diamond was worth more than a marquis – it's easier to resell.

"The cut of the diamond is measured geometrically. 5.6 is a perfectly cut round diamond. A good diamond will have six facets.

"He showed us how the reflection of light works into a

diamond. He took a diamond and put it under a table where there was no light.

"'If it still reflects,' he said, 'it's a good cut.'

"He also taught us about color. The range starts at D and goes all the way up the alphabet scale. The lower the letter, the better it is. He showed us how a diamond expert can hide a chip. They are slick. They'll hide it under a facet or put filler in there to hide it. But with the proper cut you can make an F diamond look like a D. I've seen one two-carat diamond ring go for $7,000 and another one go for $100,000. Same size, but a different cut, clarity, and color."

His education complete, Larry Lawton then discovered the mother lode of jewelry stores, H. Stern Jewelers located in the Fontainbleu Hotel in Miami Beach, Florida. He paid the store a visit, masquerading as a wealthy contractor, and after a quick inventory, he determined the store held twelve million dollars in diamonds and jewelry.

This is my store, Lawton told himself. It had so much inventory Lawton decided he needed to talk to his fence before doing anything further. The fence was well-aware of H. Stern Jewelers. Lawton told the Genoveses, "It's between ten and twelve million, and I'm going to get my forty percent. I want four million for the job."

They agreed. The deal provided that he would get a million dollars up front, and a million every two months until he was paid off. They also advised him that if he pulled it off, he'd have to leave Florida for a while, because the heat would be too great.

Lawton began casing the store from a piano bar across the hotel lobby, watching to see who was coming in and out. In the mornings he would act like a hotel resident. He'd put on his bathing suit, and he'd walk through the hotel to the pool, and as he slowly walked around pretending to be a hotel guest, he watched to see when the employees came and when they left. He saw that the store manager arrived thirty minutes before the guard to open the store. Two other employees didn't come in until after the guard arrived, he saw. He would have a thirty-minute window of opportunity. Lawton needed to be out of the store before the guard arrived.

Lawton suspected the store had a time lock on the safe. If there was one, he would have to wait until the manager opened up the safe in the morning. Lawton watched every morning as the store manager put the jewels out for display. Because of the time lock, Lawton couldn't do this job at night. If anyone tried to open it earlier than the regular time, a silent alarm would go off, and the police would be right behind it. The only way he could pull this job off, he saw, was to kidnap the manager at his home at night and go with him to open the store in the morning.

To find out where the store manager lived, one evening Lawton followed him from the Fontainbleu in Miami Beach north on I-95 to his home in Hollywood. After he saw where the manager lived – a nice house in a nice area -- he went and bought the supplies to carry out the rest of his plan.

"I went and bought sticks that I painted to look like dynamite," said Lawton. "I bought a clock and some wires.

What I was going to do was enter his house at night and kidnap the guy. I was going to stay with him all night, strap the 'dynamite' to him, and take him with me. While I did that, I was going to have my accomplice guard his wife and daughter. My accomplice would have a walkie talkie.

"I was going to tell the manager, 'Listen, you're coming with me. If you make one foolish move and this guy doesn't hear from me, he's going to kill your family even if I get caught. He's going to kill your wife and kid? Is it worth it?'

"I was going to strap the fake dynamite on him before we got into the car, and I'd tell him, 'If you do anything stupid, I'm going to run from here and blow you up. If you try to have a traffic accident with me, and the cops come, I'm going to walk away and blow you up. If you're in the car and I see you make any move to attract attention from the cops, I'm going to get out and blow you up. And your family will be dead.'

"I figured since he was only the store manager, it wasn't his diamonds, and he'd give them up.'

"I wasn't really going to kill anyone. After robbing the diamonds, I was going to call my accomplice and say, 'Leave.' I'd be out of Florida on my way to New York before anybody knew what hit him."

His four million cut was going to be Lawton's retirement score. He had no worries about the Genoveses stiffing him. Dominick Gangi's cut was $400,000, and there would have been a mob war if the Genoveses tried something funny and didn't pay.

The night before the planned robbery, Lawton and his

accomplice, carrying his bag of props ready to go, waited in the bushes of the store manager's home. The robbery was a go. The plan was to knock on the door, and when the manager opened the door, rush in and take him and his family hostage.

Lawton's heart was racing. This was to be his biggest score, but it also was his most dangerous. So much could go wrong. As he and his accomplice crouched outside the home, a neighbor came walking by with his dog, who growled at them.

"And that spooked me," said Lawton. "Call it a gut feeling."

The growling of the dog broke the spell. Lawton in an instant decided the plan was too risky, and he called it off.

"And luckily that happened, because kidnapping is a crime that has no statute of limitation."

*

Though he passed on the $4 million from the H. Stern job, Larry still had enough money to become King of Fort Lauderdale. His two favorite passions were sex and gambling, and with the money from his jewel robberies, he had hundreds of thousands of dollars to indulge himself with both.

"I was living the good life. I'd go out every night. I had a wife at home, I was getting blow jobs from my secretary, I had a *gumada,* a girl friend, I had a gorgeous hooker, Teresa, and I'd be banging other broads all day. I had orgies with couples, and I don't know how I did it."

He indulged his every whim.

"I went fishing. I went scuba diving. I did all of that. If I wanted something, I bought it. I had a gold Rolex, gold chains. I had one chain on my arm that spelled out L-a-r-r-y in diamonds. I had it all. That's why when I went and robbed jewelry stores, I looked good, and they thought, *He has money.*"

His neighbors knew Lawton was in the mob, but they didn't seem to care. Every Fourth of July he would throw a party for a thousand people. It was called Larry's Fourth of July Block Party. The entire block was closed down.

"I hired a ride company that brought The Whip, The Bounce House, a trackless train, and a bunch of rides," he said. "The mayor – I was the godfather to his son -- and other city officials came. I had so much pull with the city that they brought Port-a-Potties. They shut the street off. No permits. The fire truck came, and they don't usually bring the fire truck to parties. I had it brought there for the kids. I had clowns painting kids' faces. I had Barney the Purple Dinosaur. I had a band and a DJ. I supplied ten kegs of beer, forty cases of soda, a thousand hot dogs, a thousand hamburgers, and six hundred ears of corn. I held a car show. All free for the neighborhood. I didn't want any money, no donations. And I even donated money to charity. I knew a radio disk jockey, Larry Brewer from Melbourne, a city where my parents lived, and I'd say to him, 'Tell me a home for abused kids that's in need,' and he would tell me, and I would go to Toys R Us and I'd buy two thousand dollars worth of toys for the children in the house. One time I visited the home and saw the kids didn't have sneakers, and I bought them all sneakers.

"I was generous, and people called me Robin Hood. The neighborhood knew I was in the mob. They knew I didn't work, had all the money in the world. They assumed I was a drug dealer, which I wasn't. No one knew exactly what I did, which was the way I wanted it."

Lawton still had the bug for gambling and loved the action at the casinos. He traveled to the Bahamas, Las Vegas, and Atlantic City to gamble.

"I would go to all of these places comped. Once at the casinos in the Bahamas I lost $10,000 in twenty minutes, all the money I brought. I called Fat Tony, my right hand man. I had a safe in my house, and I always kept big money there. My wife didn't even have the combination to the safe. That's just the way we did it. My buddy, Fat Tony, had it.

"'Tony, go to the safe. Get ten thousand. Send Junior on a plane down here with the ten thousand.'

"Junior was there the next morning. And I went back to gambling."

Lawton had carte blanche at the Taj Mahal in Atlantic City. They'd fly him first class from anywhere. Any time he was in Brooklyn and wanted to go, the casino would send a limousine for him. Two of the jet setters Lawton gambled with were Roger King of King World Productions and Pete Rose, baseball great and addicted gambler.

"I was getting the suites on the 49th floor. Roger King was getting the penthouse, with butlers and cooks. Oprah Winfrey used to work for him. I used to do coke with him up in his room, and I'd gamble with him in the casino in the high roller pit.

"One time Roger and I were in the high roller pit, and we were drunk on Dom Perignon. He always had guys with him, like I did. He told one of his guys, 'Go to the cage and cash these chips in.' They were worth about $250,000. The guy came back and said, 'Mr. King, they want your ID.'

"'Fuck my ID. He's not getting my ID. I'll buy this place and fire fucking Trump.' He started climbing up on a chair."

"'Roger, get down,' Lawton said to him.

"Cameras were all over the place, but nobody said a word," said Lawton. "The pit bosses and dealers were looking at him. If you're a big shot, they don't care what you do. All they want is your money.

"I would do coke out of little bottles right in the casino, even though there were a zillion cameras. If you're a big gambler, they don't care.

"I met Pete Rose through Roger. What a fucking junkie gambler Pete was. One night Roger, Pete, and I were up in my hotel suite playing gin for a hundred dollars a hand. Pete didn't care what the game was. He just wanted to gamble.

"Pete's a competitor. I knew he gambled right from the beginning. But he gambled on his own team to win. He never bet against his team. He wanted to win at all costs. He was wrong, because he might let his pitcher go a couple more innings. You're not looking at the bigger picture. But he was such a competitor. I never met a competitor like him. He'd bet roulette, blackjack, gin. He'd bet on two cockroaches walking up a wall. He didn't care what you played. He wanted to gamble. He had a real disease."

Lawton's riches also allowed him to indulge in his every whim. As a child Lawton had been small, so small that at age

12 his grandfather sent him to Florida for a couple of weeks so he could learn how to become a jockey. Lawton always had a fondness for horses, and one afternoon while at home he was watching the movie *Lonesome Dove*, when he called up his associate Fat Tony and said to him, "Get the car. We're going to buy a horse."

"What track are they running at?" he asked.

"Not a race horse. A horse," said Lawton.

"What track?"

"No, it's a riding horse, you fucking nut."

"A trotter?"

"Shut up. Get over here with the car."

Fat Tony drove over and picked Lawton up. They were in a Cadillac, and they drove to the Triple Cross ranch in Davie, Florida. Lawton had seen the sign: *We sell horses.* The three crosses out front made it look like a KKK Ranch, but it was actually a ranch owned by devout Christians.

"We went in the back to see a guy by the name of Mike Fletcher, who was a championship bronc rider. Here came two guys with New York accents dressed in slacks and two hundred dollar loafers in a Cadillac. Can you imagine what he must have been thinking?"

"'Listen, I'm looking to buy a horse,' Lawton said.

"'Are you for real?'

"'If I buy a horse, you have to show me how to ride it. I haven't been on a horse since I was 12.'

"'Okay.'

Said Lawton, "I went looking for one horse, and he ended

up selling me two horses – I couldn't ride alone. I bought two saddles, a trailer, the whole fucking thing – ten thousand dollars later. In cash. And then I gave him $600 a month to board the horses and muck the stalls, and if I came down, to saddle them. Sometimes I'd get stoned on coke or weed and ride around like a nut. But I loved the horses. All because I watched that movie, *Lonesome Dove*."

"What are you going to buy next?" Fat Tony wanted to know.

The answer: a boat. There's an expression: the two best days of a person's life is when he buys a boat and when he sells it. Too bad Lawton had never heard that expression.

Lawton had a buddy named Nicky who owned a gas station in Brooklyn. Nicky was a mobster, and he brought Lawton to a wholesale dealer who sold him a twenty-six-foot cabin cruiser at the auction. Lawton attached the boat and trailer to his new van for a trip to scenic Lake George.

They got on the highway, and the first thing that happened was that an axle on the trailer snapped, and one of the tires fell off. Luckily the boat didn't come off the trailer.

"Here we are sitting on the side of the road not knowing what to do," said Lawton. "We called a tow service, and they towed the boat and trailer on a flatbed to a repair place, where it cost me a thousand bucks to fix it."

Continuing on the trip it turned out that Lawton hadn't hooked the trailer up right. They hit a bump, and the trailer came off the hitch, landing on the roadway, making a deep gouge in the tarmac, and when Lawton hit the brakes, the boat kept going and smashed into the back door of his new van. Fortunately, the chains held, saving the boat..

Lawton stopped, and he and his three cohorts put the hitch back on and drove to Lake George in his dented van.

"We got the boat to Lake George," he said. "We rented an island there. It was a chance to get away. We put the boat in the water, headed towards our island, but we didn't open up the sea water valve, and we burned up the motor. The boat actually caught fire.

"We put the fire out, got towed back, and it cost another $4,500 to fix it. We went back to the island, and we had a good time, but I ended up getting a ticket for not having a spotter in the boat while someone was water skiing. What a fucking disaster!"

The camping trip cost Lawton ten thousand dollars. He was so disgusted that when he got back to Brooklyn, he got rid of everything, including the boat and the new van.

*

Lawton worked at his jewelry store robbing business six weeks a year. Whenever his bankroll would drop below $40,000, he knew it was time to get back in the car, discover America, and find a new jewelry store to rob.

His biggest score came after Lawton drove around the wealthy Maryland suburbs of Washington DC, scouting jewelry stores. He settled on one in an area near Tyson's Corners. The jewelry store he was casing was closed on Monday, so on that day Lawton drove to Washington to visit the White House and do some sightseeing.

"I'm a history buff," he said. "Did you know I can name you forty-four presidents? I can name you every president who got killed in office, and who killed him. Eight died in office. Four were assassinated. I know who the longest serving was. The tallest. The fattest. I'm kind of a savant. I can tell you how many countries there are in the world, their capitals, the smallest, the largest, and their populations. I love history, and that's why I went to the White House.

"I went to the White House with my binoculars, and when I was looking up on the roof, I saw one of the secret service guys looking down on me with his binoculars.

"It was winter. A cold day, so I wore a jacket. I always made sure I had on a nice leather jacket or a long coat that makes you look like a businessman. The coat I wore that day was one of the long coats given to me by the Coast Guard."

The store near Tyson's Corners was perfect because there was construction going on in the mall plaza which made it harder to see into the window of the jewelry store. In front of the store was a boardwalk made of wood.

"The store had display cases in the window, but they were covered in felt so you couldn't see what was in there from outside the store," said Lawton. "That's good for me. That store was made to be robbed."

The owner of the store was a wholesaler, Lawton's preferred target. These were the jewelers who sold to other jewelry stores. The store owner in Maryland was selling to all the little guys all around him. As soon as the store owner showed Lawton his box of loose diamonds, Lawton knew this was going to be a *big* score.

"The Maryland job was a two-man job. My accomplice was in the car. We stayed in a shitty motel – I always stayed in shitty motels, and I kept a low profile.

"I knew when I entered the store that there were two employees, a guy and a girl. First I took down the guy. The girl wasn't going to give me any trouble. I tied them up with flex cuffs, pulled the bags out of my stomach, started filling them up, and then I walked right out the back into a construction site – a perfect spot. When there's a construction site, no one questions a thing when they see a car.

"I put the jewels in the car, and away I went. I always wished I was a fly on the wall so see how long it took them to get out of the flex cuffs and for the cops to arrive.

"I drove straight to Brooklyn, my typical MO. It was only about a six-hour trip. I called my fence on the way and told him I was coming.

"See you tomorrow at one." I stayed in a shitty, little motel in Jersey just across from the George Washington Bridge. I took the jewelry out, spilled it out on the bed, and looked at what I got. By this time I knew quite a bit about diamonds, and I could see this was quite a haul.

"I brought them the diamonds the next day at one sharp, and they handed me $400,000 in hundred dollar bills. That meant the jewels had been worth $1.1 million at least. I got my usual, around forty cents on the dollar.

"As I told you, I would always put my money aside for Dominick off the jump street. He got $50,000 in his envelope, and then I would pay off my crew. My accomplice made $70,000 for that robbery.

"I came home and counted my $300,000 on the coffee table. I told my wife, 'You can keep anything under a fifty.' There were fives, tens, and twenties sometimes because sometimes I'd steal cash out of the jewelry store's register. Sometimes I'd get as much as two thousand dollars in small bills. I gave her five grand one time, and she loved it. I'd tell her, 'Go buy whatever you want.' She never wanted for money."

CHAPTER 6

The Single Life

While Larry Lawton was living the life in southern Florida, his wife Roselyn was feeling neglected and unhappy, and with good reason. As a mob wife, Roselyn didn't dare question Larry's comings and goings. Larry had several laws he laid down for the marriage. Among them: when he was away Roselyn was never to check up on him, never to call to find out where he was, and never to even beep him.

"If I was out, I was out," said Lawton. "And I'd come in at all hours. She stood up for me during the pizza fire incident. She was a good mob wife.

"If you can't control your wife, nobody is going to trust you to control anything else. And I knew that. Some guys couldn't do it. I could. Roselyn never called the Homestetch or came in unexpected. That was the law."

But there reached a point where Roselyn couldn't stand the empty feeling of abandonment and powerlessness any longer.

Larry had flown up from Florida to Brooklyn with his brother David, Fat Tony, and another crew member named Mike to celebrate Fat Tony's thirtieth birthday. They went to the Taj Majal to gamble.

What a night it was. Larry hooked up with gambling buddy Roger King, the owner of King World. King, the distributor of

Wheel of Fortune, Jeopardy, and Oprah Winfrey, was betting ten thousand and twenty thousand dollars a hand in blackjack.

"That's when I realized what real money was," said Lawton, who was betting a thousand dollars a hand.

They attended a prizefight between heavyweights Burt Cooper and Michael Moorer. Lawton was sitting in the third row. Roger, one of the backers of Moorer, was ringside. Before the fight Roger introduced Lawton to Donald Trump, the owner of the Taj Mahal, who was also sitting at ringside.

Larry and Roger bet on the fight. Larry bet an orange and white chip – a thousand dollars -- on Cooper to win five orange and white chips. When Cooper knocked down Moorer in the first round, Larry smirked at King.

I've just won five grand, thought Lawton, who also realized that five grand to King was just a drop in the bucket.

But Moorer recovered and knocked out Cooper four rounds later. After the fight the two went back to the high roller pit.

Larry won $30,000 at the blackjack tables, and the next morning he returned to the tables while waiting for his limo to arrive to take his crew back to Brooklyn. He opened a table in the high roller pit and was betting a thousand dollars a hand. Before he knew it, he was down $30,000 when the limo arrived.

The night before Larry had picked up a hooker, and they agreed he would take her to the Homestead and put her to work. Before going to the bar, Larry had the limo take him home so he could change clothes. He walked in and walked out without saying a word to Roselyn. He and his crew drove to the bar, and when he returned that night, Roselyn was visibly angry. When he said he was going back out again, she flung a set of keys at him. The keys whizzed by his face and broke a curio cabinet filled with dozens of Precious Moments figurines. Larry turned, glared at her, and walked out. As far as he was concerned, their marriage was over.

Roselyn, badly in need of companionship, demanded that they move back to Brooklyn so she could be closer to her parents. To placate her Lawton rented her and their young son a three-bedroom apartment on 71st Street and 13th Avenue in Brooklyn. She lived there full-time, and he commuted back and forth from Fort Lauderdale, spending Saturdays with his wife and son, and Sundays with the mobsters at the Homestretch.

In 1992 Larry and Roselyn divorced. Roselyn had grown up in Brooklyn around the mob life, and she knew all too well that if Larry stayed on his chosen path, he would end up in prison or worse, and she didn't want that for her son.

They had money, and she pleaded with him to leave Florida and open a liquor store in Brooklyn. Larry thought about it. He knew he had enough mob connections that he wouldn't be shaken down like most liquor store owners in Brooklyn, but Larry was drawn to the mob life in a big way and just couldn't break the ties. By the time of their divorce Roselyn was so bitter that she refused to allow Larry to see their three-year-old son.

Larry went to see Willie the Weeper.

"When you're in the mob, you don't go to lawyers," said Lawton. "You go to your mob friends."

"Willie," Lawton said. "I want to see my son. Fuck all these people. I don't care what the protocol is. This is my son. I want to see him."

Willie knew that Larry was half nuts and feared for what he might do.

"Calm down," said Willie. "Let me call Lenny and set something up." Lenny was Larry's father in law.

Willie told Lenny, "Larry needs to see his son. I don't want any problems around here."

Willie set up a meeting with Larry and Lenny at a Greek diner at 65th Street and 7th Avenue. On this corner a lot of mob guys hung out and went for coffee or a quick meeting, and left.

They sat down for coffee. They made small talk, but there was no talk about what Larry was doing in the life, because Lenny well knew the life.

Lenny's parting words were, "Larry, come pick up your son tomorrow morning at eight."

Said Larry, "He didn't even ask his daughter, because he knew it was the right thing to do."

*

With his wife out of the picture, Larry proceeded to remodel his Florida house into a luxurious bachelor pad. He made the room upstairs into a gym with mirrored walls and a rubber mat floor. He bought a pool table with a hanging light, installed a nine-foot bar, and paid ten grand for a sophisticated sound system with five separate zones which could be controlled by a box in the living room. The parties at his house were legendary. He found any excuse to host a party. He celebrated every holiday – Fourth of July, Memorial Day, Flag Day, even Martin Luther King's Birthday. He bought a sixty-inch TV set, and invited all his friends to watch the championship fights on pay-for-view TV. More than anything, there were girls.

"I was a bachelor, and I liked it that way," said Larry. "Not that I wasn't fooling around when I was married, but it was different now. I had girls every day. This whole time I was living the large life with these girls. I knew all the girls in the bar, all the girls in the strip clubs. I'd bring over nine broads with three guys, and we had wild, wild parties."

At times nine naked bodies would be shoe-horned into his three-person Jaccuzzi. It was one long, wild orgy.

At night Lawton and his buddies went to such clubs as Pure Platinum, Solid Gold, Joseph's, and Flixx. Larry had a limo and a driver and although Larry didn't use cocaine to excess, he used the drug to party with girls.

"Most of the strippers are coke heads, and if you have coke, you can get any stripper you want."

He hung with the big shots of Fort Lauderdale. Customers were not supposed to be intimate with the strippers, but Lawton was friends with the club owners, and the bouncers didn't dare say a word.

"There's a champagne room in every strip club," said Lawton. "It's where the high rollers go. They get broads to give them lap dances. They'd be naked and sit on your balls and dick, and whatever else you wanted them to do."

One time Lawton closed Pure Platinum at two in the morning, and with five girls, the owner, and Larry's driver, laid an ounce of coke on the bar, took out his credit card, lined the whole ounce up for eight feet, sniffed coke for a few hours and partied, and then headed over to Flixx in Larry's limo.

Lawton's behavior often skirted the law, but up to this time he hadn't gotten into any major trouble until one night outside a Melbourne nightclub when Larry pulled his Caddy up over a curb and it stuck there. He had been drinking, and when he left the club and tried to leave, he couldn't move his car. Angry and frustrated, he got out of the car, pulled his gun, which he always carried, and started blasting away at his car in the parking lot. After he put three bullets into the hood, he put the pistol back in his holster, went back to the bar, and resumed drinking.

"I was crazy," said Lawton. "I shot up the parking lot, and I ended up getting arrested."

While Lawton sat at the bar, four cops entered, their guns drawn. Lawton looked up to see the guns pointed at him. He raised his hands, walked out of the bar, and was searched. When they found the gun he was handcuffed and put in the back of the police car. He had a license to carry the gun, but he was arrested for discharging a fire arm within city limits.

His parents, who lived in Palm Bay, the city next to Melbourne, bailed him out at four in the morning. His father, a sports junkie, never once questioned him about why he was arrested. Instead he began asking Larry sports trivia questions.

"He knew I knew I was wrong," said Lawton.

Lawton picked up his Cadillac a day later. He noticed the cops hadn't even checked his trunk.

"What idiots!" said Lawton. "I could have had a dead body in there."

Charged with shooting a gun in public, Lawton had to return to Melbourne for trial. His appearance was scheduled for nine in the morning. He arranged for him, his lawyer, and two friends to go on a sixty-foot Hatteras deep sea fishing boat later that morning.

Lawton had a good lawyer, who got the charges reduced, and Lawton was given two years probation. The case over, Lawton and his lawyer sped to the docks where the captain and his crew were waiting. On the boat were too prostitutes Lawton had hired for a thousand dollars a day each along with sandwiches and liquor.

The owner of the boat was showing one of Lawton's associates how nice his boat was when Lawton pulled up, jumped out of the car, and said, "Let's go. Let's get this thing underway."

The owner wanted to show Lawton around the boat.

Lawton, impatient, looked at him with killer eyes and with all he could do to control his temper, told the owner, "I rented this boat. Get the fuck off before I throw you in the fucking water." The boat captain, who knew Lawton from previous trips and knew he was a big tipper, ran down the ladder and told the owner, "I got this. Let me get under way." The captain, looking at the two girls, knew he would be taken care of quite nicely.

The boat took off. Lawton and his associate were in the fighting chairs, and the two beauties were taking off their clothes at the back of boat, showing Lawton and his buddies their comely attributes. The girls were 25 years old and very accommodating. Once out in the ocean, the emphasis wasn't on fishing

"While we're out in the ocean, the girls are blowing guys and fucking everyone," said Lawton. "I sent a girl to the captain to give him a blow job, and while I was in the fighting chair, I caught a dolphin. I was screaming, and no one was around. They were all down below having sex. I brought the fish in, and it was half eaten by barracudas. Nobody cared. All this was was a party. It's what we did. That's the way the life was: broads, good times, and good company."

Lawton's security company, meanwhile, was making big money from all the illegal payoffs he set up, but when he went to the owner and asked for $50,000 he was owed for all his hard work, the owner reneged, saying the company wasn't making nearly enough money for him to be able to pay him.

"I thought the owner and I were friends," said Lawton, "and when he said no, I took it personally."

Lawton took the company check book and wrote himself a check for $9,900. He did that because checks under $10,000 weren't reported to the IRS at that time.

Said Lawton, "I went to the broad in the bank who I was fucking on the side, and I had her cash the check, because the owner's signature was on it, which I forged. When this motherfucker found out, he went to the police and filed a complaint. The police put out a warrant for my arrest. I had no idea."

Lawton in the interim on a whim went on a seven-day cruise. After playing a round of golf with a couple of buddies, he sidled up to the golf course bar and immediately was captivated by the looks of the bartender.

"Hey, you're beautiful," he said to her. "You want to go on a cruise?"

"He's not kidding," his two buddies said to her. "If he says he's going to take you on a cruise, he'll do it."

The woman was skeptical at first but then agreed to go. A week later they boarded a cruise ship in Fort Lauderdale, and after one day she made the grievous mistake by admitting that she was falling in love with him. She was giving him google eyes, one thing more than any other that Lawton didn't want.

Lawton wasn't looking for a relationship. He went on the cruise with the idea of meeting a slew of girls. The first night out they had a toga party. Everyone was wearing a sheet that covered their underwear. Lawton had nothing on underneath.

Lawton and his bartender/date were at the dinner table, when she started to express her feelings for him.

"She wanted to love me, and all I wanted was sex," said Lawton.

When she asked why he was looking at other girls, Lawton went into a rage. He got up from the table, went over to the office of the ship's steward, and told him, "Get this bitch out of my room. I don't give a fuck what it costs. Get her her own fucking room."

Lawton enjoyed the cruise, partying every night with different girls. Little did he know he was being watched, because of the felony warrant out for his arrest. He was lucky because the night before the ship came into port he threw the bottle of coke which he used with the girls to party into the ocean.

The next morning the ship pulled into port. At six thirty in the morning Lawton heard a knock at the door.

"Steward," a man said. When he opened his cabin door, two custom agents stood there pointing their guns at him. Lawton was one of three passengers they arrested and handcuffed.

Lawton was standing on the stairs of the ship with the other two under arrest when one of them kept saying, "It's not me. It's not me."

Lawton told him, "Shut the fuck up. I'm a criminal. I know. It *is* you."

Lawton waited on the deck of the ship wearing Bally of Switzerland shoes, a Hawaiian shirt, and handcuffs.

"Hey, Larry," his friends he had met on the cruise were saying to him, and Larry would turn his shoulders and show them his handcuffs.

"I'm tied up right now," he said. They gave a look of shock and kept on walking. Lawton was laughing.

Lawton left the ship at seven in the morning before he had the chance to pay his $1,000 bar bill. He was taken to the Dade County jail, which housed 32 men in a sixteen-man pod. Larry was the only white guy, and no rookie to street life, he knew there was going to be trouble. *The Fresh Prince of Bel Air* starring Will Smith was playing on the TV. He walked up to the TV and turned it to the news.

"A big black guy came up to me," said Lawton. "In the joint they call him the House Man. He turned to say something to me, and boom, I hit him. And I could hit like a tank. He didn't go down. We got to fighting, and he hit me in the throat. I couldn't talk. My hand was broken. The guards came and took me to a different cell."

The next day Lawton, his face still swollen, was put back in the same pod wearing the same bloody shirt.

"This was the county jail," he said. "They didn't care. The motherfucker I was fighting with looked at me with respect, threw a kid off the top bunk, and said, 'That's your bunk. You're okay.'

"That jail was terrible. This was right after Hurricane Andrew. There was no electricity or hot water, and the jail was packed to the gills. I was lying in my bunk, and I could hear the patter of little feet. I looked up, and I could see a rat on a pipe over my head. I didn't make a move. I didn't want that rat to fall on me. After the rat walked past, I tied towels on each end of the pipe so the rat couldn't return. Fuck that, I don't like rats, human or animal.

"This place was a nut house. A kid tried to rob my two hundred dollar shoes. I fell off the bed hitting him, boom. I pounded his face into the concrete. Boom, boom. Nobody breaks up a fight in jail. I was smashing this kid.

"Finally someone said, 'Larry, enough.' They grabbed my

arm. I quickly turned to see who it was, and it was the House Man, the big guy. My hand was already very swollen. It had already been broken. The guards came and took the kid out. They didn't touch me, because the other inmates pointed to the kid and said, 'He's a thief.'

Lawton, unable to make a phone call, ended up staying in the Dade County jail for ten days.

"Tony and everybody wondered, *What happened to Larry? The cruise came in, and where is he?* In the county jail you can't make a long-distance call, and Fort Lauderdale is long distance from Miami. It took me ten days to get someone to make a call for me.

"Can you call this guy? Tell him I'm here."

Larry was transferred to the Broward County Jail, which enabled him to call his friend Fat Tony. He was bonded out for $20,000. Lawton ended up getting five years probation for writing the bum check.

All Lawton could think about was revenge against the owner of the security company for having him arrested for writing the $9,900 check after he had made his former friend a pile of dough.

"When I returned to my townhouse, I was thinking, *This motherfucker. How can he do this to me? We're robbing these people, and he doesn't want to give me any fucking money? Then he goes and calls the cops? This fucking cocksucker* — I was getting so mad. I could have blown the whistle on his whole operation. You know what the press would have done with a story about a guy stealing from the school board? I could see the headlines in the newspapers, "Security Company Robs School Board."

"The reason I didn't do it was that I wasn't a rat, and I was making too much money on diamond robberies. I didn't want to open the whole thing up, because if I did, I'd get myself in trouble. What if they put my picture in the newspaper? The owners of the jewelry stores I robbed might have seen it, and I would have been done for."

Lawton decided instead to burn his partner's place down.

"The company was in an L-shaped plaza on Wilton Manor Boulevard," he said. "I had hung around with enough pros to know how to do it. You put gasoline in a two-liter squeeze bottle. With a knife you jab a hole in the top of the screw cap, and then you lay the bottle right near the door. A door is never sealed a hundred percent, so you squeeze the bottle so it blows the gasoline under the door, and then you light it, and the fire goes under the door into the place.

"After I torched it, I left. I wasn't one of those arsonist criminals who watches his fires burn."

The office of the security company was destroyed. To make his point Lawton also threw a Molotov cocktail into one of the security company's cars and destroyed it. An article in the Fort Lauderdale paper the next day discussed the suspicious nature of both the store and the car fires.

The next time Lawton drove past the building he noticed that the owner had put up metal doors across the front of the security offices. This time he threw a Molotov cocktail onto the roof and another one into a security vehicle.

Lawton got a call from his lawyer.

"You're suspected of burning his place down."

"Are you kidding?" Lawton said. "Why would I burn his place? I had nothing to do with it. He has a hundred employees, and they're all low lifes. You know what security guards are."

Said Lawton, "Nevertheless, I think they had an idea I did it."

In the end Lawton was handed five-years probation on the check robbery on his promise to pay back the money. As for the fire, there was a great deal of suspicion but no hard evidence, though considering Lawton had been suspected of burning down his own pizzeria he had to be the primary suspect.

*

Around this time one late afternoon Lawton was drinking at the Colony West golf course bar. His limo was in the parking lot. A beautiful woman was sitting with another man across the bar, and she kept looking at Lawton. Lawton picked her up and took her into his limousine, and like that, she became his girl friend. Lawton named her Spanky because she enjoyed being spanked. For Christmas he gave her a television set. She gave him pajamas.

During a big New Years' party at Larry's house, Larry, Spanky and Fat Tony's father were together at the bar when Spanky made the same mistake the woman on the cruise made. She told everyone, "Larry is my boy friend."

Lawton went ballistic.

"What did you say? Get the fuck out."

"You want me to leave?" Tony's father asked. He was uncomfortable being in the middle of this.

"No," Lawton said. "You stay. She goes. Get the fuck out."

Lawton kicked her out of his house and never saw her again.

"That was how I was," said Lawton. "I was the boss, and I didn't want anything to mess that up."

Not long afterward Lawton was sitting in a country and western bar in Fort Lauderdale. The owner was a wiseguy from New York. From across the bar Lawton noticed an attractive girl with a cowboy hat on. To Lawton she looked like Shania Twain, and he sent her a note on a napkin.

The note read: "Hey beautiful, let's not fuck around. We're all adults. I'll take you for a ride on my horses."

She agreed, and as she got off her bar stool, Lawton noticed she was a cripple with a bad limp.

"I did it anyway," he said. "I took her for a ride on my horses, and we rode up a trail to spot I used to call Blow Job Rock. I considered leaving her there, but I didn't. What a psycho I was."

It wasn't too long after that that he met his second wife, Melissa.

"I used to loan shark money to a guy named Dave McKay, who owned a bar. He was in his 30s, my age, and his bar was called McKay's. The bar had a women's softball team, and I sponsored the team, which was called Larry's Ladies.

"One day there was a party at my cleaning lady's home. After riding my horses, I walked in with a drug dealer friend of mine, when I saw this smoking hot girl sitting on the couch with a loser guy. I said to Fat Tony, who was already there,

'Who is the fine girl over there?'

"He said her name was Missy. 'She plays on your softball team. She's only 19.'

"'Who's the guy she's with?'

"'Some loser.'

"I invited everyone in the place back to McKay's bar for drinks on me."

"When we got back to the bar I said to Missy, "What are you doing here?"

"I'm a player on your team."

"You can't drink here. You're aren't 21."

"Yes, I am."

"Tell you what," Lawton said. He pulled out a wad of cash wrapped in a rubber band. "If you're 21, I'll give you a thousand bucks. If you're not, you show me your tits."

"Fuck you," was all she could reply, and she walked out.

A short time later Lawton threw an Easter party on the beach for the gang at the bar. He bought kegs of beer, and barbeque for an army. Even though he weighed close to 250 pounds, Lawton was wearing a Speedo bathing suit. Lawton didn't care.

Lawton told Tony, "Go get some girls, invite them back to my house for a private party. Get Missy.' Everyone knew my house was the party house. Missy agreed to come.

Larry walked up to her and said, "You're driving home with me." She agreed. Lawton hosted what amounted to an orgy for the rest of the evening. But Missy was only Larry's.

At the end of the party Missy spent the night.

"She ended up in my room – and I didn't bring many girls up to my room," said Lawton.

The next morning she told Lawton she worked at Johnny's pizzeria and had to be at work on time.

"Why don't you take off, and I'll pay you for your day?" said Lawton.

"No, I can't do that," she said.

"I'll tell you what, if you lose your job, I'll give you a job at the bar, and I'll double your salary."

She refused. She said she was loyal to Johnny.

"And that meant a lot to me," said Lawton. "I drove her to work, picked her up at the end of her shift, and she never left my house from that day on."

After eight months, they were married in November of 1994 in Las Vegas. She had just turned 21. They were comped by the Excaliber Hotel, where Lawton won $25,000 playing baccarat and backjack. They were married in a little chapel in Vegas.

Missy, like his first wife Roselyn, had no idea what Lawton really did for a living. His next jewelry store robbery took place in Marietta, Georgia. After talking up the owner, he was shown the box of loose jewels. When he came in to rob the place, the owner didn't want to give up the box.

Lawton grabbed the owner's wife and held a gun to her head.

"Listen, you fucking idiot," said Lawton, "if you don't hand over the box, I'm going to blow your fucking wife's brains out.' The owner then gave up the jewelry.

The next robbery occurred in Palm Bay, Florida, not far from where his parents lived. He walked in, announced it was a robbery, and the girl behind the counter started to laugh.

"You think this is funny?" Lawton wanted to know.

His two accomplices came in, and they emptied the store of valuables.

Before they were finished, Lawton went out to get the car to bring it around back. He looked up and down the plaza and noticed the mailman walking toward the store. The mailman was going to come into the store, he realized, and he certainly didn't want that.

As the mailman was about to enter, Lawton interrupted him.

"The owners just left," Lawton said. "They'll be back in ten minutes." The mailman pushed the mail through the slot in the door and kept on going. Once the mailman entered the next store, Lawton got in the car, drove around back, and picked up everyone and the loot.

"The FBI said there were four people involved in the robbery when there only were three," said Lawton. "The people in the store knew there were only three. The FBI thought I was a lookout to divert the mailman. I was smart enough not to run or do anything foolish. The mailman wasn't going to wait, and he went on his route. That was a pretty quick job."

*

As part of his nouveau riche Lawton bought himself a limousine so he could travel around town in style. To house it he rented an entire warehouse. In that warehouse he paid friends in the construction business under the table to build him a clubhouse that served as his headquarters. The crew installed ceilings. A flunkie of his stole a roof air conditioner that he bought hot for $250 and had it installed. He built a small, private club with a bar. In another room he built offices for his bookmaking business. The office had a couch, big screen TV, a satellite dish, a refrigerator, and phones for his bookies.

His bookies, Fat Tony and Little Mike, a neighbor who lived with his mom in Lawton's neighborhood, was open for business Saturdays from 10 until 1 in the afternoon, and from 3 to 5 to the end of the football games. On Sunday they'd work from 11 in the morning until 1, and then reopen from 2 to 4 at the end of the games. Lawton's bookmaking operation took its betting lines directly from the computer. Computers were just becoming big in the mid-nineties.

"You could bet anything, football, basketball, fights, anything," said Lawton. "My customers were all junkie gamblers. The biggest betting, of course, came during the NCAA basketball tournament."

Little Mike knew about Lawton's jewelry store heists and wanted to become involved. Lawton knew that not everyone had the balls to go into the store with a gun, jump the counter, tie someone up, and skip out with the jewels. Lawton decided to give Little Mike his chance.

Lawton took Little Mike as an accomplice to rob a jewelry store in Coconut Creek, Florida.

"Wait in the car," Lawton told him. "When I give you the

signal at the door, bring the car around back."

Lawton gave the signal, but it turned out that Little Mike didn't have the stomach for the job. He got cold feet and ran away. Lawton always had contingency plans, and he walked out of the store like a regular customer, got in the car, and drove off himself.

Lawton drove to an apartment in Margate and emptied the bag of jewels on the bed.

"It was cool. I loved it," said Lawton. "Meanwhile, the other two guys I was with wanted to kill Mike for running off. I calmed them down."

"No one gets killed," said Lawton. "If anyone does the discipline, I do it."

But Lawton didn't do a thing. He saw that Little Mike just wasn't cut out to be a jewelry store robber.

"I just never used him again," he said. "He was just like Fat Tony, who couldn't rob anyone either. But Tony had a good memory and he didn't drink, so he did the bookmaking. I tried to use my crew to the best of their ability."

Lawton had rules for his crew. No drugs during robberies.

"If I caught you with drugs, I'd shoot you. No drinking before a job. When he drove to an area for a robbery, his men couldn't even go to the local bars.

"I'd get a cheap hotel room under a false name, and they had to watch TV, or we'd order pizza. We never made ourselves conspicuous. I learned something about hanging out with guys: they are so much better than broads. Nobody fights. Nobody argues."

One time in Brooklyn his brother Dave and Jimmy, another accomplice, came home after a job and during a party offered Lawton crack. Lawton pulled out his pistol and pointed it at them.

"If you ever come around here with that stuff, I'll kill the both of you," he said.

They knew he was serious, and they never again did drugs around him.

"I laid down laws, and I was half nuts anyway," said Lawton. "Crazy Larry. Larry Florida."

More than any other rule, Lawton believed his men owed him the same type of loyalty he paid to Dominick Gangi and Willie the Weeper: they were to show up on time with no questions asked.

One time at four in the morning he beeped Junior, one of his key men. Junior didn't answer. Junior was sleeping in the warehouse, and when Lawton went in there, he found him laying down half drunk on the couch. Lawton took a .357 and shot three bullets close to Junior's head. The sound of the gunshots reverberated throughout the warehouse. Boom, boom, boom. Junior was so afraid Lawton intended to kill him that he began to cry.

"'You motherfucker,' said Lawton, 'if you don't answer your beeper, you better be dead or in jail.' Junior learned his lesson."

*

Lawton's next heist took place in the Savannah, Georgia, area. Though Lawton didn't usually pick out chain stores, he decided to rob the Freidman Jewelers in Savannah because it just seemed too easy. There was a Home Depot around the corner, and two employees who Lawton got to know.

On the day he robbed them it was thundering. Rain was pouring down, a perfect situation, because people walking by the store holding umbrellas walked with their heads held down. They didn't look in.

Lawton asked if he could go to the bathroom. He wanted to make sure there wasn't another employee in the back. After he came out of the bathroom, his two accomplices walked in. Lawton pulled his gun, put the two employees on the ground, and tied them up. The three then robbed the place.

This store had jewelry cases going down each aisle. One of his crew went down one aisle, swooping up the loot, and the other went down the other as Lawton walked up and down like a general, pointing.

"Don't forget this. Go to the other side and take that."

Lawton was wearing a suit. He went to the front door and looked out, as though he was looking at the rain. People would walk by, and he'd nod, and they'd nod, as they ran to their cars or to another store. If they had wanted to come in, Lawton would have let them. He never stopped anyone from coming in. It took fifteen to twenty minutes to clean out a store.

They got away cleanly, but the robbery was a small one.

"I didn't get much," he said. "My take ended up being about $130,000. This was where I learned my lesson not to rob retail stores."

The closest Lawton came to serious legal problems came

in December of 1994 after a trip to New York, where he met his buddy Joey Grillo. They two men were close. Grillo made a lot of money selling cocaine, a business Lawton chose to avoid.

After one of Lawton's robberies Joey asked if he could borrow $35,000. Lawton, flush with cash, knew Grillo was good for it and made the loan. While Lawton was in New York taking care of business at the Homestretch, Joey met him there and repaid the money. Lawton was driving back to Florida by himself, and he wanted company so he flew up Junior, one of his crew, to drive back with him. Lawton warned Junior in advance, "If we should ever get stopped by a cop, just tell them you wash my limousines and you know nothing."

In addition to paying Lawton the $35,000 in cash, for the trip back Joey gave him a gift of five grams of cocaine in half-gram packets, ten little packets in all. Lawton put the packets in the center console of his rented Mitsubishi Diamante.

Lawton had been drinking at the Homestretch Bar before he left.

"It was the beginning of December, and I was freezing my balls off," said Lawton. "It was two in the morning, and I was going 80, and I got stopped by two New Jersey State troopers."

It was a rent-a-car, and the police ran his name and number. One trooper went to the passenger door, and the other ordered him to stand outside behind the car. The first trooper leaned into the car and opened the glove compartment. The $35,000 in cash fell out right in front of Junior, who was sitting in the passenger seat. There were stacks of hundred dollar bills.

The cop asked Lawton "Where did you get this?"

"I sold my Corvette," Lawton said.

"You have a receipt?"

"No, I sold it on the streets of Brooklyn. That's the way you do things in Brooklyn. A guy offered me money for the car, and I gave him the car and title. The title was in the glove compartment, and I gave him the car."

The other policeman meanwhile ordered Junior to get out by the side of the road. When his partner opened the middle divider, he discovered the packets of cocaine.

Said Lawton, "Right then and there they took me down to one of those outpost station houses they have in Jersey. I was sitting in the holding cell, and I knew what they were thinking, that I was a drug dealer. They were figuring out what they could do to me.

"No doubt they knew I was associated with the Gambinos. They called in a detective. The first thing I wanted to do is talk to my lawyer. I called him. It was two in the morning. His wife answered and said he was at a bachelor party. I beeped him. I put 911 on the beeper, a sign of an emergency.

"While I was waiting for him to return my call, they put me back in the holding cell. I could hear them interrogating Junior. They said to him, "You're involved with organized crime. That guy is no good. What are you doing up here?"

"Junior said, 'All I know is I wash the guy's limousine, and he told me to come up and drive down with him.' Junior was sticking strong.

Lawton's lawyer, Keith Belzer, called him back.

"Larry, you know the drill. Don't say anything. When you get to the county jail, you'll be out in no time." Belzer's father owned the Hound Dog bail bond company, across the street from the Ft. Lauderdale courthouse.

Lawton went in front of a magistrate judge, who sent him to the Atlantic County jail. They impounded the Diamante.

Lawton was sitting in a cell wearing his Bally of Switzerland shoes. A man in the cell with him was distraught, moaning and groaning that he couldn't raise a hundred and fifty dollar bail.

Lawton told him, "Shut the fuck up, you fucking punk. When I get out of here, I'll bail you out too. Just shut the fuck up."

"Will you? Will you."

"Sure." And he did.

"I was treated like gold there," said Lawton. "They let me make phone calls. The cops who arrested me were up all night.

"I said to one of them, 'You know I'm going to be out of here before they finish the paperwork, don't you, you prick. What do you think you got here? You got nothing. You got me with $35,000. What else you got? Five grams of coke. That's petty.'

Lawton and Junior each were given a $25,000 bond. Lawton returned to his holding cell and called his lawyer. His bail bondsman in Fort Lauderdale posted his bond, and he was out. It took all day. It was six at night when Lawton walked out of the cell.

Lawton called the Taj Mahal in Atlantic City, and they sent a stretch limousine to the Atlantic County Jail to get him..

"You want to call a cab?" he was asked.

"I got a car coming," Lawton said. He sure did. A limousine.

"I didn't have any money," said Lawton. "They took it all. I only had a few hundred dollars in my wallet, and they actually left that in there. I took the limo to the Taj Mahal, and I was so tired I almost fell asleep on the stairs.

"The next morning I flew home on the first flight from Philly. It left at seven in the morning. Missy was waiting for me.

A few months later Lawton and his attorney returned to New Jersey, and they had to go back a second time and a third. In the end his lawyer made a deal.

"I got five years probation, and in exchange the courts and the cops would steal $12,000 of my $35,000," said Lawton. "On top of stealing my $12,000, they wanted me to pay court costs and pay the probation, because I had to be transferred from New Jersey to Fort Lauderdale. Who's the real criminal?"

Lawton said to his lawyer, "Hey, what the fuck is going on? I do the extorting around here."

They dropped the case against Junior.

"I paid cash to make it go away. Over a couple years my legal fees cost me $70,000. Who was robbing who?"

CHAPTER 7

The Last Heist

Lawton decided to hit the road with his three assistants to see if there was a promising jewelry store to rob in the state of Pennsylvania. He wasn't going to bother looking in the city of Philadelphia proper, but was sure there would be a promising store in its suburbs. He found the perfect target in Fairless Hills in Philadelphia's outskirts.

"It was in a plaza, and the angle was right, everything was right," he said.

Lawton went into the store. There was only the owner. As always, he did his best to get to know the man, and when he was standing away from the buzzer, he jumped the counter, put a gun in his face, and put flex cuffs on his hands and feet.

As usual, Lawton shouted at his victim to get down and be quiet.

Lawton and one accomplice were emptying the store of all the diamonds, when they saw a woman walk up to the window, cup her hands, look in, and see the robbery taking place. Lawton would later learn that the woman had her antenna up for anything unusual because a couple weeks before someone had gone onto the roof of her store and stole an air conditioning unit. Because of the air conditioning unit robbery, Lawton found out later, she came by to investigate when she heard Larry yelling at the jewelry store owner.

"We had to leave in a flash," he said. "The owner had five guns in the safe. We had already put them in my bag along with the jewels."

Lawton usually watched the tied-up victim up to the last second, but because of the woman looking in the window, he was distracted. The owner somehow got loose, and while Larry and his crew were running out of the store, he ran and found another gun he had hidden.

"As usual we had left our car -- with a stolen license plate -- parked in front of the store," said Lawton. "We booked outside, and just as we left the store shots rang out. The front window of the store shattered right next to us. I was thinking, *Holy fuck, the guy got out of his handcuffs and found a gun. I don't know how he did it, but he did.* We sprinted a few steps to the car and jumped in."

Lawton was behind the steering wheel, and as he looked up through the windshield, he could see the store owner level his gun right at his head. Lawton ducked. The store owner shot. The bullet went right through the windshield dead center right in middle of the driver's seat. The bullet scraped the top of Lawton's head and struck his brother, who was in the passenger seat, in his back and then in his arm.

Lawton's brother screamed, "I'm hit. I'm hit."

"Where? You all right?"

"Just get out of here."

"I'm heading to the hospital?" Lawton would have dropped him there if it meant saving his life.

"No, no, get back to Brooklyn."

It was a Streets of San Francisco getaway. Lawton turned the wheel, spun the tires, raced through the parking lot, and took off heading for Brooklyn. In his rearview mirror, as he sped away, Lawton could see the jewelry store owner aiming his pistol.

He had his route all planned. He knew the plate was fake, so he wasn't worried about anyone taking down the number. Lawton remained calm. He had planned for contingencies like this.

His biggest problem was that there was a bullet hole right in the middle of his windshield, and he had to pay tolls. Lawton was sure the police were informing all the toll takers about the robbery.

Be on the lookout for an armed robber with shots fired. With a description of his rental car.

Lawton knew what to do. He pulled up behind an 18-wheeler, obscuring the view of his windshield from the toll taker, and when it was his turn to pay, he rolled a few feet past the toll booth, reached back and gave the toll taker the money. That way the toll taker couldn't see the bullet hole in his windshield.

As he was paying, he heard the radio in the toll booth announce, "Be on the lookout…."

A minute later, and the toll taker might have paid more attention.

We got away with it, Lawton thought.

It took two hours for Lawton to drive to Bensonhurst,

Brooklyn. He pulled up in front of the Homestretch Bar. There was dried blood on the top of his head and the side of his face. His brother had blood on his arm and back. His arm burned and pained him.

Lawton and his brother ran upstairs. Friends cleaned Lawton's wound. He had nothing more than a scratch. His brother had a bullet in him. They patched his brother up and were able to get the trickle of blood to stop. Lawton's plan was to fly his brother back to Florida and have him treated there.

Because Lawton's rent-a-car was from Florida, not New York, he could replace the windshield. If the car had been from New York there would have been the registration in the window, and he wouldn't have been able to replace it.

"I needed to get rid of the hole before I drove home," said Lawton, "so Willie the Weeper called Bensonhurst Auto Glass, which is all connected.

"'We need the car fixed.'"

Lawton went with the car because the diamonds were in the trunk.

"You don't ask questions in Brooklyn," he said. "They put in a new windshield, so I didn't have to worry when I brought the car back.

Lawton called a buddy, a building contractor who used to be on the fringes of Raymond Patriarca's mob in Rhode Island.

He said, "Hey, Uncle Mikey's, Davey's been hit. We have to find a doctor for him. He can't go to the hospital with a bullet."

"Uncle Mikey," who hung out at the race track, called a

doctor -- a veterinarian he knew from the track. There are a lot of knockaround guys at the track. This guy was one of them.

The vet said he could operate on his brother on a table in the home he was building. Lawton thanked him, but decided it would be better if his brother flew home so his mother could take care of him.

"I got my brother a flight," said Lawton. "This was before 9/11. You could pay cash. You didn't have to show an ID card. I put my brother on a plane and called my mother, who has been a nurse forever. My mom knew what to do, but she didn't know what I did. I said, 'Mom, Davey and I were playing with guns in a bar, and Davey got shot, and he has a bullet in him. You have to take care of him. We can't call the cops. You know I have a record from the Atlantic city bust.' I'll go to prison.

"My mother used to be an emergency room nurse in Westchester Square hospital in the Bronx. She worked in a clinic in Palm Bay. She got some penicillin, and she fixed my brother up. She could see the bullet wasn't in a bad spot and felt more damage would be done trying to take it out than leaving it there. My brother was lucky he had my mother. Without her, he might have died. Or gotten his arm amputated by a veterinarian.

"I flew my wife up to drive home with me. I drove to Little Italy, dropped off the diamonds and got my $70,000 for the job. On the way back to Florida I pulled into a rest stop along I-95, took the five guns from the jewelry store robbery we just did, and back by the picnic tables threw them into a lake."

He continued his trip back to Fort Lauderdale without

incident.

*

After the Fairless heist, the FBI flooded the area with agents and local police. They went to every jewelry store in the area. They asked, "Did anyone come in with the following MO: A nice guy coming in with a suit, asking about diamonds."

Lawton's usual MO was to case many jewelry stores in the area before robbing one. He had walked into a jewelry store about two miles away from the actual robbery. Lawton and an employee, perhaps the owner, a Jewish lady, discussed his buying a diamond worth $10,000. Lawton didn't know whether she was suspicious or just wanted to offer him a better deal after he walked out, but she followed him and took down his license plate number.

"While I was casing her place I had not yet put on the stolen plate," said Lawton, "so she got the license plate number of my rental car, gave it to the police, and they found it registered under the name of Tony Banko, my friend who rented the car for me. I had used his credit card. I was listed as the co-driver.

"Well, Fat Tony weighs 350 pounds. I don't look like Tony. The FBI saw there was an alternate driver, and sure enough, it was me. They ran my name through the data base and saw I had a record for possession of cocaine and that there had been $35,000 in the glove compartment of my car.

"Then the FBI took my picture to all the jewelry stores around the country that I had hit, and they said, 'Do you know this guy?'

There was a chorus that responded: "That's the guy who

robbed me."

"Six of twenty store owners I robbed pin-pointed me exactly, and they had a bunch more who were 95 percent sure it was me," said Lawton. "They had tapes of me buying coffee at a WaWa store in Savannah, Georgia. I never used a mask, because I never anticipated I would be caught. An eyewitness doesn't mean much if you can't tie it to anything.

"I was golfing the day I was arrested. My wife had said to me, 'I think I'm being followed.' My mind was thinking of who it might be. *Is it the cops? Is it another mob family trying to rob me?* I wondered.

"I called a friend of mine and told him to take all the guns out of my townhouse. So everything was out of the house when on a Monday afternoon at around five my wife Missy was taking a walk to the mailbox with my fifteen-month old daughter Ashley when I heard her scream, 'They're coming.'

"I was sitting around a table with my brother and another guy who was involved in my bookmaking operation. Since this was a Monday they had come down from central Florida to pick up the week's bookmaking sheets and records."

Lawton went to the door, and it flew open. The FBI came running in with guns in my face. He turned around, and he could see more agents coming through his patio holding guns and rifles. The next day the Palm Bay police surrounded his mother's house in Palm Bay, Florida. His sister answered the door.

"We have a warrant for the arrest of Lawrence Lawton."

"He's in jail," his sister said.

"When I was arrested I had about $3,000 in cash in my pocket, and I was wearing expensive jewelry," said Lawton. "I asked the FBI guy if I could give it to my wife. He said I could. The FBI wasn't bad. When they caught me, they said, 'Man, we've been looking for you for a long time.'"

The cops also arrested Tony Banko because he had rented the car. They drove Lawton to Opa locka, where they had built a new FBI headquarters. When he arrived there he saw that they also had Tony. Lawton's thought was, *I hope he shuts up.* Tony knew what Lawton did, of course, but he was never involved in a robbery. Tony said, "All I know is I rented a car for him because he doesn't have a credit card." And they ended up letting Tony go. There was no evidence for him to be arrested.

They then took Lawton to a federal holding facility in Miami. He was hoping to win bond, because if he got out on bail, I was going to flee to Costa Rica.

"My dad and I were very close," said Lawton. "I took him all over the country golfing. I even took him to the Bahamas, Hawaii, and everywhere. My father, who was crying at the hearing, offered to put up his house for bail. I would have paid him back as I had a lot of friends who I was protecting, and they would have given me the money.

"My lawyer said, 'Your honor, the government says he's a flight risk. He had a case in New Jersey in 1994, and he flew back and forth from Florida, and he never jumped bail.'"

When the judge agreed, the prosecutor jumped up and said, "Your honor, "He has ties to organized crime. He's a danger to society. You can't give him bail."

The judge was silent for a few seconds, and then said, "Okay, he's a threat to society." Lawton was remanded. No bail.

Said Lawton, "Then I was kidnapped – not exactly but pretty much kidnapped -- at three in the morning I was pulled from my cell, handcuffed, shackled, and put on a plane and taken to Harrisburg, Pennsylvania. For three days I was in transit. I was fed nothing but a bagged lunch, which consisted of an apple, a pint of juice, and a pack of outdated stale crackers. I had no shower, and I stunk.

"From Harrisburg, Pennsylvania, I was flown to Rhode Island. Why? I have no idea. My destination was Philadelphia. I was already in Pennsylvania. Go figure. I guess it's just the crazy Air Marshal Transport system. And so for two days they drove me back toward Pennsylvania in a van. My last stop was the Elizabeth County Jail in New Jersey. How stupid is that? What a waste of money!

"So I was in the Elizabeth jail, and they picked me up the next day, and I went in front of a magistrate judge. Some guy comes over to me and says, 'I'm going to represent you.'

"I looked at him and said, 'Who the fuck are you?' He was a public defender.

"I said, 'Your honor, can I speak?'

"Go ahead, Mr. Lawton."

"I said, 'I don't know what's going on. I was kidnapped by these people. I haven't had a hot meal. I don't know where I am. I have an attorney, and I smell.'"

That drew a chuckle from the other inmates waiting to be arraigned sitting in the jury box. The judge looked back to the marshals who transferred him and asked if what he said was true.

"We just picked him up from the jail, your honor," they said.

The judge said, "I'm going to suspend this hearing. I want you to put him where's he's going to be housed. I want him to have a hot meal. I want him to get cleaned up, and I want him to have a phone call, *now.*"

Even though there were signs all over the holding cell area saying, *No phone calls,* they had to give Lawton one. When a federal judge orders something done, it gets done.

"I called my wife," said Lawton. "I told her to get hold of the lawyer, my family, and Fat Tony, and let them know that I was kidnapped by the feds and where I was.

"I was then sent to Fairton, a federal correctional institution, somewhere in South Jersey and processed into the carrot unit, the unit reserved for guys in pre-trial not yet sentenced. It's an actual prison. The only difference is that the guys in orange clothes are pre-trial and the ones in khaki colored clothes are sentenced inmates.

"I called my wife back the next day, and she was hysterical, crying uncontrollably, saying how the lawyer said he needed more money because it came out in the papers that my case was big, that I was involved with organized crime, and I was facing life in prison.

"I calmed my wife down and got off the phone – furious. I

couldn't sleep that night thinking about my wife and kids, and how a lawyer could be so heartless.

"When I contacted my lawyer the next day, it took all of my self-control not to curse him out. That's why I hate lawyers. Too often they're sharks who feed on people who are down and out. When they know a guy needs them, they bury you.

"I called Dominick, the big mob boss, who said he didn't want to get involved, but he gave me the name of a lawyer. I don't recall his name, but I sent him the paperwork, and he said to me, 'You know you're going to go away for a long time.' Because they were accusing me of using a gun in the four robberies I was charged with committing. Under federal law you get five years for the first robbery with a gun. Every robbery after that you get twenty years running consecutively. I was facing eighty five years just for having a gun.

"He said to me, 'Go to the law library. Look up the statute. They never found a gun. You never shot anyone. You can beat the gun charge.'

"I had used a BB gun during the Fairless Hills robbery, and I'd turned it in. A BB gun is not classified as a firearm. I told the FBI where I had dumped the guns I had taken from the jewelry store. Divers went into the lake off I-95 and found them. And that was one of the major arguments I made to prove I wasn't a gun guy. My defense was going to be, *If I was going to use a gun, I wouldn't have thrown the five guns out.* Not only that, *As I was getting shot at, if I had a gun, wouldn't I have shot back, even in the air?* If I had had a real gun and shot back, you wouldn't be reading this book. I'd still be in prison."

In the end the prosecution dropped the gun charge, because they felt Lawton would have beaten it for lack of evidence. Then the feds offered Lawton a deal.

"The feds offered me a three-year sentence if I gave up my accomplices," said Lawton. "They wanted everyone and their mother. They wanted my fences. They wanted Dominick. They wanted Willie the Weeper. They wanted all my accomplices."

Lawton wouldn't do it. He wasn't a rat.

"There's no ratting," said Lawton. "You have to accept responsibility and do your time, and that's exactly what I did. My crew was always known for how loyal we were. A lot of mobsters, like Sammy Gravano, that prick, say they're going to be loyal and then rat. Sammy said he feared for his life, but that was bullshit. He ratted because he's a fucking rat. He wanted freedom more than anything.

"Even though I was facing a long prison sentence, I never told, and the feds punished me for my silence. I would spend a lot of time in solitary as a result.

"They charged me with four robberies, and after they dropped the gun charge I took a plea for twelve years on the condition I didn't have to rat. I had to give them a profer, meaning I had to admit my crimes and tell them how I did them."

During his profer Lawton told the court that his partner was John Rodriguez from Miami. The name was fictitious, and he chose it because he knew there had to be a lot of John Rodriguez's in the Miami area.

"Talk about being smart!" said Lawton. "It was a real smart

move until later. Do you know what the FBI did? They pulled every ID card, every driver's license, and went to see every John Rodriguez in Miami. There must have been five hundred of them. I must have cost the government a million dollars. Boy, were they pissed. Of course, there was no John Rodriguez. He was a fictitious person. He was really my brother David. Everything else I told them was true, except I didn't do it with John Rodriguez. Five years later, when my brother's wife, a fucking wacko, turned him in, they ended up throwing him in jail and convicting me on perjury. It was the same charge they leveled at Bill Clinton, filing a false statement. They gave me twelve months for that, but the sentence ran concurrently with my sentence for robbing the stores, so what did I care? My brother ended up going away for ten years."

At first Lawton thought he was going to go away forever, but then he had that glimmer of hope from Dominick's attorney, and he beat the gun charge. When he was given twelve years – under the plea bargaining agreement he received four twelve-year sentences to be served concurrently – he was the happiest person in the bullpen, the holding cell under the courthouse where inmates wait until they go back to the county jail or their assigned prison.

Said Lawton, "These other prisoners were saying, 'You poor guy, you got twelve years.' Ninety percent of them were snitches, and they only got a few years. But even after getting twelve years, I was a happy camper."

Because Lawton wouldn't snitch, the feds decided to take it out on him. Their punishment was to send him straight to

USP Atlanta, a maximum security prison.

"They say they don't do that. Bullshit," said Lawton. "I went to Atlanta, which at the time was the worst prison in America.

"The guards said to me, 'You're going to Atlanta man. Oh, I'm sorry. You're fucked. You're a white guy in that prison. There they torture you."

CHAPTER 8

Journey to Atlanta

While Lawton was working out his plea deal with the government and before he was sentenced, he was held in detention in medium-security facilities in Fairton, New Jersey, and then was transferred to Schuylkill, Pennsylvania.

The unit for pre-trial prisoners was called the carrot unit because everyone housed there walked around in orange jump suits. Lawton travelled back and forth to the court house in Philadelphia in vans that held seven to ten prisoners.

Before his hearing Lawton sat in a holding cell under the courtroom, and after the hearing, he'd be taken back to the cages down below and wait while the cases of the other prisoners were being heard. At the end of the day he'd go back to prison.

*

After a defendant is convicted, the Federal Bureau of Prisons assigns a new inmate a security level. His crimes, length of sentence, past history, and prison infractions are all factors that go into what security level he will receive, and that security level will determine what prison he goes to.

The Federal Bureau of Prisons has four basic levels: camp, low, medium and high. A fifth level, super-max, located in

Florence, Colorado, is a lockdown facility for the stone-cold killers and other menaces to society.

Camp is the level with the least supervision and the fewest rules. It houses inmates with short sentences and no violence on their records. There are no fences, no controlled movements, and very few guards monitoring these inmates. Drug offenders and white-collar criminals are usually assigned to these camps.

There are camps at all the high-security facilities, also called penitentiaries. The reason they have camps at the penitentiaries is so non-violent inmates can man the warehouses and take care of the grounds around each penitentiary.

The next level, the low-security facility, is primarily for drug dealers, ex-cops, a judge or two, and white collar criminals – serious offenders who aren't very violent and who have sentences usually less than twenty years.

Though the prisoners aren't violent, the low-security prisons still go to a lot of trouble to make sure no one escapes. The lows have double barbed-wire fences and vans with riflemen that circle the prison 24/7 to watch for escape attempts. The fences are electrified and have sensors on them.

The low-security facility has dormitory-style living quarters and group bathrooms with toilets and sinks lined up along a wall. Because it's dormitory-style living, there are no lock-downs, the periods when inmates must remain locked in their cells.

Despite the non-violent nature of their crimes, low-security prisons are no country clubs. Inmates of low-security prisons don't have a run of the place. They're only allowed to move from one area of the prison to another – from work to the cell block, from the yard back to the cell block, or from the cell block to the library, say – during certain times of day and for short, specific periods. These prisons are talked about as country clubs, but they are far from that. They just aren't as draconian as the rest of the prisons in the system.

At the next level, medium security facilities, most of the men are there because they committed violent crimes. They've been convicted of serious felonies such as armed robbery, rape, assault with a deadly weapon, or some crime where someone got shot, stabbed, and gotten the shit beaten out of them. They are sent to a medium-security facility rather than a high-security facility because their violence hasn't escalated to a penitentiary level.

They have the same precautions to prevent escapes as the low-level facilities, with electrified barbed-wire fences and constant patrols. Prisoners live two to a cell, unless the place is overcrowded, and then three live together, with one of them sleeping on the floor. Or they add another steel bunk, and they sleep as though they are in a coffin.

There's a lot of violence at medium-security prisons, and the primary weapon used to combat it is called the lock-down. During lock-down, prisoners stay in their cells twenty four hours a day for anywhere from a day to even months. Lewisburg Penitentiary was locked down for six months in 1996, after members of the Aryan Brotherhood killed four Muslims, and the prison administration feared a race riot. On lock-down all you can do is sit in your cell. The guards will search the cells, interview inmates, and do whatever they can to diffuse the situation.

While in the carrot unit Lawton considered what prison he'd have to go to if he was convicted. Lawton was sure he'd go to a medium-security facility. It stood to reason. He hadn't killed anybody. He didn't have a life sentence. Penitentiaries were for murderers and repeat offenders. Lawton didn't even have a prison record.

What Lawton hadn't counted on was how angry the government was when he refused to rat out his brother David and the others who had helped him stage his jewelry store robberies. The prosecutor decided to punish him by recommending to the judge that he be sent to USP Atlanta, a maximum-security facility.

"My points didn't justify a penitentiary but they sent me there anyway," said Lawton. "They say they don't stick it to you if you refuse to cooperate. Bullshit! Because I wouldn't rat, I went to USP Atlanta, the worst prison in the country at the time."

Before he arrived at the federal penitentiary in Atlanta, first he would have to endure the trip there. From the Schuylkill, Pennsylvania, prison he'd have to travel first to the transfer center of the prison system, located at the United States penitentiary in Lewisburg, Pennsylvania. From there he would wait for an interminable period to take a plane to Oklahoma City – the hub of ConAir -- and then – finally – fly on to

Atlanta.

It was like the slow boat to China, but so as far as the prison administration was concerned Lawton had been sentenced to twelve years in prison, so there was no rush to get him where he was going. All they cared about was that he got to where he was supposed to go, and that he didn't try to escape.

As Lawton sat in his cell in Schuylkill, Pennsylvania, he could only think, *What a fucking trip this is going to be.*

*

Not a week after sentencing, Lawton was told it was time for him to begin his journey. Because he was classified as a violent offender, he was handcuffed, belly chained, and a black box was placed around his cuffs, making any movement virtually impossible.

"You can't move your hand more than inches," said Lawton. "Your hands get numb, you lose circulation, and you feel totally helpless." On the positive side, because he was wearing the black box, the other convicts sitting around him gave him some respect for being a hard-ass.

"They look at you, and they're thinking, 'I'm not going to fuck with that guy. He might be crazy.'"

After Lawton shuffled onto the bus and sat down, he and the other convicts were driven to Lewisburg, Pennsylvania, the facility that housed what they call the "hold-over" prisoners, those waiting to be shipped to their final destination. When the Lewisburg prison came into view, Lawton couldn't believe what he saw.

"On the way up the hill to the Lewisburg prison, which

was built in 1934 and looks like something out of a Dracula movie, I could see forty-foot walls, with gun towers and a lot of barbed wire," said Lawton. "We arrived in the morning, but the place looked gloomy and drab.

"When we arrived, we didn't go onto the yard. Almost everyone who got off the bus was sent directly to J Block, where they once kept the Cuban criminals from the Mariel boat lift."

J Block was the SHU, the special housing unit, or as it was better known, "the hole," where he was kept in seclusion for almost two weeks. Lawton's cell, a big block of solid concrete, was like a mausoleum. A broken window with rusted bars let the cold weather into the cell.

"When you're in the hole, it's like you're an animal in a cage at the zoo, only the animals at the zoo have more freedom," said Lawton.

The front of the cell was a big gray, steel door. There was one narrow slot in the door that opened and closed. Any time Lawton was allowed to leave his cell, whether it was to shower, to see a counselor or a doctor, he was handcuffed.

"No inmate housed in the SHU was ever allowed out of his cell without being handcuffed," said Lawton. "Every time the guards wanted to open the main door of the cell, I had to turn around with my hands behind my back and stick my two hands through the slot so the guards could cuff me."

The slot, which was also called the "food chute," was the opening through which he received his meals, all which he ate in his cell. According to Lawton, Lewisburg, unlike most prisons, actually had pretty decent food. The prisoners at Lewisburg were allowed showers twice a week, though for Lawton taking a shower at Lewisburg was always unnerving.

"They would cuff you, take you to the shower room with three guys I didn't know, and uncuff you," said Lawton. "Then they'd lock the door. Here you were naked in a room with three strangers who had been convicted of violent crimes. You could feel the tension. Every time I went in there to shower, I knew potentially I was risking my life. I went because I stunk and I needed to wash off. But every time I went in there, I was wary."

The only way Lawton could see what was going on around the cell block was to put a mirror through the tiny ten-inch square hole in the front door of the cell that had two bars across it. Using his mirror he'd look up and down the cellblock. He didn't know a soul, and since this was a transfer unit, cellmates would come and go. He was lonely, but he knew his stay at Lewisburg was temporary, so he patiently waited out the days until he'd be shipped out.

Once a week the Lewisburg warden's crew would walk through the hole to see how everybody was doing. The inmates called it "the Dog and Pony Show."

"They called it that," said Lawton, "because the whole thing was bullshit. Like the warden really gave a fuck.

"'How you doing?' he'd say.

"We were thinking, *What do you mean, 'How am I doing?' I'm in the fucking hole, jerk-off. Give me a blowjob, and I'll tell you how I'm doing.*

"One Thursday the word went out for all the inmates in the hole to fill our shampoo bottles with shit and piss. You really don't want to know how we did that, but I'm going to tell you anyway. You shit in a cup, let it sit a day, then mix it with water or piss and liquefy it. You put the mixture in a shampoo bottle, and then you wait.

"Since the tier had only one door, the warden would walk up one side and when he got to the end, he'd have to walk down the other side speaking to inmates in all the cells. On this particular Thursday, when the warden walked to the far end of the tier, as he started walking back toward the entrance, someone kicked his door, giving everyone the signal for all the inmates from all the cells to squirt the warden and his flunkies with their mixture of piss and shit. While the inmates were squirting away, all the while they were screaming and making sounds like insane monkeys in a crazy house.

"I didn't participate," said Lawton. "I was somewhat new to the system, and my cellie, who had built up more anger against the prison than I did, wanted to do this more than I did. I had nothing against the prison at this time. As I watched through the little ten-inch window over my cellie's shoulder, I could see him squirting away with a vengeance. I could see the warden, ducking and running, his clothes ruined. He was beyond angry, scrambling to get out of there. He and all his prison staff were covered in a heavy spray of piss and shit. The smell was nauseating."

Such disobedience didn't go without punishment. Severe

beatings followed.

"Even though I wasn't involved in this, it didn't make any difference," said Lawton. "About three hours after the warden got his ass out of there, the goon squad – the special operations team – six or seven giants -- went from cell to cell and beat everyone's ass. Four big fucking gorillas, white boys who were six foot four, 280 pounds, all goons, came into our cell wailing away. Whether you were involved or just an innocent bystander, they didn't give a fuck. They went down the tier, opening every door one at a time and beating everyone's ass bloody.

"I could hear them coming, and when they came to our cell, they ordered, "Cuff up," meaning we were supposed to put our hands in the opening in the door so they could handcuff us. Of course, once we knew why they were coming, there was no way we were going to cuff up. I knew we couldn't kick their ass, but at least I wanted my hands free to protect my face. At that point they came in anyway, and all you could try to do was protect yourself. Ater you were knocked down, you dropped into a fetal position. There was no point trying to resist at that point. No matter how tough you were, you couldn't beat four giant goons. And they beat the shit out of us. Simple as that. After they left, I was spitting up blood, and my face was all puffy. You might think, *They aren't going to hit you in the face because they might leave a mark?* Bullshit. They didn't give a shit about bruises or cuts. After they beat us, they left us lying there in a heap. I was beat up bad, but it was no big deal. I had been beat up bad before."

On the day Lawton was transferred out of Lewisburg, he was handcuffed and shackled along with a number of other inmates, put on a bus, and taken to an airport near Allenwood, Pennsylvania. He was travelling on ConAir, an operation run by the U.S. Air Marshals. Once again Lawton was belly chained and black boxed, and he was shackled with ankle cuffs as well. He was then searched again by the Air Marshals.

Said Lawton, "They make you open your mouth, pat you down, check your balls for weapons or a key or a razor blade or a bobby pin, which you can use to open handcuffs, and then they send you hobbling up the stairs onto a huge plane that holds about two hundred passengers."

Once Lawton and the other inmates took their seats, they were told they were forbidden to get up for any reason. If you had to go to the bathroom, it was tough luck.

"One time I was on ConAir for sixteen hours," said Lawton. "If you have to shit, they don't give a fuck. You just hold it in. You risk constipation or worse because your shit is poison, and you can actually die from the poison in your system. Or your intestines can explode.

"I used to watch the rookies, the young kids, get on the ConAir plane and eat the lunch they were given. I'd tell them, "Are you an idiot? It's better to be hungry than have to go to the bathroom and not be able to go." But they thought they were bad-asses, and they wouldn't listen, and hours later they'd be in purgatory."

The women prisoners were kept together in one section at

the front of the plane.

"You could sit a row or two behind them and try to sneak a peek," said Lawton, "but boy, did they look nasty. Picture it, an ugly broad, no makeup, in handcuffs with a prison travel uniform. Not too appealing."

The plane's destination was FTC Oklahoma, the hub of the Bureau of Prisons transportation system. No matter a prisoner's final destination, first stop always was FTC Oklahoma.

"You might be going from Pennsylvania to Atlanta, or from Southern California to New York but you still had to stop in Oklahoma City," said Lawton. "I've gone from Coleman, Florida to Jessup, Georgia, and I had to go through Okla-fucking-homa. I even went from Jessup, Georgia, to Edgefield, South Carolina, normally a two-hour bus ride, and I had to go through the Oklahoma hub. Go figure."

His destination, the Federal Transportation Center in Oklahoma City, is a sixteen-story building located at the Oklahoma City airport. Yes, the prison is at the airport. The plane pulls up to the building, the ramp is extended to the plane, and everyone walks right into the prison. The prisoners' feet never touch freedom.

After Lawton and the other prisoners disembarked, they walked into the prison past a huge guard standing six foot eight and weighing 300 pounds. He was an American Indian, and he was a legend.

"We were all in line," said Lawton, "and the Indian ordered this one prisoner to do something, and he didn't do it fast enough, and he snatched him out of the line, took him out of our sight, and gave him a beating.

"He snatched the dude out of the line, dragged him into a cell, and beat the crap out of him," said Lawton.

Lawton was placed in a holding cell with a hundred other prisoners. Immediately he could see that that FTC Oklahoma was a zoo. Several bloody fights broke out immediately.

"An inmate might recognize someone from another prison, a guy he didn't get along with, or there might be two guys from rival gangs who recognize each other, and without warning a fight breaks out," said Lawton. "Or a guy gets sentenced, and he's pissed off, and he thinks another guy might have snitched on him, and pow, it's on.

"I saw two Latino guys get into it. This one guy knocked the other one down, and his head was up against the steel toilet, and the first guy kept kicking the guy's head against the toilet. You heard ding, ding, ding every time he smashed his head against the steel toilet.

"No one interfered. The goon squad came ten minutes later, after the fight was over.

"They won't just open the cell and help the guy, because there are a hundred guys in there. Can you imagine if they opened the door, and a hundred guys tried to escape? They had to wait for the goon squad to come in. In most instances, like this one, the fight is over before they arrive."

At Oklahoma Lawton kept to himself. No one bothered him there.

"I do my thing," he said. "I didn't have co-defendents. I'm a good convict. I know how to handle myself. A lot of inmates have bravado, and they end up getting killed."

Oklahoma housed about three hundred men on each floor. The prisoners never left the floor and never went outside. There was one little recreation area with a basketball hoop, but that was about it. The purpose of this prison was to move prisoners within the system. The guards had one goal: make sure no one escaped.

Once a prisoner arrives at FTC Oklahoma, he has no idea how long he's going to be held there. It can be two or three weeks, or it can be three months, but chances are, it won't be a quick turnaround.

On Lawton's floor there were sixty cells in his pod, three pods to a floor, and each cell were supposed to hold two men. Because there were more prisoners than beds, in some cases three men were in a cell, and one of the men had to sleep on the floor.

Lawton's main gripe with the Oklahoma facility was the poor quality of the food.

"The food is made in the kitchen, and it comes up on a cart," he said. "You get fed breakfast, lunch, and dinner on a tray. The food is shitty processed, bullshit food. Mystery meat was the norm. Was it chicken? Was it beef? What was it? We never knew. It was mystery meat, something you wouldn't feed your dog."

While housed there Lawton felt lost and helpless. He had no possessions. He didn't know when he was going to leave. He had trouble falling asleep.

"You own no property at all, are given a golf pencil to write a letter, and if you're lucky, you'll get the two stamps a week they're supposed give you, *if* they come around," he said. "The prisoners heading off are awakened at one in the morning for their flight out. You get awakened all the time. You can't get comfortable. You can't sleep. You want so badly to get to where you're going, regardless of what other hell hole that might be."

While staying at the Oklahoma City hub, he informed one of the guards he was headed for Atlanta.

Said the guard, "Oh man, I'm sorry. You're fucked. You're a white guy in that prison. They're going to torture you there."

Lawton couldn't imagine such a place could possibly exist in America – until he got there.

CHAPTER 9

The Worst of the Worst

Lawton left Oklahoma before the crack of dawn. At Oklahoma prisoners rarely see daylight. He had arrived in the dark, and he was leaving in the dark.

The plane's first stop was Harrisburg, Pennsylvania. After the plane landed on the tarmac, Lawton sat there waiting in his seat for what seemed an eternity. A lieutenant walked onto the plane and started reading off names. Prisoners got up and hobbled down the stairway at the back of the plane. Lawton could see prisoners, standing in front of their assigned busses, again being searched for contraband. The Air Marshals then reloaded the plane with new inmates heading to God knows where.

The next stop was Atlanta. After hearing all the horror stories Lawton was beginning to feel an unsettling nervousness.

"You're a white boy in a prison with all black guards. You're the shit of the shit," he was told. Another prisoner who had spent time there told him, "The guards are going to beat your ass."

Lawton thought to himself, *How am I going to survive this?*

Lawton's name was called. Handcuffed and shackled, he got up and shuffled off down the center aisle to the back of the plane.

"Name and number," barked a huge black lieutenant.

"Lawton, 52224-004," he said.

Still in irons, he hobbled down the ramp and looked around. The plane was surrounded by guards with shotguns.

No getting away from here, he thought.

He headed to his assigned bus and waited to be searched.

Lawton sat on the bus as it drove through the slums of Atlanta. There was a sign for the Atlanta zoo. *Fitting*, he thought. Then he saw the prison, which was built in 1903. He could see the forty-foot high walls that ringed the place. A series of gun towers were prominent. Underground the concrete had been poured twenty-feet below the ground level, a guarantee that no one would dig himself out. In one brick tower Lawton noticed a flock of pigeons. He envied their freedom. In 1903 the Atlanta Federal Penitentiary was the largest poured concrete structure in the world, designed to make sure he wouldn't see the outside world for a long, long time.

This place is a dungeon, he thought.

As it was supposed to be. After all, it was designed to house the worst of the worst. Al Capone had resided there in the 1930s. The Cuban criminals who made up a large part of the Mariel Boat Lift ended up there, as did Tommy Silverstein, perhaps the most violent criminal Atlanta had ever seen.

Silverstein had been one of the founders of the Aryan Brotherhood, a Nazi hate group that targets blacks and Jews. In the 1970s Silverstein was in the hole when someone passed him a key and he was able to slip his handcuffs. He murdered a Black Panther by the name of Cadillac Smith, and when the guards came after him, he killed two guards, including a lieutenant. Silverstein was put in solitary confinement, alone with no human contact, and he's been in solitary since 1983. He has since been moved to Leavenworth, Kansas.

"Friends have told me he's a totally fucking psycho," said Lawton. "Everyone was worried about bringing members of Al Qaeda from Guantanamo to the U.S.? Are you kidding me? I laugh. Put them in there with guys in penitentiaries like Atlanta and they'd be lucky to survive."

*

The bus pulled up to a garage area and stopped. Lawton could see the gate open. After the bus pulled into the garage, he could hear the gate clang shut behind him.

"Okay, file off," everyone was ordered.

Lawton walked into a huge elevator with fifteen other inmates.

"Turn around and get against the wall," came the order from a burley guard with a deep voice. "Nuts to butts, tighten it up."

Lawton, who had traveled on a plane and a bus shackled for twelve hours, ached all over.

I guess I'm not going to get any sympathy from this place, he thought.

The elevator ascended, and after it stopped, the elevator door opened, and everyone entered receiving and discharge. The prisoners were ordered into a large cell. One by one the prisoners were uncuffed. They stood body to body crushed in like cattle as each prisoner's name was called for processing.

"Lawton, 52224-004."

Once they determined that Lawton was actually Lawton, the first thing they did was conduct a thorough body search.

"You lift your cock, bend over and spread your ass, then you squat and cough," said Lawton. "They want to make sure you don't have any contraband on you. They check to see you're not suitcasing – hiding something up your rectum."

Some of the prisoners were only staying at Atlanta overnight before being transferred to another prison. Those convicted of non-violent crimes were going to Atlanta's camp. Most, like Lawton, were headed to the SHU, the special housing unit, or the hole, where each prisoner with violence in his record had to spend from a few days to a month while undergoing what is known as the Captain's Review.

For his review, Lawton had to wait ten days, and during this period he learned just how hard living in the hole could be.

"The first thing I did was size up my cellie both physically and mentally," said Lawton. "I'm good at that. I'm a pretty intimidating guy, even though I wasn't all tatted up like I am now, and I wasn't nearly as hard-looking."

His cellmate, he saw, wasn't going to be a threat. But that didn't mean he didn't feel uncomfortable over his situation. He was used to living on his own terms. He was used to having privacy. Quickly Lawton learned that having the luxury of privacy was a thing of the past.

Because he had been traveling on ConAir, the first thing

Lawton had to do when he was assigned a cell in the hole was make a bowel movement. But the toilet was not three feet from the bunk beds, and there was another inmate already housed there who he didn't know. Lawton was used to privacy in the bathroom. This was entirely different.

"You gotta shit," said Lawton. "I asked him to turn around. I didn't want him watching me. When you're sitting on the toilet, you're used to being alone. I sat down on the toilet, and he lay on his bunk, his head at the far end of the cell faced toward the wall. If I had wanted to, I could have reached out and touched his leg. That's how close we were.

"This time I was lucky. My cellie was okay. Later in other prisons I had to room with cellies who were animals. That's when you fight in the cells. One time I beat a guy until he couldn't move, because when you're locked in, it's either him or me. No referee. Lucky for him, I had a heart, or I would have killed the guy. I was worried he was going to kill me first. But not this time. I became comfortable with my cellie rather quickly. We started talking. If you don't get along, then when it's time to go to sleep, you better sleep with one eye open. Which is what I did that first night anyway. Atlanta was one place where you never got comfortable."

In the hole, Lawton quickly saw, he and the other prisoners were at the mercy of the guards.

"You find you have nothing coming to you," said Lawton. "Meaning there's no point banging on the door and saying, 'Hey man, I don't have a blanket.' What blanket? You're lucky you're alive in there. If you bang on the door, the guard comes up to the door and says, 'What do you want? You want a blanket? Now you don't get one.' They do whatever they want to do. You're under the command of the fucking Gestapo."

The inmates in the hole were also at the mercy of the elements. Temperature, both from the weather and from the water temperature of the showers, was a serious problem.

"Atlanta had air conditioning, but it was either broke most of the time or the guards were fucking with us," said Lawton. "In the summer the place was a sauna, and in the winter the prisoners froze. We'd beg for blankets. We didn't always get them."

Showering was a problem because the guards controlled the temperature of the water. If a guard felt like it, he could turn off the hot water in the winter so the prisoners would freeze. But that wasn't nearly as bad as when they turned off the cold water, because the result was boiling hot water. When the guards turned off the cold water, Lawton quickly learned you couldn't shower or you would be scalded. One time Lawton didn't shower for fourteen days because the guards refused to turn the cold water back on.

Lawton lay on his bunk in the hole listening to the mayhem around him.

"You hear everything that's going on around you," he said. "You'll hear the other inmates talking or screaming. You hear the drug deals going down. The orderly will come up to your window and say, 'Do you need anything? What you got?' I didn't have anything. I was new to the system. I didn't know how it worked. What he was saying was, If you need heroin, if you need weed, whatever you want, he could get. And if you had it, he could find a buyer for it.

"The orderly asked me, 'Who do you know?' He wanted to know if I had any connections. I was also offered credit if I wanted to buy drugs. Many times I saw guys who bought drugs on credit, and before they knew it, they had a heroin addiction.

"I kept a low profile. My goals were simple. I wanted air, food, and shelter. I told myself, *That's all you have to worry about.*"

Lawton would learn that he had one more goal; one more important even than the others, and that was survival.

Finally, after two weeks in the hole, Lawton underwent Captain's Review.

*

The captain, who is head of security, has to clear each new prisoner for his yard. He and his staff do this by asking a series of questions to see if the prisoner has problems with any particular group, or any particular inmate, or to find out if the prisoner fears for his life, in which case he might find himself in solitary confinement.

"The Captain's Review is important," said Lawton, "because if you're a wise-ass and the captain doesn't like you, you could end up in the hole forever."

Lawton's review went quickly.

"Do you have any problems on the yard?"

"No."

"Do you have any separtise?" Meaning, was there anyone

with whom he had a beef? This could be someone involved in the prisoner's case, like a snitch, or it could be someone the prisoner had a fight with in another prison. Every new prisoner gets asked, because if unchecked these feuds can get somebody killed.

"No."

"Are you scared to be on the yard?"

"No."

"All right, Lawton. Pack up."

Pack up what? Lawton thought, *What the fuck do I have to pack up?*

*

Once in the general population, now Lawton really had to watch his back. He was one of two thousand inmates at Atlanta. Most were in for violent crimes including murder, rape, and as in Lawton's case, armed robbery. About eight hundred of the prisoners were sentenced to life, meaning they weren't going to get out and they had nothing to lose if they were to commit further mayhem. Two hundred were psychopaths, who chased drugs and punks (guys who were gay or who were gay in prison) and who were intent on escape, as impossible as that might be.

Many of the inmates belonged to gangs including the Aryan Brotherhood, the Bloods, the Crips, the Latin Kings, Surenos, Gangster Disciples, and a number of others.

Worse for Lawton, most of the inmates were black guys with chips on their shoulders. Though he had no prejudice in his bones, Lawton quickly learned what it was like to be in the minority.

"Atlanta was a terrible place for a white guy to be," said Lawton. "The Atlanta penitentiary, fittingly near the Atlanta zoo, was only fifteen percent white." Of the two thousand prisoners, only 375 were white. And eighty percent of the guards were black. "And they hated white prisoners," said Lawton. Over and over he would hear, "Who the fuck do you think you are? You're a white guy. Forget it."

"The white guards weren't much better," said Lawton. "Most were out to prove themselves."

Every day behind the concrete walls of Atlanta crimes such as stabbings, rapes, robberies, drug dealing, extortion, prostitution, gambling, and pretty much any other illegal activity you can think of took place. For inmates found to be a snitch, a child molester, or someone not accepted in the minds of the inmates, the likelihood of a stabbing, a severe beating, or even murder was inevitable.

"I was a monkey in a cage," said Lawton. "The trick was to avoid the worst of the worst and survive."

*

After getting his bedroll, Lawton was assigned to cellblock A-1. Accompanied by guards, he and a half dozen other inmates had to walk past C-block, the long-term hole that consisted of five tiers of cells with old iron bars, like dungeons, from the time Al Capone was housed there. Lawton could hear the commotion coming from behind the steel doors.

As Lawton headed toward A-block down a long passageway,

he could hear all the commotion coming from D-block and B-block as well. As he entered A-block all the inmates were looking at him. Not a word was uttered. It was eerie, because A-1 had two tiers, and the inmates were hanging over the top tier watching him in silence. On every floor in Atlanta there are two guard stations where the guards often stay when not making rounds. They were looking too.

As he walked past the cells toward the guard station, he noticed one inmate who looked just like a woman, with his eyebrows and lips tattooed. These inmates who looked like women, of which there were many, were called punks, he would soon learn.

Holy fuck, Lawton thought, *this is a world unto itself.* Cells were not assigned. The inmates picked their own cellmates. It was nerve-racking because Lawton had no idea how the inmates approached each other.

Who will be my cellie? he wondered.

He was on the lookout for a white inmate who didn't appear to be a homicidal maniac.

Lawton and an inmate by the name of Lee Sharow found each other. As he walked by, Lawton was asked by Sharow, "Yo, where you from?" That was always the first question asked.

"New York," said Lawton.

Sharow then began talking, asking him questions like, "Where'd you come from? Who was on the bus? How long have you been traveling?" And then he asked, "How long you got?"

"I have four 12s," Lawton said, meaning he had been hit with four twelve-year sentences to run concurrently. Lawton was a little embarrassed. Compared to most everyone else, it was a very short sentence. Sharow, who was from Pensacola, Florida, had attacked a man with an axe handle and killed him. He was serving a life sentence.

Sharow didn't want a cellie who was a snitch or a wacko. He wanted a cellie who would live and let live. Early on Sharow and Lawton clicked, important because strangers who were going to be living in very close proximity for a long, long time better get along.

"Hey, I got some toothpaste," said Lee.

"Hey man, thanks a lot." Sharow also gave him a pair of sneakers.

Sharow and Lawton together walked over to the guard.

"We're going to cell together," said Sharow.

Sharow, it turned out, was part of the group of cool white inmates. The word went out: *Lawton's a New York guy, a white guy, and he's okay.*

*

Lawton's next order of business was to get in touch with Vic Orena, who before his incarceration at Atlanta had been the acting boss of the Columbo crime family. Oreno, convicted of murder and racketeering, received three life sentences plus 75 years in a federal penitentiary. In prison Orena was an important person to know.

Lawton asked Sharow if he knew Orena.

"I have a letter for him," Lawton said. The letter was from Jerry Chilli, a capo from one of the crime families who controlled the operations for the mob in Broward County, Florida, and in Hollywood, Florida. Lawton and Chilli had met while Lawton was on trial for the jewelry store robberies. When Chilli learned that Lawton was going to Atlanta, Chilli wrote Orena a letter of introduction letting Orena know that Lawton was a stand-up guy.

"Vic Orena is in D-block," said Sharow. "He usually goes to the yard every day. You should see him there."

His cellie situation settled, Lawton's most fervent wish was to go outside on the yard. He had just been in the hole and travelling for the past six weeks, and he was dying to see and feel some sunlight. And he badly wanted to meet Orena, one of the most powerful inmates in the prison.

Orena was on the yard, as advertised, and when Lawton gave him Chilli's letter of introduction, he was greeted like it was old home week. On day one, Lawton had found a cellmate and for his protection and for companionship joined Orena's group, which included other powerful Mafiosi including the murderous Vic Amuso, once a soldier for Joey Gallo but later the reputed boss of the Lucchese crime family. Amuso had killed several members of the Joseph Profaci crime family.

Also there was the fearsome Nicodemo "Nicky" Scarfo, the cold-hearted murderous boss of the Bruno-Scarfo Philadelphia crime family. Scarfo was responsible for twenty-eight murders, half of them members of his own gang. He was also suspected of killing a federal judge. Pasquale "Patty" Amato, another member of the Colombo crime family, also was housed in Atlanta. Patty and Larry often would sit on the yard and on Sunday afternoons would listen to an Atlanta radio station that played Frank Sinatra from two to four p.m.

"The only good thing about Atlanta was that it had good radio stations," said Lawton. "That's because we were in the city."

Lawton got to know all these men. Often he would walk the yard with Nicky Scarfo, but he got to know Vic Orena the best.

"I learned that Vic made some phone calls, found out I was a stand-up guy, and along with the note from Jerry Chilli, that's why he took care of me. Being one of the guys helped me get through Atlanta."

Lawton's first week on the yard wasn't too bad. Then he got in trouble. Lawton was standing with a group of white inmates, the cool guys, who began complaining about the food.

Lawton had eaten the food, and it was disgusting.

"This was 1998," said Lawton, "and we'd been given the meat from Desert Storm, which took place in 1992. One time I bit into the slop, and I almost chipped my tooth. The worst meat is cut right near the bone. It was disgusting. That's what they gave us. There was no way they could have sold this meat anywhere in the world.

"The guys said to me, 'Go to the warden and tell him how shitty the food is. Maybe it'll help.'"

Lawton, a newbie at Atlanta, didn't know it, but his cool friends were messing with him and leading him down a dangerous path. Atlanta was run by Warden Willie Scott, a large, hulking black man known as "Big Willie the "trouble-shooting warden." During his career Scott was sent to prisons to straighten them out and impose discipline after a riot or other disturbance. He had so much pull that he could transfer an inmate without going to the regional office. He would say, "Put him on the bus." And the inmate would be shipped out to another prison that night.

Warden Scott was a no-nonsense guy who didn't stand for backtalk, criticism, or even a wrong look, – or suggestions from inmates. Lawton's friends were having fun with him and knew what was going to happen.

Lawton walked up to the warden, and he said, "Warden Scott, the food here isn't very good."

"'Oh really,' he said calmly. 'Hold on.' He called the lieutenant over.

"'Throw him in the hole." he ordered. And into the hole Lawton was thrown.

"What the fuck did I do to be in the hole? asked Lawton. I said, 'The food's not that great.' I didn't even say it in a bad way."

The injustice of it all made him boil with anger, an anger he had no way of dissipating.

During his time in the hole he was banging on the door to get the attention of the counselor on the floor, a decent man by the name of Farley.

"I said to Farley, 'What kind of place is this, Disneyland?'

"Farley was a big black guy who was pretty cool," said Lawton. "'What the fuck is going on?' I said to him. 'This place is a fucking zoo.'

"'Larry,' he said, 'Just be quiet. Don't say anything.'

"I always bitched. I couldn't help myself."

And because he couldn't help himself, three of the eighteen months he resided at Atlanta was spent in the hole. Unlike his stay in the hole before Captain's Review, this time Lawton was sent there as punishment. This time his treatment wasn't as humane. He was put in a cell, stripped naked, and as punishment the guards made him sit naked in the cold for a couple hours before they brought him his orange jumpsuit.

"It was winter, and you're on the floor in a fetal position freezing your balls off," said Lawton. "You're at their mercy." Two weeks later he was returned to his cell on the yard. All the while Lawton was learning what it took to survive.

He learned to eat Ramen noodles raw, which when raw look like a chunk of straw.

"Then you drink a glass of water, and the noodles expand in your stomach, and you're full. When you go from being a millionaire riding around in a limo to eating Ramen noodles raw to keep from being hungry, you truly understand the big picture."

He also learned that to survive, he had to be vigilant every day.

"Imagine waking up every morning fearing for your life," said Lawton. "I never slept past six o'clock in the morning.

Every single morning you put your boots or sneakers on. You never know when you'll need them in a fight. You never look into a cell. One time I noticed an inmate being stabbed by two other inmates, and I just kept on walking. Another time I watched four inmates run in on a guy and stab him thirty times. The guy came staggering out of his cell, blood dripping everywhere, screaming. The four ran to ditch their shanks, because they knew the guards would come running, and there was going to be an investigation. Everyone knew who did it, but no one was ever able to prove it."

Another time Lawton saw a guard attacked by an inmate. That doesn't happen in most prisons, but in Atlanta the inmates with life sentences would go crazy, and they didn't care. Lawton watched an inmate slam a guard to the ground and then kick him repeatedly. No one came to stop him until the other guard on the floor hit the alarm button, and then dozens of guards and staff came running to his defense.

"I'm sure that inmate got the beating of his life," said Lawton.

Lawton once heard the guards break the leg of the inmate in the next cell. He didn't' see it, but he could hear the snap of the bone and the blood-curdling screams through the vent.

"You have no idea from where the danger will emanate," said Lawton. "It could be from one or more of the guards or another inmate. It could come from looking at someone the wrong way, bumping into someone and not saying 'I'm sorry,' or a slight real or imagined. Maybe someone thought you looked into his cell and saw something you shouldn't have seen like a guy stashing his drugs or hiding his wine. Or perhaps a guy was fucking a punk. Or maybe the guy with the shank was just mentally ill, like an inmate by the name of Ozzie.

"Ozzie was a black inmate who went crazy," said Lawton. "He taped two shanks, one to each hand, and he ran down the tier stabbing anyone who was in his path. By the time he got to the end of the tier, all the guards came running. They were screaming, "Drop the knife." But the shanks were taped to his hands. They surrounded him, and they sprayed him with mace. He didn't kill anybody. He just went crazy.

"There's a different code in a penitentiary than in any other prison setting," said Lawton. "It's all about survival. Psychopaths rule the prison."

CHAPTER 10

An Atmosphere of Violence

One fear Lawton had to overcome was that of rats. Not the human snitching kind of rat. The rodent kind of rat. Atlanta had such a major rat infestation it allowed cats, dozens of cats. One of the rats even had a name.

"There was one rat in the kitchen the inmates called Big Ben," said Lawton. "He was so big he could get on its hind legs and get up on a chair. That rat was fearless and wouldn't run from you. The inmates tried to poison and trap him, but nothing worked. I once ran up to Big Ben with a broom, but he just turned his head and showed me his teeth. He held his ground. I was so freaked out that I backed away. You didn't fuck with Big Ben."

Another time Lawton was in his cell, and he heard chewing.

What the fuck is that? Lawton wondered.

"I got up and opened my locker, and the sound stopped," said Lawton. "I closed the locker, and I heard the sound again. I opened the locker a second time, and a rat jumped out on top of me and ran out of the cell. I freaked out. Ahhh, motherfucker. I hate rats, all kinds."

But his fear of rats was nothing compared to his feelings of loneliness and failure. Lawton had married Missy in November of 1994. He and Missy had a daughter, and he also had a son with his first wife. He and Missy lived together until December of 1996 when he was arrested.

While he was robbing jewelry stores, they were living high on the hog. In his six years he had cleared about four hundred thousand dollars a year, but he never figured he'd get caught, so he never stashed any of his money.

"If I had stashed thirty percent, that's three quarters of a million," said Lawton, "but no one in my business does that. You just don't. You live on the edge. You live a different life. Nobody I knew lived the life of a regular person.

"People took advantage of Missy and the money dried up. She had everything, and suddenly she had nothing. All through my time in prison I would send her two or three hundred a month, but that wasn't nearly enough to live on. She ended up living with a guy and having his baby.

"Losing Missy drove me crazy. I knew it was my fault and that she had to move on. We had lived a wild life, but we were starting to look like a family. I would sit in my cell and cry uncontrollably, want to call her every minute, but I had to be strong. My heart was truly broken.

"Your brain is amazing. It keeps working while you're sleeping, and sometimes that isn't a good thing. I would wake up in a sweat. I was locked in a cell and couldn't do a thing about my situation. You truly start going crazy. You also have to appear tough, because in prison the first sign of weakness could be the last sign you see. The place was full of animals and vultures.

"Once you're in prison, your marriage is over. You can't

expect someone to wait for you. Ninety five percent of all marriages dissolve this way. It's the norm. I could never blame Missy for our divorce. Hell, I put myself in prison. It wasn't her fault. I blame nobody but myself."

*

Lawton quickly learned about currency in prison. In all the years as a prisoner he never once saw any money. Instead, in prison the main currency was postage stamps.

"An inmate is able to buy postage stamps at the commissary at face value but on the prison yard, the value of a book of twenty stamps was five dollars," said Lawton. "It cost twenty-five cents for one stamp. Inmates would amass hundreds and even thousands of dollars worth of stamps gambling or dealing drugs.

"If you wanted to buy a grilled cheese sandwich from the kitchen, it would cost you four stamps worth a dollar," said Lawton. "A hamburger would cost four stamps.

"I watched an inmate get killed for a book of stamps, which he had used to buy drugs. I didn't know much about him. He was a black guy in his early 30s, kind of muscular. When you owe money, everyone knows it, and they stay away from you. Because the inmates know you're trying to get money from whoever you can in order to pay off the debt."

The other currency at Atlanta was drugs.

"In Atlanta, if you went into the hole, you would suitcase some heroin," said Lawton. "Once you arrived at the hole, you could then trade the heroin to the orderly for things you wanted like a toothbrush, soap, or a radio. If a prisoner owed money to members of his group, that group might send him to the hole with heroin suitcased to make money. He'd then trade the heroin for stamps, and he'd use the stamps to pay off his debt.

"Most of the guys who did this were junkies," said Lawton. "They were told, 'If you use the heroin and don't come back with the stamps, we're going to kill you.' Some of them used the heroin anyway and then ran to the captain to keep from getting killed."

It wasn't long before Lawton saw that there were more drugs in prison than there were on the street. Quickly he learned which inmates sold what and in what amounts. His friend Reno, a member of the Latin Kings, earned $10,000 a month selling heroin.

"If you're on the streets and you want to buy heroin, you might have to drive two miles," said Lawton. "In Atlanta you only had to go five cells down. On the streets you might have one or two heroin dealers in your neighborhood. In Atlanta, we had fifteen dealers. Everything was readily available – heroin, crack, coke, acid, weed, you name it."

He also discovered how the drugs made their way into the prison.

"There are several ways," said Lawton. "A girlfriend of an inmate will wrap the heroin in cellophane, put it inside a plastic Kotex, and put it inside her vagina. She'll come in for a visit, go to the bathroom, take it out, and pass it to the guy. He'll then suitcase it -- slide it up his rectum.

"Or someone on the outside would take heroin or coke or

weed and put it in a condom in little balls. He'd make thirty of those and put them in an M&Ms bag. Then during the visit, he'd go up to the candy vending machine, buy M&Ms, and then switch them. The inmate would sit there eating what the guard thought were M&Ms, but really they were the little balls of heroin, coke or weed, and later he'd shit them out.

"While I was there one inmate was caught with seventy little balls of weed. If the guards think you have something in your system, they will put you in a dry cell. A dry cell is a totally empty cell with no running water. They then wait until you take three shits into a bucket before you can get out. If there's anything in your system they'll find it. Someone watches you the whole time.

"I never had to go through this ordeal," said Lawton. "I wasn't a drug pusher."

A third -- and most prevalent method of bringing drugs into the prison -- involved the guards, who brought them in. The drug kingpins in the prison contact their people on the outside, and those people would send the guard money and drugs to a specific PO Box. The guard would then bring the drugs right into the prisoner's cell. Lawton saw guards bring in a pound of weed at a time. If a pound of weed was worth $1,000 on the streets, it was worth ten times that in prison.

At Atlanta, most of the debts were drug debts. If the debt dragged on too long, you could get killed.

"This guy had borrowed books of stamps, and he used them to buy drugs, and he didn't pay the guy back, and sure enough, three guys go into his cell and stab him to death," said

Lawton. "Just like that. Everyone knows the identity of the killers, who have life sentences. What did they care?"

One time an inmate acquaintance of Lawton's borrowed money from a loan shark, who made the loan because Lawton had vouched for him.

"I gave my word that he was good for it," said Lawton.

Several months went by, and when the inmate by the name of Streeter didn't pay back the debt, Lawton knew if he didn't do something to urge Streeter to pay the money back, he would be the target of the guys who had lent him the money. Lawton decided that the impetus Streeter needed would come at the business end of a shank.

"You can make a steel shank out of anything," said Lawton. "You can make it in a machine shop. You can make a shank from the edge of a foot locker or from bed springs. Shanks go for big money in the joint."

Lawton, like most inmates, had numerous shanks planted all around the prison. He had one shank outside his cell on a pipe above his door. He had another shank inside a coffee creamer can inside his locker. He had another one hidden on the yard. The guards often found the ones on the yard, so Lawton was never sure it was there.

"Why did I need a shank? For self-protection," Lawton said. "Death was a common occurrence. There were more murders and overdoses in the Atlanta prison than anywhere in the system. You never wanted to be caught with your dick in your hand. Your dick isn't hard enough. It better be steel."

Lawton took a shank and went looking for Streeter. He

found him, and when Streeter saw Lawton, he must have realized that Lawton was after him, because he began running through the unit up the stairs to the second level where he lived to get away from him.

"I'm chasing him, and he's running through people, and I take two stabs at him with my shank, and I get him on the side," said Lawton. "He made it to the second level, where I wasn't allowed to go."

Lawton ran back to his cell, ditched the shank, and was all hyped up waiting to see what would happen. During count time, Streeter walked past Lawton's cell in handcuffs. He had blood on his shirt from where I got him. He looked right into the window where Lawton was standing and never said a word.

"I give him that," said Lawton.

Another time Lawton was certain that another inmate – Lawton never knew his name -- was out to kill him. When Lawton went out on the yard, he made sure he carried his knife with him.

"I knew he was going to have a knife, and I had to protect myself," said Lawton. "If I pull out my knife, he's going to stop for a second, and that'll give me enough time for the guards to shoot down on the yard. It might save my life. In prison you do what you have to."

The problem Lawton had was that he had to get through three sets of metal detectors to reach the yard with his knife. Lawton knew exactly what to do.

"I put the shank in one half of a plastic toothbrush holder, taped the open end, and put it up my ass. I made sure to put it *way* up. Did you know you have seven extra inches in your ass to hide something? You do. I knew one guy who put six quarter-rolls of weed up his ass.

"To get to the yard you have to pass through three metal detectors. When the detectors go off, the guards pull you out of the line, and they strip search you. You have to lift your nuts, turn around, spread your ass, but the knife is past your sphincter. They can't see it, and they won't find it. They don't know if you have a metal knee or a bullet still in you. After you get through that third metal detector, only then do you take the shiv out of your ass, put it in a wooden handle hidden on the yard, and you have your shank. Wooden handles don't get found as much because the guards run the metal detectors everywhere and wood isn't detectable.

"We confronted each other. The guy pulled a knife, and I pulled mine. The guards came out of the tower and leveled their rifles screaming over a bullhorn for everyone to get down. The situation was diffused. The shank up my ass saved my life."

Off to the hole both went.

In another incident Lawton and a buddy stealthily followed an inmate he had a beef with into the gym, a space so dangerous that the guards rarely would enter. There were two handball courts and a regulation basketball court and bleachers on either side of the court. Inside the gym was a bathroom, located behind the wall, and Lawton watched the inmate go inside.

Lawton noticed that one of the orderlies had left a mop bucket and wringer near a supply closet, and Lawton told his friend, "Watch the door." He picked up the mop wringer and held it by his side as he stood by the outside entrance to the bathroom. Lawton heard the toilet flush, and when he saw the shadow of the inmate as he was walking out, he swung the mop wringer like it was a baseball bat, and he smashed the guy in the face. The guy dropped like a stone. Lawton dropped the mop wringer, left the gym, and blended into the crowd as he headed back to his unit.

"I hit the guy at three thirty in the afternoon," said Lawton. "That was the time they had recall, which was when you had to go back to your cell. Every day in federal prison they have what they call four 'clock standup count, when every single inmate has to be on his feet locked in his cell. They do that because for three days they had counted an inmate who had died on his bunk.

"So every day at four o'clock they count, and if everyone is counted, they open the doors about four-thirty, and then they allow the units to eat. Sure enough, four-thirty came, and they didn't open the doors. At five, they still didn't open the doors. Holy shit! I was sure it was because the guy I smashed wasn't accounted for.

"I wondered whether I had killed him, but when someone in prison dies, the word gets out fast, and no one had said anything. Someone found him, all fucked up. At about five fifteen they opened the doors. I never heard about it again, and I never saw the guy again."

*

After several months of incarceration at Atlanta Lawton was learning how to become a convict. There are two types of men living in Atlanta. There are the inmates, who follow the rules and do everything they're supposed to do. They aren't trusted. And there are the convicts, those who question authority, stand-up guys, who understand how to do prison time. Usually old timers.

Lawton was a convict, and one of the illicit enterprises he became involved in was the making of wine and alcohol. Stealing from the kitchen was a part of the prison culture, and Lawton, who worked in the kitchen, became very good at it.

"Every week we would make thirty gallons of wine," said Lawton. "We'd take fifteen gallons and break it up into sixty quarts, and we'd sell each quart for five dollars. That's one book of stamps. That's $300 a week or 60 books of stamps.

"Making wine involved stealing fruit and sugar from the mess hall. Stealing sugar was an art. You can't just walk around prison like you own the place. You have to hide things, because the guards are constantly patting you down. One of my co-conspirators had a size 10 foot but he stole size 13 shoes from the laundry. He looked like Bozo the Clown with his big feet, and he would stuff sugar packets and Ziploc bags full of sugar into the space in front of his toes in the shoes, and he'd bring it back to our unit.

"We mixed the fruit we stole, and the sugar, and we'd put a little yeast in there and let it ferment, and viola, it became wine – wine that could make you drunk as a skunk.

"To make the wine, we had put the wine in a bag, hide the bag behind the cell wall, and let it ferment. To make the hiding place in the wall four or five of us used nail clippers to chisel a foot-round hole behind the shower in our cell. We'd put a large bag in the hole and pour the wine into the bag. Getting the wine out of the wall required us to steal a hose from a clothes washer or dryer. We'd suck on the hose and siphon the wine back into a bucket. As soon as the wine was ready, we'd sell it, and within an hour everyone was roaring drunk.

"One time we didn't give the wine enough air to breath, and it started to cook, and it exploded, making a big hole in the bag. You could smell the alcohol throughout the whole cell block. The guards looked for the wine everywhere.

"The other fifteen gallons we'd cook off and make into white lightning, pure grain alcohol. To do that you have to boil it, and we did that by taking a piece of electrical cord from a typewriter or from the light in the counselor's office, we'd then take the device that boils the water – we called it a stinger -- two small metal drain covers or any two pieces of thin metal, take a little piece of rubber or wood, something not conductive, and face the two pieces right next to each other without allowing them to touch, maybe a quarter or half inch apart, then put one wire to one, the other to the other, and you boil water or any liquid real fast. The key is to make sure the metal doesn't touch, and you plug the electrical cord in when the device is in the liquor -- or you'll blow the fuses in the area of the prison you are in."

Which Larry did. "If there's no power or lights, the administration and guards freak. Using that little device, I was able to make the liquor. We took the wine we made, and we put it in a mop bucket. We put the mop bucket in a big trash bag, and we stuck the stinger inside the wine. The bag expands as the heat from stinger cooks the alcohol. The alcohol rises and ends up on the sides of the bag where it drips down to the bottom of the bag. The pure grain alcohol is at the bottom of the bag. For every gallon of wine, we made one pint of hard liquor, and that stuff was the real deal. It could really fuck you up. In prison that pint sold for forty dollars.

"Guess what happens when you have a lot of drunk inmates in prison? Fights, stabbings and total mayhem. I was told that one time in Florence, Colorado, three guys were put in a cell because of overcrowding, two had life sentences and the other a 10 year sentence and was due to be released soon. They all got drunk and the two with life sentences used a razor they stole previously and cut out the liver and intestines of the other guy. They hung the intestines around the window in the cell door. Did they hate the third guy? Who knows? They had totally lost it."

About four months after being incarcerated in Atlanta Lawton was caught with a shank by the guards. He had it for his own protection, but getting caught with a shank was an offense punishable by a stint in the hole.

Soon after going to the hole, Lieutenant Catret, who was in charge, wanted to know where Lawton got the shank. Lawton, who wasn't a rat, refused to tell him. Catret, like the prosecutor, made him pay for his silence.

"Catret, the head of the SHU, was an Italian asshole guy from New York City who had a team of goons with him," said Lawton. "Catret was pretty big, but he didn't do his own dirty work. He was the motherfucker who used to beat everybody's ass. The goon squad would go into a cell, and you would hear inmates begging for their lives. You could hear them screaming on the end of the tier. And you knew it wouldn't be long before they were coming for you."

Catret was heartless. Because Lawton wouldn't tell him what he wanted to know, Catret sent his goons in to exact punishment.

"When you hear them open the door at the end of the tier, you know they're coming to get you, and that's the most fear you have in prison. You really believe you're going to die. It's not the beating itself. The door opens, and your juices are flowing, and your adrenaline is up, and then you work yourself up, get mean, fuck you, and get ready to fight.

You get ready to fight, but the outcome is always the same: a severe beating.

"Four guards the size of gorillas came in and no words are said, they just start beating on me, and you can't fight that many guys. No way. All that movie stuff is bullshit. As I was trying to cover up, all I can hear the guards saying is, 'You're a smart ass, huh?'"

They knocked Lawton to the floor, kicked him, and pounded on him over and over again with their fists until they figured he had enough. Other than screaming in pain, Lawton took his beating in silence.

"There's no telling on them," said Lawton. "Who are you going to tell? Nobody cares about you. I'm a pretty tough guy, but there were times when I wondered whether I was going to survive to the next day."

While in the hole Lawton made various objects, to make what little life he had more bearable. Like having a straight-edged razor blade from a disposable razor to sharpen a pencil or cut a piece of bed sheet. The trick, of course, was stealing the blade without the guard finding out.

"An inmate is given a razor to shave once a week," said Lawton. "An hour later the guard comes and retrieves it and makes sure the blade is still in the razor. I learned how to fool the guards by taking a silver-colored advertisement from a magazine, cutting it into the exact shape of the razor, and putting the silver-colored paper in the razor in place of the actual blade. The guard would check, see what he thought was the blade, and throw it in the trash. I then kept the actual blade in my cell, a blade which I used for various reasons. "

One of the other items Lawton learned how to make at Atlanta was a rope, which only had two uses: either it was a means of communication in the hole or a way to commit suicide.

Each cell in the hole had a solid door, but there was a one-inch gap underneath it. The inmates figured out an ingenious delivery system to pass messages – known as kites -- through that gap under the door.

"They give you a sheet, and you cut it lengthwise into

strips," said Lawton. "Then you tie them together to make a long rope. You attach a message to the end of the rope along with a weight – usually a flat, empty toothpaste tube to give it enough weight to travel far enough to go down the tier and get under another inmate's cell door.

"If you miss, you pull it back in and try again. Until you reach him."

Lawton got so proficient he could shoot a kite along the floor into just about any cell.

"I can also make a rope out of a pair of underwear. It takes me eight hours. You take the cotton that goes up and down, up and down, and you twist it and twine it into a rope. That rope makes a better kite because it's smaller and lighter, but it takes a lot more time to make."

The other use for a rope: an inmate can hang himself with it. In that so many of the prisoners were sentenced to life and never were going to get out, some decided to end their lives, or as the prisoners described it, check out.

"I'd see guys, and then they'd be dead," said Lawton. "Guys hanged themselves. When you hang yourself, you don't have to actually be hanging. You can hang yourself on a rung of a ladder on your bunk. You tie your rope around your neck, sit down, and die. What happens, the air is cut off, and you die. People check out. They say, 'What the fuck. I'm done.'"

Hanging wasn't the only means of suicide in Atlanta. A drug overdose was another means of leaving the prison world behind.

"One time I was in my cell," said Lawton, "and I was with

another inmate, who was a drug dealer. A guy walked into the cell and said to him, 'Listen; I need five papers of heroin.'

"My friend said, 'You owe me money. Get the fuck out of here. You better give me my money, because I'm going to fucking stab you.'

"'I'm not going to pay you back,' the guy said.

The stare of the drug dealer was intense.

"'What are you talking about, you trying to fuck with me?'"

"'I'm checking out.' The guy had a life sentence, and he wanted to die.

"'Are you kidding me?' asked the drug dealer.

"'No.'

"'Okay, good luck,' the drug dealer said, and he handed him the five papers of heroin.

Said Lawton, "I sat on my bunk watching this thinking, *Is this for real? Where the fuck am I? Is this real?*" It was.

"The guy went back to his bunk, OD'd on heroin, and died."

*

Lawton saw the need to be tougher. To become physically strong, he invented a workout program for himself befitting a heavyweight champion boxer. His workouts, which he did in his cell usually by himself, were physically punishing. Five days a week he'd do six hundred sits-ups and six hundred push-ups in 45 minutes. He would do a hundred and fifty hand-stand presses where he'd get up against the wall with his feet pointing to the ceiling, and he'd press his entire body weight. He also did burpees by the thousands.

"It's an up-down pushup kick-out routine that would make you so soaked with perspiration that you'd look like you just got out of the shower with your shorts on," said Lawton.

To look tough Lawton also took advantage of the fact that Atlanta housed some of the finest tattoo artists in the world. Today tattoos cover most of Lawton's body.

"Each tattoo means something, whether someone was killed in the institution, whether I wanted to honor my nephew, or if I just wanted some beautiful art. One guy, Andre, an expert at tattooing, was a heroin addict, and for one paper of heroin, worth about twenty-five dollars, he would give me a tattoo that would be worth hundreds of dollars on the street. For some guys, tattooing was a very good hustle."

Larry also learned how tattooing, which was against the rules, was done in prison.

"Inmates are the most resourceful people in the world," said Lawton. "You can make a tattoo gun in a number of different ways. You can take a toothbrush, heat it, and bend it into an "L". Then you steal the motor from an electric typewriter or a pencil sharpener out of the counselor's office, you tie the motor to one end of the "L", and you take a barrel of a pen and put that on the other end of the "L". For the needle you might use a guitar string filed down to a sharp point or a needle from a sewing kit. You put that through the barrel of the pen. You attach two batteries to the motor -- you get the batteries from a radio or from the commissary -- and you've got a tattoo gun.

Said Lawton, "We got the ink from melted chess pieces, or you can take a plastic chair, melt it down, and get ink from that. The black guys would buy hair grease, burn the grease, and black smoke would rise and they'd catch that on a piece of paper or cardboard. They'd scrape the black soot into a jar and put water in it, and they'd have black ink."

Never far away, Lawton saw, was violence. One evening while Lawton was lying on his bunk he could hear a number of the black inmates screaming through the vent, "We're going to kill the white guys tomorrow."

"You just never knew what was going to happen," Lawton said. "You never knew who was going to get killed. You don't know if the cell door is going to open, and they were going to come into your cell or whether they were just saying that. Atlanta was such a tension-filled place, though rarely did the whites and blacks have any problems, because *everyone* was against the guards. It was a convict joint. People got stabbed all the time, so we never knew whether race was the cause or not. I could hear the white guys screaming back, 'Fuck you, nigger. Come and get me, you scumbag.'

"But nothing happened."

Sex was one of the major causes for violence. Rapes occurred. Not every day.

"You don't see them," said Lawton. "You only hear about them. You'll hear about a guy who gets raped in his cell by a bigger, meaner guy or one time five guys with pillowcases over their heads ran into a cell and raped a guy.

"Rape is not a crime of sex, but rather a crime of violence.

It's to show superiority, to demoralize the person, or to keep him down. You can fight it, but you rarely can stop it. If a guy is intent on rape, he might knock you out before he rapes you.

"There are two tiers in Atlanta, and one evening I could hear the screams of a guy who I knew by the name of Shane coming from the top tier," said Lawton. "The guard hit the deuces, and the other guards came running. They screamed, 'Lock down. Lock down,' and everyone returned to their cells. The guards went upstairs and we never heard from Shane again.

"The next day at six in the morning we were sitting around the unit waiting to be called for chow when an inmate friend, who had just come from the infirmary, said to us, 'Hey, you gotta see this.'

"It was Shane's medical report, and it said, 'Inmate Shane was cut with a sharp object from the top of his anus all the way to his scrotum.' He had been cut from the top of his ass to his balls, and they found seminal fluid in there. Don't ask me why someone would do this. But then again, rape is not a sex crime. Rather it's an act of violence."

There's also a lot of consensual sex in prison, says Lawton.

"You hear it all the time from your cell, the banging on the walls, the moaning. It's man on man, but nobody calls it homosexual sex. If you call a dude who's fucking some punk gay or a faggot, he'll kill you. That guy doesn't believe he's gay. They don't use the term."

A certain percentage of the men in prison liked to look, dress, and act like women. These men, who are called punks, had women's names like Princess, Goldie, JLo, and Alicia Keys, named after the singer. They tattooed their eyebrows and lips, and tattooed on blush. They took their underwear, re-sewed them into panties, and dyed them pink with Kool Aid. Goldie, a black punk about 50 years old, wore a button-down shirt, and he'd pull the shirt through his top so it looked sexy, and wore red lipstick and a bandana on his head like Aunt Jemima.

Most of the punks, who were usually very thin, wanted to be women, and they ended up with a lover, said Lawton.

"They do everything a married person would do, do the laundry for him, cook for him, clean for him, and anything else he wants."

Princess was a punk who actually took part in a marriage ceremony in prison.

"Two men had been fighting over him," said Lawton, "and after they fought, the winner, whose name was Charles, and Princess were married."

"Talk about a psycho situation," said Lawton. "The cells are small, but a large group of us gathered round. They had a guy from the Odenist religion who performed some bullshit ceremony. The groom made a ring from folded, intertwined paper. We were chuckling but not too loudly. You never fuck around with a punk. In prison a punk will get you killed.

"Afterward they had a party and made a cake out of honeybuns. You could never look at Charles and say he was a gay guy. And how do you tell a guy with a life sentence what to do? I never told anyone what to do."

All the inmates may have been men, but jealousies arose

exactly as with heterosexual couples. Lawton saw inmates die from lover's quarrels. Punks could be extremely violent if crossed.

One afternoon Lawton was in D unit watching TV with his white Italian buddies. He was sitting with his back against the wall, as he always did, when an inmate everyone knew walked in and stabbed another inmate in the neck right in front of him. The guy who got stabbed started fighting back. All the other inmates left the TV room, and then the guard, a woman, locked them in the TV room and hit the deuces, a little orange button on the intercom radio.

"You hit 2,2,2 on any phone, and the guards come running," said Lawton. "That's why they call it the deuces."

While the two were fighting, a punk ran up to the female guard, threw her on the floor, took her keys, and opened the door. He ran in and smashed the attacker in the head with a lock.

"The punk thought he had attacked his lover," said Lawton, "but it turned out it wasn't his lover; it was someone else."

The inmate who was attacked was taken out on a stretcher. The inmate who did the attacking and was slugged by the punk suffered a concussion and also had to be carried out on a stretcher. The punk was taken away in handcuffs.

Another time Lawton witnessed a punk who took a bowl of water, put a Snickers bar in the water and then put it in the microwave until the Snickers bar was melted and the water boiled. He then threw the concoction in another inmate's face.

"The caramel and the chocolate of the Snickers bar stuck

to his face, and I will never forget the scream as long as I live," said Lawton. "It was a love triangle, and the jilted lover took out revenge on the winner. The victim had to be air lifted to an outside civilian hospital."

Gay inmates could be real trouble.

"There was one inmate we called Mountain," said Lawton, "because he was six foot six and weighed about 350 pounds. He was gay, and you didn't want him to like you." Lawton avoided him as much as possible.

One potential danger in Atlanta was that AIDs was rampant among the inmates taking part in sex.

"The HIV rate was very high," said Lawton. "Who knows if they have AIDS or not? I knew punks who had AIDS, and guys would fuck them. I asked, 'Why would you do that?' I didn't get an answer, but it was probably because they had given up on living. These men think, *What the fuck do I care about dying?* Otherwise, why would a person do that? Prison is a very depressing place."

Serving a long term in a place like Atlanta can make a person go crazy. This happened to Dave Collingsworth, Lawton's cellie during his last six months at Atlanta.

One day Collingsworth told him, "Larry, I just won my appeal. I'm getting out." Collingsworth had been convicted of robbing a bank.

"I was excited for him," said Lawton, "but he was freaked. He started putting laundry detergent in a bag.

"I have to bring it home," Collingsworth said.

"What are you doing?" asked Lawton. "Leave this shit and get out of here."

"Maybe my mother doesn't have laundry detergent," Collingsworth said.

"He was really freaked out by the thought of returning to civilian life."

"Dave," said Lawton, "just get the fuck out of here."

After beating the bank robbery charge, a year and a half later Collingsworth was back in Atlanta. He had robbed another bank and had gotten caught.

*

After being incarcerated for eighteen months at Atlanta, Lawton's counselor suddenly "discovered" that he didn't have enough points to be housed in a maximum security prison.

"Just like that," said Lawton, "I went to a meeting with my counselor, and he said to me, 'You have low enough points to go to a medium.' And they transferred me to the Coleman Correctional Institution in Coleman, Florida, which to me was a country club in comparison."

But in order to transfer, Lawton had to survive his last few weeks at Atlanta. There was no guarantee. Every day at Atlanta Lawton faced potential danger. Ten days before Lawton's scheduled transfer, he had a beef with an Indian inmate called Bonnie. Their set-to could well have ended up with Lawton committing murder, or getting killed. That it didn't happen was as much a matter of good fortune as anything else.

"On our unit we had TV rooms," said Lawton. "For a hundred and sixty inmates there were four TV rooms -- a black TV room, a Spanish TV room, a white TV room, and a sports TV room.

"We were in the white TV room around six thirty in the evening," said Lawton. "I had brought a chair in there. You have a chair in your cell, and you can bring it to the TV room. I always put my chair up against the wall, because you don't want anyone behind you. And Bonnie walked over and sat in my chair.

"Bonnie," I said, "That's my fucking chair."

"He grumbled, but he got up.

"I walked away, and I came back, and Bonnie again was sitting in my chair. He obviously was trying to pick a fight with me.

"Bonnie," I said, "What the fuck?"

He said, 'You fucking guys,' meaning the Italians, 'think you own the place.'

"Before he could move, I hit him with an uppercut, boom. He fell against the wall, and I grabbed his long hair and I kept smashing him. I must have hit him fifty fucking times. Each time he tried to slide down the wall, I pulled him back up and hit him again.

"The leader of the Aryan Brotherhood, one of the most notorious groups in the prison, tapped me on the shoulder and said, 'Enough, Larry.'

"Bonnie, beat to shit, was all fucked up. He needed stitches under his lip. He was able to get up, and he went back to his cell. The guards never knew what happened, and Bonnie wasn't a snitch and didn't tell. Still, I was worried what he or one of the other Indians might do to me.

"I went back to my cell. I was all hyped up. Reno, who was a Latin King, came to see me. Reno, a psychopath, liked me because I had taught him how to be a bookmaker. Reno stabbed people. He had three life sentences. He didn't give a fuck.

"Reno said, 'Larry, we have to kill the Chief. They're going to try to kill you.'

"My life started flashing in front of my eyes. You have to picture Chief, who was the head of the Indian inmates: he was six foot seven, 300 pounds. Every group had an inmate who called the shots, and Chief was that guy, and Reno wanted me to kill this giant motherfucker.

"The eight o'clock move is the last move of the day, and then they have lock down for the nine o'clock count. Reno was saying, 'Let's kill the Chief when he comes in.'

"I knew the Chief was going to come and see me. I got a knife and put it behind my leg. Reno, who was crazy, stood out in front of my cell. The cells have two-feet-by- six-inch windows in the door, and I could see a shadow come across the window. It was the Chief.

"In prison you never, ever enter another man's cell. Chief gave me the courtesy of knocking. He held his hands in front of him and said, "Hey Larr, we know what happened. You're all right. It was Bonnie's fault.'

"'All right, Chief,' I said. And that was it. But for the next ten days until the day I left Atlanta, I put my chair in front of the door. I didn't go into my cell until they locked me in, and when I got up, I was sitting there waiting with my knife. There wasn't one time when that cell door was open that I wasn't ready.

"Atlanta had been the worst of the worst, and I survived it, but barely. When you survive the worst of the worst, nothing else can make you fearful -- to this day."

PHOTOS

Larry Lawton December 1961

Larry 7 Years old

Larry 12 years old

Bronx NY - Throgs Neck Little League 1970

PHOTOS

Lawton Family Picture 1972

Grandmother 2003

PHOTOS

Larry Coast Guard 1979

St Frances De Chantel Report Card - Mrs. Armelleno 1972-73

Coast Guard Sandy Hook NJ - 1981

PHOTOS

Angela Cusano childhood date 1979

First wife Roselyn 9-11-1987

PHOTOS

Coast Guard ship running a gambling night 1985

Lukes Piano Lounge - Queens NY 1987

Tommy, Louie, Me 1992

Louie, Cruiser Weight Champ Mark Randazzo, Larry 1992

Joe Fraumeni 1993

Uncle Louie Constantino 1993

PHOTOS

Joe Fraumeni and me golfing 1994

Larry with sisters Lynne and Debbie 1993

Larry Lawton & Tom Ferrara with his wife - 1996 Larry's Block Party

Second marriage to Missy 1994

2nd wife Melissa visiting in prison 1999

PHOTOS

Larry Jr. age 11

Daughter Ashley age 4

PHOTOS

Parents visting 2000

Joe and Louie visiting 2002

Federal Prison ID's

Wife & Daughter visit 2003

PHOTOS

Me at my sister's pool 2007

John Oliver Daily Show 2009

Doing RCP 2010

Huckabee Show 2010

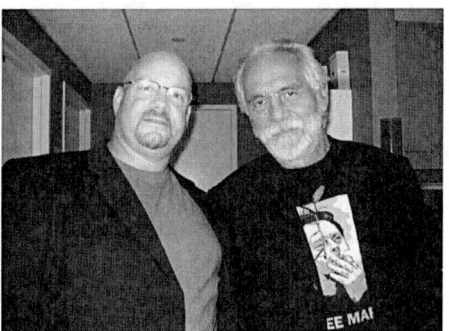

Tommy Chong 2010

PHOTOS

Governor Huckabee 2010

Parenting Program 2011

Fox Anchor Keith Landry, Larry, Judge Babb and Lt. Governor Kottkamp Orlando Matters 2011

Theresa and Me 2011

Today

CHAPTER 11

Coleman and Jessup

When Larry Lawton learned he was leaving Atlanta and heading to the federal correctional institution at Coleman, somewhere in the middle of Florida, he started questioning other inmates to find out what Coleman was like.

"Oh lucky you," said an inmate. "You're going to a country club."

Lucky Lawton, indeed.

He travelled by bus from Atlanta to Coleman. Surprisingly, he didn't have to go on ConAir. Though he was handcuffed and shackled, this time he wasn't black boxed, so he had a tiny bit more mobility during the trip.

The bus looked like a Greyhound without the markings. The prisoners entered the bus from the back, and in the front in a cage sat the driver and next to him a lieutenant with a shotgun. In the back of the bus there was also a guard with a shotgun sitting in a caged area. The guards didn't talk to the prisoners. Apparently they weren't allowed to say a word.

The prisoners were given a bag lunch consisting of an apple and an outdated packet of cheese and crackers. The bus stopped, but only for the guards, who went to eat at McDonald's and Wendy's. The bus had a toilet so the prisoners could pee, but because of the shackles that was all they could do.

"I saw prisoners try, but inevitably they shit their pants," said Lawton. "Thank God they didn't sit next to me."

After about six hours the bus arrived at Coleman, the biggest federal prison in the country, home to 8,000 inmates. The first thing Lawton noticed was the tall barbed wire fence. When the bus stopped in front of the lobby, two trucks with armed guards pulled up in front of and behind the bus. The prisoners shuffled into the lobby and then went to receiving and discharge, where they did the usual routine of lifting their balls, squatting, changing their clothes, and going through the usual inspection routine. Most of the inmates were going to the compound. The others, including Lawton, went to the hole to undergo captain's review.

After a week Lawton was assigned a new dorm.

"I had just come from a prison built in 1903, the worst of the worst," said Lawton. "My housing unit at Coleman was built in 1995. It was beautiful. I was told it was a country club, and I felt like it was a country club."

Coleman, like most prisons, was forty percent black, forty percent Hispanic, and twenty percent white.

"As a white man, you're never in the majority," said Lawton.

Because Lawton came from Atlanta, he arrived with a bad-ass reputation.

"When you tell them you come from Atlanta," said Lawton, "they don't want to fuck with you."

Once he settled in at Coleman, he was courted by the baddest of the white inmates to join their little group. As a result, he became buddies with an inmate by the name of

Pinball, the leader of the Fort Lauderdale Outlaw motorcycle gang and another inmate by the name of Meaty, another Outlaw. He also became buddies with Tommy Farrisi, a mobster, and Frankie Turino, a gangster from the Bonanno family from the same area back in Brooklyn from where he came.

"When you're accepted into a group in prison, you feel okay," said Lawton. "They introduce you to other guys. When you go to the chow hall, you sit with them. You're a new guy coming in, and it's good for them too.

"*Oh new guy, what's going on?* It's like a fraternity rush."

Before long Lawton was living large. Because he had a small pension from the Coast Guard, he always had money, and Lawton spread his money around to make his stay as comfortable as possible. He paid one prisoner to clean his cell. He paid Frankie Turino fifty dollars a week to be his cook. Frankie, who was hyper and nervous, worked in the kitchen, and he would prepare Lawton's meals and deliver them to his cell.

Lawton discovered that Coleman had a lot of amenities. It had a music room, an aerobics room, a beautiful track, and a softball field. Coleman even had a six a.m. step aerobics class. Doing aerobics Lawton got his weight down to 185.

What a difference from Atlanta!

Lawton should have kept his nose clean, but after spending time at Atlanta, he had learned to become a convict, and it had become a way of life. To keep himself in action, Lawton started running a small bookmaking operation as he had once done on the streets of Brooklyn. He printed up pro football betting tickets, and he had runners who sold them go to every unit. Instead of money, the inmates bet with stamps.

At Coleman Lawton met inmates who had been jailed for stock fraud. He would sit with them in front of the TV watching the stock ticker. One of the inmates advised Lawton to buy a company called Advanced Radio. Lawton made a phone call to a friend on the outside and bought 1,000 shares at $11 dollars a share. As it started to climb in value, Lawton was sure Advanced Radio was going to be the next Microsoft.

"If you had bought 1,000 shares of Microsoft in 1975, you'd be worth $10 million today," said Lawton. "This was 1999 when the market was going crazy, and everyone thought they were geniuses."

At Coleman Lawton also began to study law in earnest. Lawton's study of the law began when he beat the gun charge against him. The Coleman prison had a law library, and Lawton was an avid reader, and the more he read, the more knowledgeable he became. Other inmates started coming to him with their grievances, and Lawton would research the casebooks to see whether or not they had the law on their side.

Lawton never once took a dime for researching their cases. It was a matter of principle. He saw that there were other prisoners, jailhouse lawyers they were called, who took money and didn't know what they were doing.

"These people were grasping for their lives," said Lawton. "They wanted to get out. Their freedom was at stake." He didn't want to be like the "scumbag lawyers," as he called them, who charged a lot of money and lost the case.

Though Coleman may have been a country club, Lawton never let his guard down. Violence could still erupt at any moment.

One time Lawton was out on the yard when one of the older mobsters, an inmate named Georgie Matorano, took a chair a smashed it over the head of another mobster.

"They were looking at each other funny," said Lawton.

The other difference between Atlanta and Coleman was that at Atlanta the guards only cared about two things: not getting killed and not letting anyone escape. At Coleman, where the guards had more control, the rules were stricter. The rules against such things as tattoos and stealing food were enforced more rigorously.

"The inmates had more respect from the guards at Atlanta," said Lawton. "Although the guards at Atlanta would beat you, the guards knew who ran the prison and let them be. In Coleman the guards had big balls. I considered Coleman to be a petty joint. We'd get in trouble for the pettiest of infractions."

Lawton's fifteen months at Coleman abruptly came to an end as a result of his breaking one of those infractions. The SIS, which is like the FBI of prisons, investigates drug deals, sex, and other illicit activity within the prisons. The SIS also investigates activity by the prison staff.

"SIS officers were about as popular as typhoid," said Lawton.

An SIS lieutenant by the name of Figeroa became aware that Lawton was sending his chief cook and bottlewasher,

Frankie Turino, fifty dollars a week. Figueroa was sure it was to pay off gambling debts. He called Lawton in for an interview.

"You're sending money to Turino," said Lieutenant Figueroa.

"Yeah," admitted Lawton.

"What do you owe him?" asked Figueroa.

"I don't owe him anything," said Lawton truthfully. "He helps me out in the kitchen."

"No, this is gambling," insisted Figueroa.

"Frankie doesn't gamble," said Lawton. And Frankie didn't.

But Lawton wasn't trusted or believed because he had come from Atlanta, the worst of the worst. His reputation had preceded him, and some guards, including Figueroa apparently, were suspicious of him.

"Throw him in the hole," ordered Figueroa.

Before he knew it, Lawton was being transferred.

"I think they got scared of me in that prison," said Lawton. "They thought I was trying to take over the place. But really I wasn't a bad guy there. I gambled a little bit, but I passed the time. I was really good in there. I got into a groove. I had survived Atlanta, and now I was in Lalaland, and all of a sudden I get locked up by Figueroa for sending money. He thought it was a gambling debt. And he wanted to make a big deal out of it.

"I told the guy, 'You're fucking nuts.'

"But into the hole I went." For four months.

Inmates in the hole at Coleman were locked up 24/7 with one or two cellies with an hour of rec five days a week – unless the administration decided to withhold it.

"You never get out," said Lawton. "The hole at Coleman wasn't that bad, but don't let anyone kid you: the hole is the hole is the hole."

First he was put in the hole during the investigation, which lasted forty days. Then once the administration determined that Lawton was to be transferred, it took another two months for them to actually move him. Lawton spent that whole time in the hole.

"They don't put you back on the yard," said Lawton. "Oh no. Once you're in the hole, you're there. People ask me, 'Don't you have an appeal?' I love that question. No, there's no appeal."

During his time in the hole, a time when Lawton didn't have access to a telephone, his stock in Advanced Radio fell back to under what he paid for it. Lawton was able to read USA Today in the hole, and he watched helplessly as the price of the stock took a nose dive.

"I didn't know enough about stocks to put in a stop-loss order," said Lawton. "I ended up losing money. What a fucking idiot I was!"

*

Lawton was transferred to a medium security prison in Jesup, Georgia, about a five-hour bus ride from Coleman. But a simple bus ride would have been too easy. Instead Lawton was taken by bus to Jacksonville where he was put on ConAir to Oklahoma City. After sitting in a cell in Oklahoma City for a month, Lawton was put on a plane back to Jacksonville, and he then was bussed to Jesup, which was just outside Brunswick, Georgia, just an hour north of Jacksonville.

"Idiots," said Lawton.

For Lawton the prison at Jesup turned out to be an even cushier place than Coleman.

"Jesup was a prison manned by white, redneck guards," said Lawton.

"Sometimes the redneck guards didn't like New Yorkers, but they still treated me better than any of the black guards."

Jesup wasn't as new as Coleman, but it had amenities Coleman didn't have. The cells in Jesup had electrical outlets, a rarity in prison. Most new prisons don't even have on-off light switches. Guards turn the lights on and off in the newer prisons.

Lawton made friends quickly at Jesup, and before long on Friday nights he was cooking pasta for a dozen of his best friends.

"All good convicts," said Lawton. "There was Carlo Martino, Barry Meely, a couple of Outlaw gang members by the names of Steve O and Jack. They'd come to my unit, and I'd feed everybody. I'd keep forty pounds of spaghetti stolen from the kitchen hidden in different cells. I made a pasta dish called *aglio e olio*, garlic and oil. I had people steal the parmesan cheese, the oil, and of course, the pasta. The cops knew about it, and they'd ask me for a bowl.

"Some of the guards wanted my food so badly that they would look at the paperwork of the incoming prisoners and tell us the names of the rats. Cops like stand up guys too.

"One night I blew a fuse, and the whole unit went black. I had two pots going, big bowls of pasta. I cut up the garlic with a stolen razor blade. I put the garlic in the oil, put the oil in a microwave that I borrowed, and the whole unit smelled like an Italian restaurant.

"The day I blew the fuse, I went to the cop – what we called the guards in prison

-- and told him to get someone from the maintenance department to trip the breaker. He called down, and he was able to get the power back up before anyone was the wiser."

Lawton was at Jesup when the bombing of the World Trade Center in New York on September 11th occurred. He was laying down in his cell when Barry Meely, a buddy from New York, came over and said, "Larry, come out here. A plane hit the World Trade Center."

Lawton though, *Oh big deal, a little plane hit the World Trade Center.* Ten minutes later Barry came back to his cell and said, "Larry, you have to see this."

Lawton strolled over to the TV just as a plane hit the second tower.

"I was mesmerized watching it," said Lawton. "I didn't leave the TV for two days. After it became known that Osama Bin Laden was responsible, a lot of the Muslim prisoners began talking bad about the United States and started cheering the bad guys. This happened in prisons all over the country.

"After that happened, Muslim inmates were stabbed and had to be transferred for their safety. I saw one inmate smash a

Muslim inmate with a steel mop ringer, and I heard of another fight in the yard where a Muslim was beaten up.

"They had to lock these guys up in protective custody throughout the American prison system because these guys were cheering. You don't do that. We're Americans. We may be fuck ups, but we're American fuck ups."

*

Lawton spent eight months of his time at Jesup in the hole. The event that put him in the hole for six months came just before Christmas 2002 when he was caught stealing pork chops from the kitchen. Lawton had ten minutes to make it back to his cell, and on the way guards patted him down and discovered the contraband under his shirt.

They threw him in the hole for two weeks. He got out of the hole, and when he came out he learned that Jeremy Poe, his cellie, was given a shot – an infraction – for having pasta in the cell.

They interrogated Poe, asking him, "Who belongs to the pasta?" Poe refused to rat Lawton out, and he was scheduled to go in front of the disciplinary committee.

Lawton was incensed that Poe, his cellie, should be punished for something he didn't do, and so Lawton stood up for him, telling his unit manager, a black woman named Mrs. Tubb, "That's my pasta. Not his. Give me the punishment. Put me back in the hole."

Mrs. Tubbs wasn't persuaded to forgive Jeremy Poe.

She said, "He had the opportunity to tell us whose pasta it was."

"Listen," said Lawton as he became more and more agitated, "He didn't tell on me. He couldn't have, because I don't hang around with snitches."

The woman made a circular motion with her hand, as if to say, *Don't go there*, and when she did that, the sense of unfairness washed over him, and so did a strong feeling of helplessness, and Lawton snapped.

He went berserk, ripping the telephone off the wall. He picked up the paper shredder off Mrs. Tubbs' desk and threw it at her. She ducked, and the shredder smashed into a computer. Lawton, out of his mind with rage, punched a hole in the wall and on the way out of her office smashed the glass door. In all he caused $2,000 in damage to her office.

As a phalanx of officers came running, Lawton ripped his shirt off,

"Let's get it on, motherfuckers," he screamed.

The guards surrounded him. Lawton was ready to fight them all. The guards saw a psychopath, and it could have ended badly for Lawton had not one of the guards, whose name was Spells, talked him down.

"Lawton, I have to lock you up," Spells said. Meaning it was his job to handcuff him and take him to the hole.

Lawton, shirtless and surrounded by guards, felt chilly. His anger cooled as well.

"All right," he said, "you can lock me up." And he allowed Spells to handcuff him and lead him to the hole. For Lawton it was back to maximum security.

One of the inmates Lawton met in the hole was Jose

Linares, who was working for Unicor, the company that hires prisoners. Unicor pays forty cents an hour to prisoners who make mail bags, battle dress uniforms for the military, furniture, and other useful items.

"What they do," said Lawton, "is take real jobs away from people on the street. It's a real scumbag outfit. Who can compete with them when they pay slave wages?"

Linares worked as a clerk for the company, and he told Lawton he had uncovered the code to get into the authorized payment for procurements. The associate warden who ran the company was Bill Young, and Linares started a company cleverly called TYBY – it stood for Thank you, Bill Young.

"Jose figured out a way for the government to pay TYBY $135,000 for material that never existed," said Lawton. "He was caught because one of his people on the street stupidly sent $30,000 to his prison account. That raised red flags. He only got eighteen months, but he had to return his Ford Explorer.

"The hole was wild and crazy, and things happened in there all the time. Gay orderlies giving blow jobs through the chute door. A guy would stick his dick through the chute door, and get blown. Guys would also jerk off in front of the guards. The women guards like it, and so did some of the guys. It would look like the woman guard was talking to the inmate, but the inmate would be jerking off to her.

*

During the time Lawton was in the hole he was being harassed by another inmate, who constantly gave him a hard time.

"The guy was talking shit to me, just being an asshole," said Lawton. "We would curse each other through the door like animals in a zoo. They call that door warriors, and I usually ignore it, but I told myself, *I'm going to get that motherfucker.*

Each day at Jesup the prisoners in the hole were allowed one hour on the yard. They were handcuffed and led to the yard.

"Come to the yard, motherfucker," Lawton screamed at him.

At Jesup the rec area for the prisoners in the hole was a small cage.

"They brought me to the yard," said Lawton, "and I had a paper clip hidden in my hand. I went into the cage, and they let him in, and I slipped my cuffs with the paper clip. He was handcuffed and I threw him a severe beating. He thought nobody could get to him, so I beat him until I was pulled off of him. He was bleeding and screaming while the guards were yelling, 'Lawton, get back. Get back.' But I just kept beating the guy."

Lawton was given a longer stint in the hole, but he didn't care. His mentality was, *It's me or the other guy.* He was just trying to survive.

"By now I was in prison five years, and I had learned how to live, how to hustle, how to beat people, how to do everything just to survive."

Again, he was transferred, and his next stop would be a hell hole in South Carolina twenty-five miles north of Augusta, Georgia, called Edgefield prison. His country club existence had come to a screeching halt.

CHAPTER 12

The Abu Ghraib of America

Larry Lawton had to leave the cushy environs of Jesup prison because of the extensive damage he did in the unit manager's office. There may have been another reason as well in that the Jesup administration, as at Coleman, feared he was gaining too much power with the other inmates.

Lawton was beginning to see that prisoners in American jails had absolutely no rights. A prisoner who kept his nose clean, he saw, could be railroaded just because someone in power dictated it be so.

"The arbitrary nature of it all is enough to drive a man insane," said Lawton.

Unfortunately for Lawton, he was sent to Edgefield, South Carolina, a maximum security prison every bit as bad as Atlanta had been. The inmates were more dangerous than at Coleman or Jesup, and so were the guards. Lawton was forced to revert back into survival mode.

When he arrived at Edgefield, Lawton continued to pursue his study of the law. He was befriended by an inmate by the name of Pauly Tallini, who was serving a thirty-year sentence for cocaine trafficking. Tallini, who was originally from Boston, was living in Miami when he was caught with fifty keys of coke. Pauly had spent years in the law library trying unsuccessfully to appeal his conviction, and he encouraged Lawton to keep learning what he could about criminal law so he could be a successful prison advocate. Little did Lawton know that his learning the Code of Federal Regulations would help him in a four-year campaign to publicize the abuses of Edgefield prison.

*

Lawton was in the Atlanta holdover unit heading to Edgefield, his new prison, when he learned that his beloved grandmother had died.

"I was real close with my grandmother," said Lawton. "When I was out running the streets in Ft. Lauderdale, she lived in Hollywood, and I used to take my limo down to see her and take her to shows and out to Denny's. She liked that a lot. My grandmother was healthy when I went to prison and was never told the real story of why I went away. She was told I was a bookmaker, and that was it.

"My grandmother was going to be 100 on May 7, 2003. She already got a letter from the President of the United States. I didn't know this but when you turn a hundred you get a birthday card from the White House."

Lawton's mother had called the prison and asked them to send down a pastor to tell him that his grandmother had died. They never did. On March 30, Lawton called home and asked his mom how grandma was doing. His mother became silent.

"Didn't they tell you?" she asked.

"Tell me what?"

"Grandma died eight days ago."

Lawton dropped the phone and went back to his cell. He lay down on his bunk. All he could think about was how much he had messed up his life. How he had messed up his kids lives and his whole family's lives. *For what! Money and power? What a waste,* he thought. It was a real turning point.

"I didn't blame the prison, didn't blame the system," said Lawton. "I blamed myself and had to come to grips that it was my choices that got me here. I wasn't able to attend my grandmother's funeral or my nephew's funeral, and I wasn't around to be with my kids during their most precious years. I wasn't around to see my son play basketball, go to his graduation, listen to my daughters' recitals, and all those things. It's sad, and the system has no heart at all. I was about to find out how bad the system really is."

*

Lawton's approach to how he was going to spend the rest of his time in prison changed dramatically one day when he was playing horseshoes in the yard with an inmate by the name of Jim Arch who began complaining about chest pains.

"Arch," said Lawton, "Go to medical."

Arch went to the infirmary and told the staff he had chest pains and that his left arm was hurting. All signs pointed to his having heart failure.

"There's nothing wrong with you," said a member of the prison medical staff. "Get out of here. You're all right."

Arch complained for a whole week about not feeling well. He went to his job in prison maintenance, and when his boss saw how terrible he looked, he called over to the medical department to say that Arch needed to be seen immediately.

"You have gas," the medical staff told him. "Get out of here. Here's Maalox," he was told.

The distance from the medical department to the unit where Arch lived was only about a hundred yards. After making it back to his unit, Arch said to an inmate friend of Lawton's by the name of Jimmy Brown, "Jimmy, I'm dying."

Lawton was there when it happened. Lawton and Brown helped Arch into a chair. Arch then keeled over, fell face-first onto the floor, and died. Arch was only 46 years old.

*

Arch was the third friend of Lawton's to die needless in Edgefield. One friend, an inmate by the name of Shifflett, had cancer, and for the last week of his life he complained about how badly he felt.

"He never should have been in prison," said Lawton. "He should have been in a medical care center."

On the night Shifflett died he was banging on the door of his cell in pain for thirty minutes, but no one came. He was vomiting up blood, and that night he bled to death in his cell.

His cellmate, a redneck who had been around slaughterhouses, at the funeral service described it as "the worst death I ever saw, worst than killing an animal."

Lawton's other friend who died needlessly went to the prison's medical facility to get medication for a heart problem. He was so sick he had to be brought to medical in a wheelchair. The patient should have remained in the prison medical department, but the administration didn't want to have to pay for a nurse, so he was sent back to his cell. . The medical staff gave the medication to his cellie and told him, "Give him the medication at night."

When his cellie woke in the morning, the inmate was sitting in a chair stone cold dead.

"Have you ever seen a man die?" asked Lawton. "They shit and pee themselves. The stain is what tells you he's dead."

*

After Jim Arch collapsed onto the floor, the guards came running.

"Lock down, lock down," the guards screamed. All the inmates scrambled to return to their cells.

Lawton's cell was facing the front of the unit. As Lawton watched the guards place Arch onto a stretcher and then onto a golf cart, Lawton became angry when he saw them laughing as they drove off toward medical.

Heartless bastards, thought Lawton.

SIS did an investigation and went cell by cell. The administration, afraid of liability, immediately tried to cover up what happened. One of the investigators said to Lawton and Brown, "You saw Arch hit his head, right?"

Shouted Lawton at the investigator, "Fuck you, you killed that man,"

Lawton was ordered taken to the hole.

Lawton, who was close to Jim Arch, was incensed at the injustice. If any of the medical staff had taken the time to examine Arch or the other two inmates who died, they could have diagnosed their conditions and could have taken steps to save them.

"There's no medical care in prison," said Lawton. "They are heartless."

*

Even in the hole Lawton had access to law books. A friend on the outside, Steven Lander, mailed him the books he needed for his studies. Lawton also had the right to mail letters, and mail letters he did.

"The worst thing you can do is fight the system," said Lawton. "You're telling the brass how incompetent they are, and they don't like it one bit. Never mind that they are the worst people in the world."

The primary reason Lawton began his letter-writing campaign was that he himself was in a lot of pain, and the prison medical staff was doing nothing about it. While enforcing fishing regulations on the Bering Sea as a member of the U.S. Coast Guard, in rough seas Lawton fell into a cargo hold and was severely injured. Lawton retired from the Coast Guard with fifty-percent disability due to the severe condition of his back.

At both Atlanta and Coleman Lawton was on light duty status because of his bad back. At Edgefield, however, the administration doctored Lawton's records and forced him to do heavy lifting. They also put him in a top bunk, a difficult task for a man with severe back pain. Lawton sought fair treatment.

Equally important, he wanted the world to know that the people who ran Edgefield prison killed Jim Arch and his other two friends, and he wanted the world to learn of the abuses and inhumane conditions at Edgefield. Prisoners in solitary weren't getting any recreation despite federal regulations that demanded it. Prisoners in the hole at Edgefield weren't getting psychiatric attention despite other regulations that called for such treatment.

Prisoners have rights, Lawton told himself. *This is America, not a third-world country.*

In July of 2004 Lawton mounted a furious writing campaign to senators, congressmen, media outlets, and others in power in Washington and across the country.

He wrote to senators and congressmen. He wrote to The Progressive, the Human Rights Watch, The Southern Center for Human Rights, Frontline, and even the American Friends Service Committee.

He didn't get any coverage from the publications or TV, and most of the politicians didn't respond. But a few did. Lindsay Graham, the U.S. senator from South Carolina, wrote back to say he would look into his case with the Bureau of Prisons.

Lawton's letter writing made him an enemy of Edgefield's warden, John LaManna, who was so angry about what Lawton was doing that he told one of his lieutenants, "I'm going to get that man."

"He sure hated me," said Lawton, "and for the next four years he made my life even more of a living hell than it had been. LaManna was running a prison of 2,000 inmates, and I was causing him a lot of problems. I was getting the attention that was needed at a prison where they were killing people."

On August 17, 2004 Sen. Graham replied to Lawton with an attached letter written by warden LaManna. In the letter LaManna refuted every charge Lawton made. Lawton had complained he wasn't getting medication for his bad back. LaManna said that Lawton had been examined, was prescribed medication, but that Lawton "failed to report to the pill line." Later when he was prescribed medication, "he failed to pick it up." Another time, said LaManna, "he was prescribed Tylenol."

The warden concluded, "Please be assured that our Health Services staff are providing appropriate medical evaluations and treatment for Mr. Lawton." LaManna invited Sen. Graham to give him a call any time.

LaManna's answers were enough to keep Sen. Graham at bay.

On August 26 a woman friend of Lawton's wrote a follow up letter to Graham and other senators. The gist of the letter was that Lawton's back hurt him so much that he belonged in a cell for the disabled. She charged that the prison was doctoring records, ignoring requests for help, and sweeping Lawton's complaint under the table.

Sen. Ernest Hollings wrote to say he was contacting the Bureau of Prisons. He too received the same response from LaManna.

LaManna struck back. At Edgefield Lawton initially had been placed on chronic care, but then on September 1, the clinical director, a Doctor Serrano lied about his condition and took him off chronic care.

Lawton then filed suit. He was then thrown in the hole when he wouldn't accept a program assignment. Even when a handicapped cell became available, he wasn't assigned to it. LaManna instead kept him in isolation.

Lawton went to see his unit manager, a Mrs. Hobbs, who went to see Doctor Serrano, who told her, "We know about it. Forget about it."

*

As punishment for his war of words Lawton spent most of his last years at Edgefield in the hole. He was thrown in there for imaginary, made-up offenses. One time he was charged with having bookmaking equipment in his cell. Another time he was accused of having contraband. The contraband cited was a pair of knitted socks. The charges were made up, Lawton swears. Lawton spent the next eleven months in solitary confinement. "All because I was fighting the abuses," said Lawton.

*

For part of the time Lawton was in the hole, the inmate in the cell next to him was named Jack, a black man who was doing life for selling drugs.

"When you're in the hole for a long period of time you get to know your neighbor," said Lawton. "You talk to one another through the vent. You can actually have a normal conversation without yelling too loud if you jump up on the stainless steel toilet and sink combo and talk right into the vent."

The inmates, who were nothing if not resourceful, would also communicate through their kites.

"Jack and I would use kites to pass magazines back and forth. Using a kite you could also pass things like a stamp, a piece of paper, or a little coffee, if you were lucky to have it in the hole. I got so good at it that I was able to shoot the rope way down the hall to communicate with a lot of the inmates on the tier."

Like Lawton, Jack was a physical fitness devotee, and using kites they would send their workout schedules back and forth so they could coordinate them. Simultaneously Lawton and Jack would do burpees, a totally exhausting full-body workout.

"One day Jack and I were doing burpees through the vent," said Lawton. "I would do mine and yell, 'Go', he would do his and yell, 'Go,' and we did this back and forth for an hour. At the end of the hour we were drenched. On this day we finished our workout about 3:30 in the afternoon when Jack said to me, 'Hey brother, I love ya. I'm checking out.'

"I said, 'Where the fuck are you going? You're in the hole with me.' Then it dawned on me what he was going to do.

"I jumped up on the toilet sink combo and shouted into the vent. 'Jack, relax man. After count we'll talk about it.' He didn't reply."

In the federal prison system every inmate has to stand on his feet at 4 p.m. until the guards make a head count The guards will open the door at the end of the tier and scream, "Count Time." They then walk past every cell and count the inmates.

"They passed my cell and stopped at Jack's," said Lawton, "and I could hear them screaming in their radio, 'Man down.'

They also hit their body alarm. Everyone came running.

"Jack had hung himself. It isn't hard to do. You can hang yourself from a chair, the rung of a ladder, even a shower head – any place where you can tie a rope around your neck and cut off your air. You don't even have to be hanging.

"The guards removed Jack's body from his cell, recounted, and then they started chow," said Lawton. "It was as if nothing had happened.

"I couldn't eat and laid back down on my bunk. I was in shock. It was at this time I actually heard God speak to me. I was starting to question my sanity, and wondered if I would make it. His death was so unnecessary. Being in prison is so dehumanizing. Nobody cares about the inmates.

"In the hole, guys go crazy all the time. There was this totally crazy guy at the end of the tier who would sing all day and night. He drove everyone on the tier crazy. The other inmates would be screaming for him to shut-up, and when he kept singing, they'd kick the doors and make it seem like the tier was going crazy.

"The guards didn't give a fuck. Why should they? They weren't on the tier. They didn't have to listen to his constant craziness. They only came on the tier to feed us and make rounds. Like a dog in a kennel, in the hole you are totally forgotten.

"To block out all the distractions I used to get in a groove by working out and by reading. Even when I was doing that there were times when I couldn't help but feel sick about what was going on around me.

"One time the staff was putting on its usual bullshit dog-and-pony show where the administrators walk around ask if we're okay.

"Fuck no, we're not okay. We're locked in a hole, forgotten with no sunlight and no fresh air.

"On this particular day one of the inmates after the breakfast meal wouldn't allow the guard to close the door of the food chute by hanging his arm through the slot. This is called "jacking" the food chute. I've seen an inmate who was doing this get his arm broken when the guard got mad and slammed the chute door down on the guy's arm.

"No one knew it, but the inmate who jacked the food chute been storing up feces, urine and sour milk. On this day the unit manager making the rounds came from the adjacent camp, and he was being a real jerk saying things like 'You deserve to be in prison. You're an asshole, and 'your wife is out fucking around.' He wanted to piss everyone off. Who knows why? I think he just liked the power.

"All of a sudden I heard the unit manager make a loud scream. I could see the guy running past my cell. His suit was covered with a disgusting mixture of piss, shit, and curdled milk. It was disgusting. The smell on the tier was almost unbearable.

"The crazy guy who jacked the chute had thrown this concoction all over this guy. I will never forget that smell. Everyone was cheering because everyone hated this guy. The orderlies had to clean that up.

"A few hours later we could hear the doors open at the end

of the tier. A bunch of people started coming down the tier, and they start covering the windows of everyone's cells, which is what they do when they don't want anyone seeing what's going on.

"They ordered this guy to cuff-up. I knew he was going to get a serious beating.

I had gone through this a bunch of times, and my stomach started getting knots.

"There are a lot of crazy people in prison, and I often wonder why some of them aren't in a mental hospital or a medical prison. Another guy in the hole wrote messages on the wall and drew pictures using his own feces. That is so crazy. He was a mental case and the system isn't built for them."

*

On Sept. 27, 2004, Lawton had seen more abuse of inmates – himself included -- than he could stand, and he decided to do something about it. He wrote to the Justice Department, President Bush, Sen. Ernest Hollings, Sen. Lindsay Graham, Sen. Joseph Lieberman, Senator Chris Dodd, and Robert Stock of the Bureau of Prisons Internal Affairs. In it he charged that the medical staff of Edgefield prison was conspiring to withhold proper medical treatment as punishment for his letter writing.

"I feel this prison administration is out to retaliate against me," he wrote.

After spending 62 days in the hole, Lawton finally received some relief on Oct. 5, 2004. Dr. Serrano and Dr. Blocker told him surgery probably wouldn't make the pain go away, and they gave him a cane, soft shoes, new medications, and they promised they would send him to a pain specialist.

*

Lawton, who could never forgive the prison for the death of James Arch, continued writing. On January 15, 2005, he wrote to Florida Congressman Debbie Wasserman Schultz, complaining about his treatment and the treatment of other prisoners.

On May 13, 2005, Warden LaManna wrote to Congressman Wasserman-Schultz, explaining that his condition had been thoroughly evaluated and appropriate medication had been prescribed. He told her their orthopedist soon would perform a special procedure to manage his pain. He denied that putting Lawton in the hole was a punishment but was richly deserved, and he assured her his staff at Edgefield was doing all it could to provide "a safe and secure environment for staff and inmates alike."

Despite all the letters, no investigation took place.

Lawton's letter-writing campaign was a real threat to warden LaManna, who decided the only way to silence him, was through intimidation. He did his best to break Lawton. LaManna sent four burly guards – the goon squad – into his cell.

"Cuff up," they ordered. Lawton refused.

"What did I do? Fuck you."

The four gorillas opened the cell door and charged at him. They jumped him, beat him, and broke his ribs. Blood streamed from his mouth. While they were sitting on him, Lawton was having trouble breathing. He thought he was going to die.

Despite the brutal beatings Lawton's letter-writing continued.

On June 8, 2005, he wrote to attorney general Alberto Gonzalez, saying he had been thrown in the hole for five months for complaining about the medical treatment. He told Gonzalez about "the gruesome deaths" at the prison. He asked that the retaliation against him stop along with the lying and doctoring of records.

The next time the goons were even more violent and sadistic.

"After they beat me they carried me out to a room," said Lawton, "stripped me naked, strapped me down in a four-point position so I was spread-eagled, and they cuffed each leg and arm to a post.

"A white guard stood over my head. I was looking up, my eyes half-closed from the beating. He zipped down his fly, took out his dick, and he peed in my face.

"As he was peeing, he was saying, 'Lawton, you keep writing senators. You think you're going anywhere?' Lawton closed his eyes, and he could feel the pee running down his face. One of the guards then spit on him as they walked past, a big gob of spittle, and they told him, "You think you're bad. Keep writing senators."

This may well have been the lowest point of Lawton's life.

"The taste of pee is salt, and it was in my face and mouth," said Lawton. "And my heartbeat must have been going 170 beats a minute. I was livid. There's no worse feeling in the world than being strapped down like that. And that was for writing senators and exposing the abuses of the prison."

Lawton came to and was carried back to his cell. Was he dreaming? Of course not. He was aching and still smelled the urine. They tried to break him, and Lawton was more determined than ever to fight the abuses of the prison. Instead of breaking him, they made him stronger.

*

On June 14, he wrote to Sen. Charles Schumer of New York. In it he said that the warden had lied in an earlier letter when he said Lawton was getting proper medical care. He said he was in terrible pain, he hadn't seen a prison doctor in nine months, and all nurses would proscribe was ibuprofen. He again charged that prisoners were dying because of the lack of proper medical care. He called for an independent investigation.

"Please send an investigator to see me," he wrote. "We are a nation founded on compassion and fairness. Sometimes some people forget that."

The war on Larry Lawton was a relentless attempt by LaManna to break him. In addition to sending goons for periodic beatings, he was put in the hole by himself and subject to torture and humiliation. At times the guards would turn off the hot water so it would be freezing.

"That wasn't so bad," said Lawton. "I could take that. What I couldn't handle was them turning off the cold water, which made the water so scalding that you couldn't take a shower. It was so hot you could actually put instant coffee in it and drink it. Or they would skip feeding me. Or they'd turn off the suction in my toilet so the waste wouldn't go down and they made me beg to turn it on. And believe me, eventually you do beg.

"When the guards delivered my food, I could see that someone had spit a big gob on my food. And I had to spoon it out and eat the food, because you had to eat. A person doesn't know what he can take until he has to.

"But the toll on your psyche is terrible. I had thoughts of suicide. I even thought of a scenario where I would fight the bastards to my death. But my will to live was stronger than anything else."

*

Lawton did what little he could to thwart the goons. He poured shampoo on the floor in an attempt to have them slip and fall. For his trouble the guards maced him in the eyes and face. He would be lying in a fetal position in his cell with snot coming out of his nose and his eyes burning from the mace when the goons would wail on him with their boots. Lawton, a tough man, cried like a baby.

"They were protecting their jobs," said Lawton. "They had families to feed. And they were sadists. They enjoyed beating me."

Deep down Lawton was sure they would kill him. The goons would tell him, "Nobody cares about you. You're a lonely piece of shit." He was beginning to believe them.

But Lawton was lucky. In addition to the senators and congressman who responded to his letters, he had friends on the outside like Joe Fraumeni, Louie Constantino, and Larry's dad, David Lawton, who all wrote letters on his behalf. The letters let warden LaManna know that people cared and were watching.

During his ordeal LaManna and his staff tried to silence him by stopping his letters from going out.

"That's a crime in itself," said Lawton. "They have a right to look at my mail, but they have no right to stop it unless there's something illegal about it. Through his dad he was able to contact the postmaster general and tell him what LaManna was doing."

Lawton sat in his cell when there was a knock on the steel door. It was Warden LaManna in person.

"I'm a lowly inmate, and I have the warden at my door," said Lawton, "and I could see *he* was mad."

"Lawton," LaManna said, "I have a lieutenant here, and I'm here to tell you that your mail is going to go out. The lieutenant will be picking up your mail every day. Is that okay?"

Said Lawton, "Once the postmaster got involved, every time I got a letter from a senator, I had to sign for it. The guards had to come to my cell, and I had to sign a book stating I got a letter from such and such person, and I had to sign for it. That way, they couldn't fuck with me."

Lawton discovered he wasn't alone in his quest for decency.

"When I was in the hole, other guards would tell me, 'Lawton, keep fighting. Don't give up. Keep doing what you're doing.' The good guards saved my life."

One of those on his side was a man by the name of Butch Lewis, the head of safety at Edgefield. He said to Lawton, "'Keep fighting. Ask your senators who's guarding the hen house."

"If a prisoner dies," said Lawton, "who do you think does the investigation? The prison itself. That prevents any abuses from being exposed. The guards are going to protect their own."

One of the guards who believed in decency was a Lieutenant Finnery. In the hole across the cell from Lawton was an inmate with no legs. The guards put the food in the chute, but often because he had no legs, he had no way to get to it. The guards saw this, but didn't act. Because he had no mobility, he also peed and defecated all over himself. The poor guy was such a health hazard that the guards went into his cell with white surgical masks covering their faces. Lieutenant Finnery, who was in charge of the hole, tried without success to get him out of the SHU and transferred to a medical facility.

As Lieutenant Finnery was filming the cell with the disabled man in it, he backed up to Lawton's cell and said, "Lawton, if anybody ever saw this video, somebody would be in handcuffs." Lawton took it to be LaManna.

In subsequent letters Lawton wrote about the prisoner with no legs and no medical care.

Only because the relentlessness of his letter writing, Lawton after eleven months was let out of the hole. Even so, every day Lawton walked on egg shells, continuing to fear for his life.

His letter-writing campaign was teaching him a lesson that would affect him for the rest of his life.

"I'm a physical man," he said, "I'm not a lightweight, but I learned there you can never beat them with physical force. They were the ones beating me. But once I started writing letters and got the senators and congressmen involved, they understood I had people on the outside fighting for my rights.

"The prison staff didn't respect me when I put the shampoo on the floor, but I sure got their attention when I wrote those letters. I learned you can get more accomplished with intelligence and words than with physical force."

*

In August one of the people Lawton wrote to was Greg Szymanski, the editor and producer of *The Arctic Beacon*, a radio and internet magazine which bills itself as "the last frontier of truth."

Lawton had written to members of the media for two years, and Szymanski was the first to publish Lawton's charges and complaints. In the article Lawton was quoted as saying three inmates were dead because of improper medical treatment. Szymanski wrote that Lawton was "stuck in a federal pen worse than Abu Ghraib."

The article described the grisly death of inmate Shifflett, who died on March 25, 2005. Szymanski wrote how he was suffering from cancer, spit up blood and tissue for more than a week, and then was left unattended by prison authorities until he died in his cell. He also described the unnecessary death of James Arch on September 15, 2004. Finally, news of their untimely deaths reached the public.

In the article Szymanski quoted Lawton as to how a third inmate, a man by the name of Harris, died in his cell after receiving inadequate treatment. And finally he told the story of the inmate with no legs who was left to sit in a pool of urine and feces.

Concluded the article, "I want people in America to know that we have our own Abu Ghraib right here in our own backyard."

The article concluded with Lawton's address in Edgefield.

*

After the publication of the article, Lawton became the talk of the prison, even by the guards. With the reputation of the prison at stake, in a last-ditch attempt to stop his letter writing, the prison staff tried bribery.

One day Lawton was sitting on the yard smoking on a cigar when one of the prison administrators came up to him and asked him, "Why are you doing this? Why don't you stop?"

"What are you talking about?" said Lawton.

"You keep writing these people."

"I'll stop writing when you do your job right," said Lawton.

"Just stop writing," said the administrator, "and we'll give you your own cell in another prison. Anywhere you want. A single cell. We'll even give you a get out of jail free card." In other words, the next time Lawton was caught breaking prison rules, he'd get a free pass.

"Just stop writing," said the administrator.

"Why are you coming to me?" asked Lawton. "I'm a lowly

inmate. Why don't you just answer those senators who are talking about me now?"

On September 7, 2005 Lawton wrote to Sen. Graham about yet another death at the prison. John Moore died in the SHU at age 43. Lawton didn't know why he died, but he requested an inquiry.

On September 8, he wrote to Sen. Bill Nelson asking to see a prison doctor. He also said he found out the prison has egg-shell mattresses for prisoners with bad backs. But the prison had refused to give him one.

In the letter he wrote, "A while back the executive assistant to the warden told me, 'I don't give a fuck who you write. Go write your senator. They never listen to inmates.'"

He concluded, "I have two years left. Please hold someone accountable for the crimes being committed here."

*

Once Lawton's claims reached the public, the beatings stopped. The bad treatment stopped. Warden LaManna's only remedy was to transfer him, which he did. LaManna sent Lawton to the medium security prison in Yazoo City, Mississippi.

The policy was that an inmate was not supposed to be sent more than five hundred miles from their home. Longer than that was considered a hardship for relatives who might want to visit. Yet Yazoo was more than a thousand miles away from Lawton's relatives in Florida.

"I really thought I'd go to Yazoo and do my time quietly and get out," said Lawton, "but LaManna figured out a way to continue to make my life miserable. He decided I needed to be fucked with a little longer, so Rick Brawley, the unit manager at Edgefield, got promoted to head of SIS at Yazoo."

Lawton, keeping his nose clean and minding his own business, was on the Yazoo yard for a month, when Brawley trumped up a charge and threw him in the hole.

CHAPTER 13

Yazoo and Forest City

To get to Yazoo City, Mississippi from Edgefield, South Carolina, Lawton first had to travel to his former home, the Atlanta Penitentiary, where he wondered whether his harsh treatment would continue. He didn't have long to find out. He was crowded into a two-man cell with five other prisoners. He had barely had time to get comfortable when a staff member barked at him, "Take that towel down."

The towel was lying on his bed. Apparently having a towel on the bed was against regulations.

"Are you kidding me?" said Lawton. "You're worried about that towel when we have five guys in a two-man cell?"

The staff member called the guards.

"Take him to the hole," he ordered.

Lawton was taken from his cell, not knowing whether he was going to the hold-over hole, or to the much more restrictive prison hole. When he got on an elevator, he knew he was in trouble. He was headed, he knew, for the prison's hole.

As a holdover inmate, Lawton was not supposed to go to Atlanta's hole. Lawton was only a holdover prisoner, but Lawton was sure someone must have seen his record as being a troublemaker, and they put him in a cell by himself naked. The temperature hovered around 55 degrees. His teeth were chattering.

Sure the goon squad was going to come in and beat him, he was filled with fright the entire time he was there. They never came.

The next day he was relieved when he was put back into the holdover unit. A week later he was finally transferred to the prison in Yazoo City, Mississippi, a medium security facility.

When Lawton arrived at Yazoo City, he became aware that gangs ran the place.

"You always felt tension on the yard in Yazoo," said Lawton, "because you never knew when something was going to jump off. You could feel the tension in the air. When you're a convict you can feel something is going to go down. It's like a sixth sense. You watch the way the inmates dress. If a guy usually wears flip flops at night, and all of a sudden one evening he's wearing sneakers, look out. Or if he has two tee shirts on, maybe he's hiding a magazine under there as body armor against getting stabbed."

Lawton, as usual, hung out with the white prisoners. In Yazoo City, only fifteen percent of the 2,000 inmates were white, and many belonged to gangs such as the Aryan Circle, the Texas Aryan Brotherhood, and the Dirty White Boys. Blacks and Hispanics made up the rest of the inmate population. The Crips and Bloods were black gangs, and the largest gang, the Pisa, made up of Mexican inmates, was the toughest gang of them all.

About a week after Lawton arrived at Yazoo City he witnessed a violent brawl. The doors of the cells opened at six in the morning, and all 110 prisoners in Lawton's unit came out of their cells. Because money was tight, Yazoo City only had one guard for the late shift. After opening the cells in Lawton's unit, the guard then headed to open the cells of the adjoining unit. With the prisoners milling around, suddenly two large prisoners, one black, one Hispanic, confronted each other like gladiators. Lawton would find out later that the two men had had a beef the night before, and this was how they were going to settle it.

As Lawton watched the two men square off, he was visited by a friend of his by the name of Big Ron. A quiet man in his fifties, Big Ron came from California. He liked to walk on the yard for exercise, and it was there that they met.

Ron's original crime was bank robbery. After getting out of San Quentin, he moved to Missoula, Montana, where he was arrested for being a convicted criminal in possession of a gun. He was sentenced to ten years in Yazoo City.

Ron learned that Lawton knew his way around the law library, and he asked Lawton to investigate his case, to see if there was some way he could get out sooner. Lawton did that for a number of prisoners. Quickly Lawton became known as a stand up guy, a go-to guy. He had everyone's respect.

After Big Ron walked over to Lawton's cell, from there the two watched as the two rival gang members went at it. It was like a heavyweight fight, and it was brutal. After exchanging punches that met their mark, the black inmate managed to wrestle the Hispanic inmate to the ground, and began kicking him in the head. The bloody fight was broken up when the heads of the two gangs waded in and broke them up.

As they did, the guard, who was new to the job, returned. He had no idea what had gone on. It was time for breakfast, and the entire unit headed for the mess hall. When breakfast was over, the entire unit was put on lockdown. The prison officials learned of the brawl and were afraid that something major was going to happen between the two gangs, so they locked the place down tight for a week until they were able to find out what the fight was all about.

In an attempt to confiscate weapons, the guards went through every cell with a fine-toothed comb. A number of inmates were caught making wine in their laundry baskets. Lawton, who was an old pro, used fresh dryer sheets so the guards couldn't smell the alcohol.

"I knew right off the bat this was a gang prison," said Lawton.

Another time a member of one of the gangs arrived at the prison. That day he walked out of receiving and discharge onto the yard only to be attacked by ten members of a rival gang wielding knives. The yard was locked down immediately. The prison had screwed up. It should have known the rival gang was laying for him and kept him safe.

Gang fights could break out at any time for different reasons. One gang member disrespecting another was a common cause. A drug deal gone bad was another. If one guy didn't pay up, before you knew it, inmates were beating on each other.

One time two of the white gangs were feuding, and the

administrators went to Lawton and said to him, "You know these people. Can't you talk to them?"

The Dirty White Boys, the minors of the Aryan Brotherhood, was feuding with a bunch of inmates from the Aryan Circle. The shot-caller – the head of the Dirty White Boys -- was in Lawton's unit. Lawton called him and the shot-caller for the Aryan Circle together for a meeting.

He told the heads of the two gangs, "Are you fucking idiots? We have 2,000 people here. There are only 350 white guys, and you're stabbing each other?"

"I got them thinking," said Lawton. The violence abated.

*

One of the favors Lawton did for the other prisoners was "pull paperwork" on incoming prisoners. The inmates didn't want to room with stool pigeons or pedophiles, and so they went to Lawton, who would make a phone call to a lawyer friend of his on the outside. The lawyer friend would pull the docket sheets in the case, find out the nature of the underlying crime, and mail the information to Lawton.

Most of the time the information got through, because Lawton might well have been helping the inmate out. But the reason the prison system does not allow prisoners to bring in their paperwork is to prevent the identification of the rats and the pedophiles. As a result, the prison staff sometimes would call the prisoner and ask him, "Did you ask for Lawton to see your paperwork?" If he said no, they would immediately move him to give him protection. If they didn't move him even though he knew someone was checking his record, he might make what the inmates called a "check-in" move. Worried he'd be targeted, he'd go to a guard, curse the guard out, and get himself thrown in the hole. It was really for protection, but he tried to make it look like he was a stand-up guy.

At Yazoo a new inmate came onto the prison yard. He was about 40 years old, white, and "dumpy-looking." Lawton had been asked to check him out, and after the paperwork came back, sure enough, the inmate had been convicted of having sex with young children. The worst inmates are the ones who have sex with kids under 12. The scum of the scum, even lower than rats. They are targeted by everyone.

"When that happens," said Lawton, "the cellie is the guy who hits him. This guy was watching TV in the middle of the TV room. His cellie came in, and he smashed him with his fist in the back of the head. The guy went down, and his cellie began kicking him in the face. Blood was everywhere. The guy was out of it. He layed on the floor, and everyone just left. There weren't any cameras in the TV room, so no one knew who did it. The cops came running, and they took three inmates up to the office and put them in the hole.

"I didn't have any feeling for those guys, so I didn't give a fuck. But I didn't want to get involved in a conspiracy charge to commit murder either.

"I have to say I was very well respected on the yard at Yazoo. Word got around the prison system that I was fighting for them, that I knew the law, and that I wouldn't cave, that I would keep fighting. That is so rare. People break, and I can understand why. I never broke. I took everything that warden LaManna and that prick Rick Brawley threw at me at Edgefield, and I survived."

After three months of living in relative peace, Rick Brawley, warden LaManna's right hand man at Edgefield, was transferred to Yazoo City as its head of SIS, the investigation arm of the prison. Lawton was sure LaManna had sent Brawley there to continue the punishment for his letter writing campaign, and so for the next nine months Lawton once again was subject to abuse. Once Brawley arrived, he was in the hole most of the rest of the time spent at Yazoo City.

"Again, they were trying to break me," said Lawton. "Every time they let me out of the hole, they found a way to put me back in. It made me stronger."

"I was in the hole so long I started another letter-writing campaign, complaining about what they were doing to me for some bogus bullshit. I told senators, 'The man punishing me was transferred here. This is a blatant disregard for my rights.' I stayed in the hole in Yazoo for nothing."

Lawton tried conciliation with Brawley. Lawton told him he would never be intimidated and would never quit, but if Brawley stopped the harassment he'd stop writing letters.

"All I want is to be left alone for the rest of my sentence," Lawton told him. "Nobody cares about inmates, and you're not going back on the yard," said

Brawley. Lawton stayed in the hole.

"Finally, I was transferred out of Yazoo. I had less than a year to go, and when you get close to your release date, they are supposed to transfer you closer to home. Where did I go?

Forest City, Arkansas, farther away still from Florida. They didn't want to do anything to help me. Not a thing."

Finally away from the clutches of LaManna and Brawley, Lawton did the rest of his time quietly at Forest City. He never once was put in the hole. Forest City, located eighty-five miles east of Little Rock, was brand new and was run well, even though Forest City was the worst gang prison of them all.

Though he was a short-timer with less than a year to serve, at Forest City he got a lot of respect from the prison system. He had easy access to the law library. The gangs knew about him, and inmates would ask him for legal advice.

"I had a lot of respect from blacks, Spanish, everybody," said Lawton.

One of his friends at Forest City was an inmate by the name of Bruiser, the head of the Aryan Circle. Lawton would pull paperwork for Bruiser to find out why new inmates were in prison. Whenever one of the new inmates asked to join the Aryan Circle, Bruiser would ask Lawton, who never took money for his services, to pull paper on the guy.

"I was sitting in the mess hall, and an inmate passed me a piece of paper with the new inmate's last name and number. They wanted to know his background and what he was in for. I called my lawyer friend, and he sent me back the guy's docket sheet.

"Bruiser and his cellie came to see me in my cell. This young kid wanted to become part of their gang. They join because of protection. And the kid was thinking they weren't going to find out he was a pedophile.

"I told them, "This kid is no good." When they found out, they got really mad. They said they were going to stab him, really fuck him up.

"I said, "Bruiser, I did this for you. Don't kill this guy. I was adamant, because if he killed him I could be brought up on a conspiracy charge, and here I was, six months to go before I got out.

"Sure enough this guy was standing below the top tier, and they dropped a heavy buffer machine down on his head and crushed the whole side of his body."

As at the other prisons, violence could erupt at any time. One day a group of ten Mexican inmates attacked a group of whites from the Aryan Circle on the yard. The fighting was fierce, and Bruiser was stabbed. Lawton was in his cell with him when the guards came to arrest Bruiser, who wasn't hurt badly, and put him in the hole for fighting.

Lawton had a routine where he would get up at six in the morning, when the cell doors cracked, and go down to the white TV room. After Bruiser returned from the hole, he would join him and they would watch Country Music Videos.

"I started watching country music videos in Jesup," said Lawton, "bus I became a huge country music fan because of Forest City prison. We would watch CMT every morning from six o'clock until eight o'clock. I very rarely went to the chow hall. I'd have a cup of coffee and maybe a little oatmeal that I bought in the commissary. I'd bring my plastic chair from my room, and I'd sit there and watch.

"One day this black guy with long dreadlocks came in and

without asking us, turned on BET.

"What are you doing?" I asked him.

Lawton without saying a word grabbed his dreadlocks and smashed his face right into the wall. The inmate, bloody, fell to the ground.

"I had to do that," said Lawton. "In prison you don't ever want to be perceived as weak."

Bruiser knew if he didn't do something that Lawton would face retaliation from the man's gang. Bruiser, who was the white gang's shot caller, had a meeting with the black gang's shot caller. Bruiser told him, "He came into our TV room and disrespected us." The incident was squashed.

With only a few months to go, Lawton decided it was time to stop pulling papers on new prisoners.

"Even when I knew they were dirty, I wouldn't say anything," he said. "I didn't want to get into any conspiracies for killing a guy. Right before I left, I had a docket proving one of the new guys was a bad guy, and I shredded it. I had to make up excuses why I hadn't gotten it. I stalled."

Lawton left Forest City on a violent note.

"Right before I got out, seven white guys from another unit came into our unit and started fighting," he said. "One guy was stabbed. I was playing chess in the common area, and I knew what was going on. They had a hit out on somebody, and the other gang fought back."

In February of 2007 Lawton threw a Super Bowl/going away party for twenty of the regular guys who watched the tube in the white TV room. He even held a raffle.

Now he was counting the days. But never once did he let his guard down. He was very well connected with the Aryan Circle, so he wasn't worried about gang violence, but he was concerned about jealousy from long-term inmates.

"You're getting out, and they have thirty or forty years to go, so you don't go around boasting about your getting out," said Lawton. "You don't go around prison saying, 'Yeah, I'm getting out. I'm leaving soon.' You could get killed doing that. You stay very low key."

With one week to go Lawton's mind was racing. He needed to keep busy so as not to go crazy, and so he spent the time playing games – chess, pinochle, backgammon, and gin rummy. He sat in the TV room and watched show after show. He'd sit in his chair up against the wall and eat a bag of Dorritos or a bowl of soup, and he continued to work out like a demon. In 45 minutes in the yard or around the unit he'd do 600 sit ups and 600 push ups. He'd do 150 handstand presses with his back to a wall. He was down to 187 rock-hard pounds.

The night before Lawton was to get out he called over all the people somewhat close to him – "I always say somewhat because you don't have too many real friends in prison." – and gave away most of his possessions.

"You don't think it's a big deal, but I was giving away a radio, a cooking bowl, my cup and spoon, a sweatshirt – it becomes a big deal. People – big drug dealers -- were rifling through my crappie clothes."

That night Lawton didn't sleep. He was awake when the

guards came for him at five in the morning.

"You're on Cloud 100," said Lawton. "You've been in prison for eleven years, and all of a sudden you're going to be a free man."

Before he could get out, he had a go through what they call a roundabout. He had to visit the medical department, the law library to return materials, the commissary to close his account – he had to go to each department of the prison -- and he had to be signed out.

The morning of his final day in prison a guard came to Lawton's cell an hour before unlocking the general population and he told Lawton, "Pack up and head to R and D."

Lawton got dressed, said good bye to his cellie, and on the way out of the unit he threw the rest of his prison clothes in a heap on the floor. In R and D Lawton was processed out and given civilian clothes -- a pair of jeans, a polo shirt, a pair of boots, and a military-style belt.

"Everyone in the world can spot a guy coming out of prison," said Lawton.

At R and D he was also given his released papers, a bus ticket, and the $275 he had in his commissary account. Most inmates who are released leave with $25. The clerk counted out the bills and handed them to him. Lawton, who never trusted the system, was leery.

"While I was in prison I had been reading USA Today, so I thought I was keeping on top of things, but there was so much I didn't know," he said. "Remember, in prison you don't see real money."

In the eleven years Lawton was in prison the look of American currency had changed drastically. The president's picture was enlarged, and color had been added to the bills.

When they handed me the new bills, I asked the cashier, 'Where do I exchange the bills?' I thought it was monopoly money."

"What do you mean?" asked the clerk.

"Do I take this to the bank and get real money?" asked Lawton. "Where do I get the real money?"

"That is the real money," said the clerk.

"What do you mean it's real money?" asked Lawton.

"I was skeptical," said Lawton. "I thought they were trying to fuck me. I thought, *These guys are stealing my money.* I was very distrustful – of everyone."

"To me it looked like Mexican money," said Lawton.

Lawton's family and friend wrote and asked if he wanted them to drive to Forest City to pick him up, but Lawton said no. He wanted to feel his first taste of freedom by himself. He wanted to get on a bus without handcuffs. He wanted to be free to see the world. Oh, what a mistake that was.

In March of 2007, after eleven years of incarceration, finally Lawton was out of prison. He was 46 years old.

CHAPTER 14

Free At Last

After Larry Lawton walked out the front door of the Forest City fortress with a bus ticket and two hundred and seventy five dollars in cash, the prison van was waiting to take him to the bus station. The van dropped him off right on time so he didn't have to wait around long. When the van drove off, Lawton stood there all alone.

The Greyhound bus pulled up, and Lawton handed the driver his ticket. From this small town in Mississippi he was headed to a halfway house in Tampa, Florida, a trip of about a thousand miles. He walked to the middle of the bus on the aisle and took his seat next to a good-looking blonde in her early twenties.

"I got on the bus and sat down, and I felt good," said Lawton. "I took my hands and raised them up like I was signaling victory. I thought, *Oh my God, I can move around. I can get up. Nobody is telling me what to do.* When I raised my hands, I was cheering inside, because I had been in handcuffs and shackles for so long. The people on the bus must have thought I was a wacko.

"The girl I sat down next to had a cell phone in her hand. I knew about the new cell phones from reading about them, but I had never seen one before. It was so small. When I entered prison, cell phones were big and gray with large antennas. I had to be looking at it like I was a nut.

"'Can I see that?' I asked her. Think of how that sounds. If anyone asked you to see your cell phone, you'd look at them like they were crazy. She was a beautiful little girl, and here was this burly tattooed guy bothering her. She handed it to me. It was a flip phone, and I held it in my hand, and it was like a little baby to me. I was afraid I might break it. I was thinking, *How do my fat fingers touch these little buttons?* After a few minutes I closed the phone and gave it back to her. She looked at me without speaking, and I know I must have weirded her out, because at the next stop, she got up and moved. If you ever want to ride a bus with your own row of seats all to yourself, just do what I did.

"I'm on the bus, and I'm looking out the window, and I'm experiencing sensory overload. I was overwhelmed. I'm looking at cars. And every few minutes I would lift my arms over my head and grin. The people around me must have thought I was nuts."

Lawton was daydreaming, staring at all the cars and scenery, when the Greyhound bus pulled into a gas station. The driver announced that everyone had forty-five minutes to get something to eat.

Get something to eat? Lawton thought. *At a gas station?* When Lawton went to prison in 1996, a gas station was a gas station. This gas station had a Subway sandwich shop, a McDonalds, and a food mart. Lawton knew what Subway was from watching the commercial starring Jared and his huge pair of pants on TV in prison.

"I went to the Subway store and got in line," said Lawton. "I was really excited. I wanted to get a sandwich – a real sandwich. I looked up, and there seemed like a thousand choices to make. I started to feel the hair on the back of my neck rise. I knew people were looking at me. I didn't want anyone behind me. I was getting panicky.

"When it was my turn to order, I froze. I couldn't make a decision. My body started shaking. People were standing in line behind me, and I could feel the tension as they started to get antsy waiting for me to order.

"I left the line, went back to the bus, and I sat in the back of the bus crying like a baby. I thought to myself, *I can't even order a sandwich.*

"After the incident at the Subway, I called my Cousin Cheryl in California from a pay phone. She's a life skills coach who helps people with psychological problems. As I talked to her I stood with my back to the wall.

"'This is normal, Larry,' she said. 'You are having what is called sensory overload. In prison you didn't make a hundred choices in a day. A person on the street makes between 1,500 and 2,000 choices a day. You're like a newborn baby in this big body.' Thank God she was able to calm me down."

Lawton, shaken, didn't eat for the entire twenty hours it took for him to reach the halfway house.

"Sitting in the back of that bus, I was a vegetable," he said. "I wanted to get back to prison. I had a very bad feeling about being free.

"I wanted to be confined again, because when you're confined you feel safe. Sitting on the bus, I felt like I was going crazy. I was totally freaking out. Bad thoughts were going through my mind.

"Someone's looking for me, that the police were coming to get me, I kept thinking. *The cops are behind the bus, and they're going to take me back to prison.*

"I had been so looking forward to getting out of Forest City and going to the halfway house. Before I got on that bus I was thinking, *Take your time. Look around the world.* But on the bus I was sitting there feeling nervous, sure that people were after me.

"Let me tell you something about prisoners. They have a sixth sense. They can feel tension. You can tell the way a person looks, the way he walks, what he wears, the air about him, the way he might move his neck, the way he might move his hand. If there was tension all around me, I could feel it.

"The first thing I do when I look at a person is determine: *Can I take him? Who's around? Can I take three of them?* I was a fighter, a street guy, and you think, *What can I do to him real quick?* Your mind plays nutty tricks on you.

"I was in a defensive mode, ready to hurt someone. In prison they call it *ready to go.* I was ready to go.

"After a while as a sat there I got a grip on myself and calmed down."

Lawton's release address was Palm Bay, Florida, his mother's house, and so he was sent to the closest halfway house, which was in Tampa on Hillsborough Boulevard. It's run by Goodwill

Industries not far from Raymond James Stadium, home of the Tampa Bay Buccaneers.

The bus dropped him off at the Tampa bus station. Wanting to get to the halfway house where he'd be locked up as quickly as possible, Lawton hailed a cab and was driven there directly. When the cab pulled up, he literally ran to get inside.

Said Lawton, "It wasn't in a great neighborhood, but that didn't mean anything to me. I'd been to Atlanta and Edgefield. I'd lived in the worst neighborhoods in the world. This was paradise."

But being free was scaring him half to death.

"I needed to get back into confinement," he said. "I felt safe there, as crazy as that sounds. After eleven years of incarceration I was in a new world."

During his first day at the halfway house Lawton was given four hours to go and buy toiletries. At first he didn't want to go. The sensory overload was too great.

"You would think that in four hours you can do a lot, but you have to take the bus to Walgreens, and I was all nervous because I didn't know exactly which bus to take or where it went."

When he finally arrived at the store, he walked up and down the toothpaste aisle. He couldn't believe how many different brands of toothpaste there were and how many different kinds of toothbrushes were being sold.

"I almost fucking freaked," said Lawton. "In prison there are two kinds of toothpaste, Colgate and Aim. And you have three days to decide which one you want. There are two flavors of Ramen noodles, and you have three days to pick what you want. You sit down in your cell, figure out how much money is in your commissary account, add the cost of the items, put them down on your list, and two days later it arrives.

"Here I was standing in Walgreens in the toothpaste aisle, and there must have been thirty types of toothpaste. *Holy fuck, what do I pick? Do I want to buy the one that's best for whiteness or best for my gums or best for tooth decay? Do I want the one that's a dollar eighty nine or the one that's three ounces more for two dollars and something?* You try to do the math, but you're a vegetable. You really can't function."

He finally picked a toothpaste, a toothbrush, and a dental floss, and he took his items to the checkout girl. The total came to four dollars and twenty six cents. He handed her a five dollar bill, and she rang him up, bagged the items, gave him a receipt, but didn't give him his change.

Said Lawton, "I was sure she was stealing my money, so I looked at her and in a real mean voice said, 'Where's my fucking money?' I could see her getting nervous. I was feeling the tension of the people around me.

"A guy tapped me, and very defensively I turned to face him real quick, and he pointed.

"It's over there," he said. It had come down the coin chute at the end of the counter in an arm of the cash register. I went over, collected the coins and put them away in my pocket, and I just about ran out of the store. I was not ready for society.

"I got on the bus and got back to the halfway house, and when I told the other former inmates what happened, they laughed, because they all had experiences like that. Some guys left their purchases at the store. Or they walked out without paying, not meaning to steal it. You just don't know how to function in society."

Technically, when an inmate is staying at the halfway house, he's still in prison. The rooms had six bunks to a room. There were two showers and two toilets. It was a lot better than prison. There was a community kitchen. A lady came in and cooked for them.

"They gave me the rules and regulations, and I was happy," said Lawton. "I was used to following rules. Rules gave me structure.

"At the halfway house the inmates were not allowed outside their door after eleven at night. You can't drink. If you have a job, you have to bring your money back and show them what you earned. You can't get laid in the rooms. All you can do is go out and work."

While staying at the halfway house, Lawton was allowed to go to the Department of Motor Vehicles and get his driver's license back. Larry did that, and so he was able to drive his dad's 1994 aqua colored Buick Skylark to and from work.

He was given a job working for Verizon calling its wireless customers.

"If people ever knew they were giving their information to ex-cons! said Lawton. "We asked for the last four digits of their social security number, for instance.

"I did that for a month and a half. I wasn't very good on the phone, but I'm an outgoing guy, and I got laid for the first time with a girl named Tiffany in the next cubicle. She was 36 years old, hot, and she had been in prison, but she no longer was on probation."

Quickly Lawton became disillusioned with how the system worked.

"The function of a halfway house should be to help you get acclimated back into society," he said. "But it's not. It's a moneymaker. You have to give twenty five percent of your salary to the halfway house. If you make two hundred dollars, you have to give them fifty. And then you have to pay taxes on the whole two hundred. The system sets people up for failure."

Everything was going well for Lawton, but then the federal prison system opened a new halfway house in Orlando, and he and twelve other former convicts were summarily sent from Tampa to this new facility.

"We were the first inmates ever sent there, and since then it's had seven directors in a year and a half," said Lawton. "They were taking people out of college and putting them in charge when they needed someone like me – an inmate – to run it.

"They had petty inspections. They had stupid rules. You can't talk to this person, you can't do this. They made it so hard on you.

"The director was a Spanish guy who was out of his league. He was fired after eight weeks."

Lawton didn't last that long. He was only there one week.

"It was run poorly, fucked up, and I told the people in charge that I hated it so much that it was hurting me and not helping me. I told them, 'You need to send me back to prison or it won't be pretty.'"

While living in the Orlando halfway house Lawton had gotten a job as the manager of an electrical service company. The owner was the father of one of the young ex-convicts in the halfway house. The son had known Lawton when they were in Coleman prison together. They had been transferred together from Tampa. He told his father about Lawton, and his father paid him ten dollars an hour.

"I was going to be an account representative," said Lawton. "My job was to make sure his accounts were good, but the guy running the halfway house did what he could to make it impossible for me to do my job.

"He told me, 'You have to report to us. You can't go from this place to that place.' They didn't want to let me work. What's a halfway house for if you can't try to adjust to society? I went to the director and told him, "This is crazy."

"If you don't like it…." he said to Lawton.

"Just send me back to prison," Lawton said.

That day the halfway house director called the marshals and had Lawton taken to the Seminole County Jail. Lawton should have gotten a shot – demerits -- but they didn't give it to him, he said, because they knew how badly the halfway house was run.

"The Seminole County jail was a scum hole, but I had been around," said Lawton. "I was a veteran."

Lawton was sent to the felony pod that housed murderers. One inmate had killed his wife. But Lawton had dealt with murderers and killers for eleven years, and he fit right in.

"It doesn't impress me," said Lawton. "It means you got caught and you're stupid. The other prisoners respected me because of the way I looked, my tattoos and my demeanor. I know how to walk into a prison and scope out the place.

"I walked into my cell. There was a kid in the lower bunk. He was in his twenties, and I told him, 'Get off the bottom bunk.'

"He looked at me.

"I said, 'Get off the fucking bottom bunk. Don't make me do something I don't want to do.'

"And he got off and transferred to the top bunk. He knew I was mean and had been around."

Lawton was in the Seminole County Jail about two months when they sent him back to Coleman prison.

"I had three weeks to serve," said Lawton. "It was like old home week. It was the best time I had. Vic Orena, the old mob boss from Atlanta, and I hugged. A lot of inmates had known me from other prisons. I was hugging everyone. Through the grapevine everyone knew the battle I had fought for prisoners' rights. I was very well respected. The inmates were yelling, 'Hey, Larry. We heard about you, man. Keep fighting the motherfuckers.'

"Even though I only had three weeks left, I still had to be careful and watch my back, because of jealousy. Some of them had life sentences, and they were never getting out. After being there only a few days, I could see the politics of the place. Guys would say to me, "Don't talk to this guy. He's no good. He's in that gang." All that bullshit. A lot of guys came up to me and wanted me to join their gang.

"I thought to myself, *I only have three weeks to go. These people are crazy. I'm going to keep to myself.* And my spirits were high because I knew that when I got out I wouldn't have to go back to a halfway house. I kept thinking: *I'm finally going to see my Mom and Dad.*

"So I didn't join anyone. I pretty much stayed to myself. I was thinking, *Get out. Just get out.*

"After three weeks they once again gave me those shitty clothes, and this time I got on a bus and headed straight home to Melbourne. But I was a little better off emotionally this time. I knew what to expect. I believe that everything happens for a reason. I'm not a religious guy – the priest took care of that – but I do believe in God. When I got to Melbourne, I took a cab to my parents' home, because I wanted to surprise them.

"I knocked on the front door. My dad answered. This was at the very early stage of his getting Alzheimer's. He was still sharp, and I was very lucky I could talk to him.

"My Mom was ecstatic and hugged me. I was shaking like a leaf. For no apparent reason either. After speaking to my parents for a while, I drove over to surprise my dear friends Uncle Mikey and Phyllis in West Melbourne."

It was Uncle Mikey's 79th birthday. Phyllis cried as she gave Larry a big hug. They had coffee, chatted, and arranged for Larry to surprise some other old friends at a birthday dinner at Carrabba's restaurant that night.

Larry showed up at the restaurant with balloons and flowers. Joe Fraumini, another of Larry's long-time friends, did a double-take when he saw Lawton. It had been a long time. There were hugs and wine all around.

Finally, thought Lawton, *I am free.*

"That was August 24, 2007, my out date," said Lawton. "Within seventy- two hours I had to report to my probation officer, Dave Lubinsky, who was an asshole sometimes, and sometimes was okay. He was my probation officer, a typical government employee who questions everything and never believes you're going to do good.

"I went to see Lubinsky, and he told me I had to get a job. I'm lucky because I had a roof over my head living with my parents, and because I was getting a pension of $1,021 a month from the Coast Guard. A lot of ex-cons don't have that.

"I had to go back to the VA to set up my medical services. I had to get acclimated to society. *What am I going to do for a living?* I know I'm not going back to my old ways. *What am I going to do?*"

The week after Lawton arrived home, he saw an acquaintance of his who lived on Tortoise Island in a well-to-do section of town. The man invited Larry to a house party about six weeks later. During the party one of the other guests, a golf pro he knew by name of Ronnie, said to Larry, "I need a big favor."

Immediately Lawton figured the guy had a beef with someone and wanted him to rough him up. .

"What the fuck," was Larry's initial response. "I just got

out of prison.

I ain't into that shit anymore. You want to get me back in the business? You want me to break someone's legs or something?"

But that wasn't what the man wanted.

"Larry," he said, "I caught my son smoking weed and stealing, and when I confronted him, he told me, 'Fuck you, dad. Where have you ever been?' I was hoping that you could talk to him."

Larry didn't know the golf pro's kid very well at all. His son had been a little kid when Larry went to prison.

"If that's all you want," Lawton said, "I'll talk to him."

"Talk to him about prison, what it's like," Ronnie said.

"Don't worry," he said. "I will."

Lawton started thinking about what he wanted to say to the boy. He went home, and looked through his pictures from prison. He had put the photos in albums, and as he looked at them, memories came flooding back. As he flipped through the pages he began to cry, because some of the men in the photos were dead, no good, fucked up, or never getting out.

The golf pro lived in a beautiful house. Lawton walked in, and they shook hands.

"Larry, I really appreciate this. I know you just got out. If you need anything…"

"Okay," Lawton said, "Let me ask you and your wife about your son."

The golf pro had a gazebo on his property, and Lawton went there to talk to the parents to find out about the kid.

During their talk Lawton told them stories about what he had endured in prison and showed them pictures.

'If you don't mind," Lawton said, "I'm going to tell this kid some tough stuff."

"You can beat the shit out of him if you want," said the father, who was at a loss as to what to do.

"I won't touch the kid," Lawton said. "I won't have to."

Said Lawton, "The kid was in his room. He was sixteen, a big kid, bigger than me, though that doesn't mean anything. He was sitting on a futon bed when I walked in, and he looked up at me. I was wearing a sleeveless tee-shirt to reveal the tattoos on my arms. I wasn't a guy in a suit trying to tell him what to do. He had said to his father, 'Fuck you, dad, where have you ever been?' That resonated with me because he was right. He was wrong to say that, but how could his father tell anyone about prison. Where had he ever been? If you want to know about prisons, talk to a prisoner."

Lawton scowled at him and said, "You told your father, 'Where the fuck have you been?' Let me show you where the fuck *I've* been."

Lawton could feel the boy's fear, and he wanted to capitalize on it.

He sat down, calmed himself, and lowered his voice.

"I'm going to show you some shit," he said to the kid. "I spent eleven straight years in fucking prison, and I just got out. I lived the life that you think is so glamorous. I did drugs." Lawton started showing him the pictures.

Said Lawton, "I was in the room with him for two hours.

His parents must have been thinking, *What's going on?* I'm sure they were waiting to hear yelling and screaming. But I didn't want this to be *Scared Straight*, a program that doesn't work very well because when you yell and scream at a kid, he closes his mind and shuts you out. He actually puts up a barrier. He will see me, but he won't hear me. The way you get to a kid to listen is to educate by telling the truth. I gave the man's son education along with reality, and I treated him like an adult.

"I told him, 'Look at this guy.' I showed him a picture. 'He's dead. He was a good kid, good family, he thought he was invincible, and now he's dead. All for nothing.'

"I told him a story about the guards abusing me. I said, 'I don't care how big you are or how tough you think you are, in prison you can't beat four guys. I was strapped down naked and peed on, and that was by the guards. What do you think is going to happen to you? At your age you're going to be sucked into a gang. If you can't control your drug habit out here, in prison they're going to get you hooked on heroin, and they're going to fuck you in the ass.'

"His face turned pal white. I knew I was getting through to him without raising my voice.

"When I was done, the kid walked me out. He was respectful. I said to his father, 'Okay, Ronnie, I'll see you on the golf course.'"

Two weeks later the dad called Lawton at home. Larry had gotten his paralegal certificate while in the hole in prison, and he had received offers from law firms. While in prison he had been successful with cases relating to ineffective assistance of counsel. He had success gaining writs of habeas corpus – they were freed, resentenced or given a new trial. He had been practicing law, in a sense, for ten years. Law firms wanted him.

Ronnie said to him, "I don't know what you're going to do with your paralegal degree, but whatever it is, don't do it. You have to work with kids."

"What are you talking about?" Lawton asked.

He said, "Whatever you did to my son, he's changed. He's respectful. He talks to us. He talks about you all the time. Whatever you do, you have to work with kids."

Said Lawton, "He asked me if I needed money. The guy was wealthy. I was living at my parents' home getting a pension, and I was surviving. I'm hard-headed and proud. I refused his money. But he got me to thinking. *I can do this.* And I started putting together a program modeled after what I had said to his kid.

CHAPTER 15

The Beginning of the Reality Check Program

Until Larry Lawton got out of prison, he didn't realize how much he was missing: family and friends, spending holidays with loved ones, hugging a woman, and smiling, but also small things like being able to change the channel on the TV without having to get into a fight with someone, or getting up and going to the refrigerator. He was eating real food again for the first time in a decade, and he savored every bite.

"Everyone asks me what I missed most," he said. "It wasn't sex, though I love sex and love my girlfriend dearly. It's food -- real food. For eleven years the prisons fed me garbage. To me McDonald's is gourmet food."

Lawton was living with his parents in a small 1,100 square foot house in Palm Bay, Florida. He lived in a ten-by-ten bedroom in the back of the house, but after living in prison to him his room was his castle.

It was in that little room that Larry Lawton built his Reality Check Program. He bought a laptop computer and began learning the basics. Lawton was in a new world. When he went to prison in 1996, computers were on phone modems, and laptops were in their infancy.

He needed help, and he got it from his 22-year old nephew Brendan, who showed him how to write using PowerPoint.

"My goal was to help young people understand just how bad prison really is," said Lawton. "I was sitting in my room thinking, *These kids think prison's a joke. They think it's a rite of passage. They watch the reality shows on TV like Lockup on MSNBC, and they don't know that what they're watching is phony because they aren't shown the real deal. They don't show you what happens when the camera isn't there. They don't show what the hole is really like, don't show them turning off the hot water or beating your ass. They don't show guards making you beg to turn the toilet back on, spitting in your food, pissing on you.*

"I said to myself, *These kids need a reality check. They should know how sadistic the guards can be, though I also let them know that some guards were sympathetic and saved my life.*

"Whenever I hold a class the first thing I say is, 'How many of you watch *Lockup*? the TV show that portrays various prisons and the inmates in them.

"Most kids and adults raise their hands.

"'It's all bullshit,' I'll tell them.

"'Huh?' is the usual response.

"They have no idea, and I decided it would become my mission in life to tell them why."

Lawton received a phone call from Dennis Broderick, a childhood buddy from when they were kids living in the Bronx. When Dennis was 12, his father was murdered in a robbery. Dennis and Larry were very close. As boys they gambled together, stole together, fought together, and in general caused trouble in the neighborhood. They grew up being gangsters. But as Broderick grew older, he changed his ways, abandoned the life, went into the Air Force, and became a highly respected vice-president of Primerica, a financial company. Broderick was heartsick when he learned that Lawton had been sentenced to eleven years in jail for robbing jewelry stores. When he learned Larry was out of prison, he called to be there for him in any way he could.

"He wanted to help me," said Lawton. "He understood where we came from, and he didn't judge me. He bought me a set of golf clubs, and on the way to playing different courses we'd talk for hours. To this day he probably doesn't know how much he helped me just by talking to me and not judging me.

"We were in the habit of eating out after golf, and Dennis would always order the same thing, a chicken sandwich, no cheese, with lettuce. It was a really bland lunch, and I tease him about it to this day. But when the waiter asked what I wanted, I would always say, 'I'll have what he's having.'

"One time we were at the Harmony Golf Course, and he said, 'Larry, you can't make a choice, can you?'

"'What?' I answered defensively.

"He said, 'You have all day. I'm going to sit here and make sure you read over the menu and you order something *you* want. Nobody is going to say a word.'

"I thought to myself, *Does he think I'm an idiot and can't read?* I was getting angry inside, but I didn't say anything. I knew he cared and wanted to help me.

"Finally I ordered a hamburger the way I wanted it. I

ordered it with onions, cheese and bacon, the way I like it, and it was a relief. I hadn't even realized what I was doing. That broke me of the habit of doing that."

*

Lawton was out of prison about three months when he learned just how fragile his freedom was. His day began when he left his home to play an early round of golf with Dennis.

"We're both early birds when it comes to golf, and we had a tee time for 7:00 a.m. at the Harmony Golf Course about forty five minutes from where I live," said Lawton. "Dennis's birthday was coming up, so I decided to stop at the 24-hour Walmart to buy him a birthday card.

"Dennis and I were going to meet for breakfast at a Denny's restaurant on US 192 at 5:30, so I was out of the house at 4:45. It was pitch dark, and I was driving the old blue Buick Skylark my father gave me when I got out of prison.

"As I approached the light on Palm Bay Road and Hollywood Boulevard, a cop car pulled in front of me. With his lights flashing over the bullhorn he ordered me to pull into the parking lot of a 7-11. I wasn't speeding, so I was wondering what was going on.

"Stay in your car," the cop ordered.

"When another cop car pulled up, I started getting nervous. I could see the two cops talking, and they then headed towards my car, one cop on each side with hands on their holsters. One asked for my driver's license as the other looked inside my car. They then backed away. Seeing I had only been out of prison for about three months, I was sitting there really getting agitated.

"The minutes seemed like hours, and then yet another cop car pulled up. And then another. There were four cop cars, and four cops who were all outside their cars talking and looking at me. I knew they had checked my record, and of course it came back that I was a convicted felon. The time seemed to stand still while all these crazy thoughts were going through my head.

Do I run? What did I do? I'm not going back to prison. This is a nightmare. Are they going to arrest me? What do I do if they arrest me?

"It was crazy. I was sweating.

"A fifth car pulled up, and out came a cop and a civilian. They all talked. Two cops headed towards my passenger-side window, while the civilian and the other two cops headed to my window. I about shit my pants.

"The civilian looked in my window and clearly said, 'It's not him.'

"The cops ordered me to wait, and a few minutes later came back with my driver's license and said I could go.

"As I was driving away I realized how easy it would be to get arrested for something I didn't do. I thought, *Who would believe a guy with my record was going golfing at 4:45 in the morning?* Another golfer might have understood, but not many other people. I later found out a Circle K was robbed, and the robber had a car like mine. I couldn't help thinking, *What would have happened to me if the guy who robbed the place was bald and had a goatee?* To this day I remember how I felt.

It was like it was yesterday. God was on my side that day. I don't know what I would have done if the cops had tried to arrest me.

"When I got to the Denny's, Dennis said to me, "You look like you just saw a ghost." I told him what happened, and we talked about it. Incidents like that keep me thinking about ways to help ex-cons readjust back into society.

*

Dennis's wife Glenda, it so happened, worked with at-risk school children at a place called the Brevard Achievement Center. Some of the kids had learning disabilities, and others had discipline problems. They were between the ages of 11 and 22. Glenda felt these were perfect kids for Lawton to talk to.

Glenda, like Dennis, was very caring and compassionate and never judged Lawton. She felt that having Lawton come and speak to her kids about what he experienced during his years in prison might just save one or two of them from pursuing a life of crime.

"Larry," she said, "I'd love to bring you to my school to speak to the kids."

After talking to the golf pro's son, Lawton was sure that the best way to get into a young person's head was through telling stories of his real-life experiences. A police officer, teacher, or parent could try to give the same message as Larry, he felt, but the kids wouldn't take them nearly as seriously because the kids would know they weren't talking from experience. Larry had eleven years of horror stories to tell, and when he told them, they registered with the kids in a big way.

"If you want to know how to fix a water leak," says Lawton, "call a plumber. If you want to know how to put handcuffs on a person, call a cop. But if you want to learn about the consequences of making bad choices, you should go to a man who has made those bad choices and has suffered the consequences by going to prison.

"A cop can't tell a kid what prison's like. But I can. I'm not reinventing the wheel, but I have found that young people listen to what I have to say. In the end my message is one of hope and change. If I can get them to see themselves as people who have made bad choices but are good people, they can turn their lives around."

When Lawton arrived at Glenda Broderick's school, he could see that her class was a bad-ass class of kids, the worst of the worst. They were a restless group of kids, but as soon as he began telling stories of what really goes on in prison, they didn't make a sound. The kids sat there enthralled, and a little scared. Lawton could see that the kids hadn't just shown up and ignored his message. He could tell they were drinking in what he was saying.

Glenda was moved and impressed with the effect Lawton had on her kids. Glenda began telling others about what he had said and how her kids had reacted, and Dennis offered Lawton a meeting room in the back of his Primerica office so he could hold classes for other kids.

Lawton started getting calls from parents who were at a loss about what to do about their teenage children. He held his first class in March of 2008, a mix of students sent by their families to help them understand the consequences of their actions. For some parents, it was a last resort.

The person Lawton needed to talk to, he was told, was Jean Bandish, the juvenile court coordinator for Brevard County. Lawton called her and after he explained to her what he was doing, she asked if he would speak at the drug court. He spoke to a group of juveniles between the ages of 12 and 18 in the courtroom of Juvenile Court Judge Morgan Reinman. As Larry stood in front of the courtroom, he couldn't help but experience a strange feeling. The last time he had spoke in court, it was as a defendant. On this day he was an advocate for law and order.

After his presentation, Bandish set up a meeting for him with Judge Reinman, who asked him to give a presentation to a group of court personnel involved in the juvenile justice system including two judges, prosecutors, public defenders, and others who were involved.

"It was an important meeting," said Lawton, "but I wasn't nervous. I never get nervous because I've been through so much in my life. I say to myself, *I believe in myself. What's the worst thing that could happen? They don't like me? I've already survived the worst of the worst.* So to this day when I speak in front of important people, I don't really care who they are. We are all the same. They put their pants on just like me, shit like me, and you will either like me or you won't. I am a free man either way."

Lawton walked into Judge Reinman's chambers, set up his

computer, and connected it to the projector. Everyone entered the room, and Jean Bandish introduced Lawton.

"Your honor," said Lawton, "Do you want me to talk the way I'm going to talk to the kids? In my program I use some pretty tough language."

"By all means," said Judge Reinman. "Say what you want, and do it the way you do it."

Lawton gave his talk about what prison life is really like, and those in attendance were as enthralled as the kids he talked to. When he was done, Lawton was invited to stay for the rest of the meeting. He declined and excused himself. This was a Friday, and Lawton was sure nothing more would come from it, but on Monday the phone rang. It was Jean Bandish.

"Judge Reinman loved the program," she said, "and I wanted to give you a heads up, because she just sentenced two kids to your program. The judge told them, 'You need to hear what this man has to say.'"

Lawton thought to himself, *What program?* He didn't have a formal program, and here was a judge sentencing people to his "program."

Said Lawton, "What a judge wants, a judge usually gets, and so I structured my formal program around the PowerPoint presentation I had showed her. I told Jean the fee for attending the program was $100 (later reduced to $50). The judge felt the parents could afford that and in addition to ordering them to take part in the program, they were ordered to eight hours of community service.

Once Lawton had court approval, his Reality Check

Program had credibility. Whenever he would walk into Judge Reinman's courtroom, she would say to him, 'Mr. Lawton, I'm glad you're here.' There were times when she would ask him to have a talk with a young offender. He always did, even when he wasn't getting paid.

*

The word spread as the program gained more and more exposure. He went on a local Melbourne radio station with several kids to talk about the program. He was invited by Karen Locke, the chief operation officer of Crosswinds Youth Services, an organization based in Cocoa, Florida, working to help families and at-risk kids, to speak at her facility.

For the first time Larry was taking the Reality Check Program on the road. Over sixty kids aged 9 to 17 sat before him.

One young boy, aged 9, touched his heart. During a break Larry asked the kid what he had done wrong, and he sheepishly admitted he had stolen a bicycle. He wore baggy pants, and his hat was on backwards. Larry thought he looked like one of the dead-end kids. Larry was concerned for his future because he could see that because he was only nine, he had no understanding of how his wrong choices had led him into trouble.

"When I talked about going to prison and what will happen to him in prison, he was lost. The boy just couldn't grasp the consequences. In essence, he was too young for the program.

"You can teach a child not to touch a hot stove," said

Lawton. "You can tell him he'll get burned. But at too young an age will he understand what getting burned means and what a scar would mean for his future? Absolutely not."

At that point Lawton determined that his program would not work for children under the age of eleven.

"I want to make sure that when I'm speaking to a child that he will understand the consequences of his actions," said Lawton. "It's not enough to know the difference between right and wrong. Everyone knows it's wrong to steal, to do drugs, to disrespect people, but do they understand the consequences of stealing and robbing? I found that most children under eleven don't understand and children eleven and older do.

"It's not enough to talk to a child about right and wrong. You must also talk about the consequences of his actions. If you can do that, you have a much better chance of saving that young person."

Lawton also saw that kids in their early 20s could be helped and set on the right path as well as teens, and he made the decision to include young adults in his program as well.

"Just because a person turns a magical number, say age eighteen, it doesn't mean he's an adult," said Lawton. "Young people mature at different ages, and the older generation needs to understand that and stop with the 'When I was your age' shit. Times have changed. From technology to labor, a child today will know ten times more than his parents.

"Parents need to educate themselves on the things a child will know. A child will spot bullshit a mile away. I tell the truth, and often the truth isn't pretty, and the kids respect that."

Lawton often will start by asking an audience of kids, "Can you hide a knife up your ass?' Inevitably the kids will giggle nervously. Then Lawton will tell them, 'I did.' And he will explain why and how, and that will set the mood. Lawton has not only spoken truth to these kids, he has opened his heart to them, and they respect him for that.

"I never judge kids, no matter what they did," said Lawton. "I am not there to judge them. I am there to help them change and make better choices in the future."

Lawton tells them, "I don't care what you did before you entered the room. You can change, and change starts *now*."

In talking to these at-risk kids, Lawton also determined that one of the biggest hurdles to change is a drug addiction.

"We have to address that first," said Lawton. "I'm not talking about a kid who smoked pot once or got drunk a couple of times. I'm talking about the kids who have an addiction. I've seen kids as young as eleven with drug addictions. Those kids need to detox and get help for their addiction. Only then will they understand what I'm talking about and then understand the consequences of what they are doing."

For the first few months of the Reality Check Program, Larry Lawton was a one-man gang. In no time speaking was becoming a full-time job. But Lawton wanted to be able to expand the program to reach kids he couldn't speak to personally. He needed an angel to back his program in order to make it grow. Finding one wouldn't take long.

CHAPTER 16

The Reality Check Program Takes Off

Larry Lawton was doing well getting at-risk kids to enroll in his class when his friend Joe Fraumeni said to him, "You need help and a business mind behind this. Your program is getting too big to be run by one person."

"I knew Joe was right," said Lawton. "Yes, I could do this out of my house, but would I be doing the most I could to help people? Probably not. A friend told me that if I didn't grow the company, I would be doing a lot of kids a disservice. He said, 'Larry, you have a talent and a gift. You can help millions of people. You need to grow and let it go where it's supposed to go.' With that comes responsibility. I told Joe I was open to the idea of taking on a partner.

He said, "I want to introduce you to someone who used to work for me."

Fraumini set up a meeting for Larry with a man by the name of Joe Reilly. Lawton had gone to bars Reilly owned so Reilly knew him, but not well. They sat down for dinner at a waterside restaurant in Melbourne called Ichabod's, and they hit it off. They were both from New York, and Lawton began telling him stories of prison and what he had been through and how relating his experiences was making a difference with these at-risk teenagers.

"I really think I can make something big out of this," said Lawton.

Near the end of dinner Reilly asked him what he was looking for.

"I'm looking for an investor and a business partner," Lawton said. Lawton hadn't asked Reilly to be that person. He just said he needed "someone."

They got up to leave. Reilly said to Lawton, "Hold off looking for an investor. I want to do a little research. I'll get back to you."

A few days later Reilly called back and asked for another meeting. They returned to Ichabod's, and during the meal Reilly showed Lawton a list of pros and cons with respect to investing in his company. Lawton could see Joe had done his homework.

"I'll invest $100,000 for ten percent of the company," said Reilly.

"Only if you come in as my partner, and if you do that, I'll give you another ten percent," said Lawton. Reilly said he had recently sold his drug-testing company and was to leave it in three months. They talked about the possibilities: a movie, a TV show, a series of DVDs, and this book.

Reilly said, "Larry, there's no way you can be everywhere all the time. It'll be the downfall of the company. The first thing we have to do is develop a DVD about the program."

"Joe totally got it," said Lawton. "He saw the big picture

and understood where we could go with it."

They agreed to become partners.

(After about a year, Reilly offered another $100,000 for an added seven percent, bringing his total holding to 27 percent of the company.)

"With Joe's money it was time to rent an office space and start a *real* company," said Lawton. "Although I was gaining credibility and more and more people were calling to ask me for help with their children, I was still just one guy working out of my mom's house."

Lawton found office space in a building not far from where he was living. The building was old and rundown, but it served the purpose. He was tucked away on the second floor in a corner office. His rent was two hundred dollars a month.

His first hire was his girl friend, Vivian, but after a month of mixing work and romance, the relationship fell apart, and she left. He then hired Erica, a woman who had worked for Reilly in his drug-testing business. Erica was young and savvy on the computer. Erica allowed Larry to spend a lot more time giving classes.

Lawton was asked by radio talk show host Carol Nelson to appear on her show on WMMB in Melbourne with several of the at-risk kids he had counseled. He and three teens discussed the hard issues parents have to deal with when it comes to their children: drugs, making bad choices, truancy, and a lack of respect, among others.

The show turned out to be a smash with the audience. Lawton turned out to be a natural on the radio. Eventually

Lawton would have his own weekly show.

By early in 2009 Joe Reilly was ready to start work. He and Larry decided to make the 67-minute DVD now known as the Reality Check Program DVD. They hired an old pro by the name of Chuck Bennett to produce the film and do the voice-over. There was no script. Lawton did it from his heart, and on the video it's easy to see his raw emotion spilling out.

Taping the DVD was a grueling process for Lawton, who had to relive the pain of the harsh moments during his eleven years in prison. When it was finished, Joe Reilly threw a launch party at his home, and more than a hundred guests attended.

The little company was growing, and in July of 2009 it received its biggest boost when Larry received a phone call from *The Daily Show* with Jon Stewart. Lawton had been a guest on the New York radio show *Crime Prevention 101* hosted by Susan Bartelstone, and someone on *The Daily Show* staff heard it.

Stewart wanted to do a piece on a Montana prison. The prison had just been built and hadn't yet been open, and the idea was for Larry to give viewers a tour. Stewart wanted Lawton to wear his cut-off tee shirt to better show off his tattoos and big arms. With his bald head and goatee, Larry looked like a crazed ex-con, perfect for the bit.

Initially Lawton wasn't sure he should do it. Lawton was a serious guy. He wasn't a comedian, but he figured this would be fun, and he agreed to fly to Montana to meet Stu Miller, one of the producers. Miller gave him some funny lines to say and told him to "look mean."

He did the piece, and a few weeks later *The Daily Show* called him back. They liked Lawton so much in the Montana bit that they wanted him to fly to New York and play a convict who yells at a group of Harvard and MIT MBA students who were refusing to sign an ethics oath. Lawton was given a suit that was designed for him to rip away when he entered the room. Underneath were his red tee shirt and his tattoos. Again he looked like a crazed ex-con. When he started screaming at the students, he scared them but good. The bit was based on the Bernie Madoff scandal, and Lawton used words like Harry Potter, British fuck, and Susan Boyle in his diatribe, and it was hilarious. Skit member John Oliver cracked up laughing.

As part of the skit Lawton showed the cast, producers, and staff how to make a shank, make a fire using batteries, and explained how to hide the shank in his anus.

The skit aired on August 12, 2009. It was a hit, and since then more than 150,000 people watched it on *The Daily Show* website.

"One of the Harvard students in the skit, Leland Chang, is now a Cambridge councilman," said Lawton. "We keep in touch to this day."

During the summer of 2009 Larry was still living with his mom. Joe Reilly owned a furnished three-bedroom, two-bath condo on the beach which he rented to a regular winter tenant. Joe asked Larry if he wanted to rent it for the summer. He was thrilled. Larry would wake up at the usual time of 6 a.m. and watch the sun rise over the Atlantic Ocean. The Kennedy Space Center was only ten miles away, and he watched the space shuttle whenever it blasted off.

"Living in this condo showed me what freedom was all about," said Lawton. "It's the little things that didn't cost anything. Sitting on the beach soaking in the sunshine. Watching the waves hit the beach and seeing dolphins frolic a few yards off the beach. I'd sit on the beach, smoke a cigar, and just relax. It was the best six months I had since I've been out."

That summer Lawton also met his future love. He was going to a gym in Palm Bay, working out strenuously as he had in prison. He'd wear headphones while he was listening to the radio, and he'd sing some of the songs, and he was hard to miss. One of those whose eye he caught was Theresa Nunez. Theresa was drinking coffee in the gym while Lawton was talking to friends, who introduced them. Theresa told Lawton she was a school teacher, and as she talked about her students and her love of teaching, Lawton was struck not only by her beauty but by her passion for helping young people.

It was just Lawton's luck that Theresa was married, so at first they were just friends when one day in November she called Larry crying. She was going through some tough times with her husband, and she wanted to talk. They talked for hours.

"I knew then that Theresa was perfect for me," said Lawton. Theresa was separated in November and they started a relationship. Her divorce came two years later.

While Lawton was living in the condo his ex-wife Missy was going through a tough time with her longtime boy friend, the father of her second child. When Missy and their daughter

Ashley needed a place to stay, Larry decided to rent a place in Melbourne. It had rooms on two floors, perfect for two families.

What made this arrangement work was that Missy and Theresa got along famously. It certainly could have been an episode on Jerry Springer: "Ex-wife lives with ex-husband and ex-husband's girl friend comes over a lot."

For three months they all lived together, and when Missy and her boy friend reunited, she and Ashley moved back to Ft. Lauderdale.

*

Once the DVD was completed, the question became how best to market it.

"You can have the best product and idea in the world, but if you can't get anyone to look at it, it dies in a garage or attic," said Lawton. "Our mission was helping people, and our marketing strategy was to build a strong foundation around what I do. What really makes a company, product or business great is having a product that works and is needed. I knew we had that. Helping people is what drives me every day. When I see a kid change, a parent cry with happiness as I get through to her kid, it's the most rewarding thing you can imagine.

"One of our top priorities was to gain credibility by going on TV and radio shows and to get written about in the newspapers. "

Their first order of business was to update the Reality Check Program website. They were frustrated because they were paying $500 a month to a woman who had control over the content. When they wanted to add articles, they had to do it through her, and so they changed to a company that allowed them to post articles themselves.

"I'm a workaholic," said Lawton, "and I wanted to be able to learn the system myself. I was always a writer. In a sense that's what law work is, putting words on a piece of paper and telling a story. I love to write and do my own articles. In prison I'd write articles for magazines and make a few bucks. All the articles you see on the site I have written myself."

Lawton took a course in web design, and he and Joe started buying website domain names.

Joe Reilly searched for planning conventions and association seminars to attend. They went to the Police Chief's convention and to the Sheriff's convention, the school administrator's convention and other similar national conventions. The word of the Reality Check Program was starting to spread.

In 2010 Lawton was asked to film a pilot for a reality TV show. A man by the name of Richard Wortman, the vice-president of development for Cheri Sundae Productions , called to talk about it. At first Lawton was skeptical, because he thought Cheri Sundae Productions sounded too much like a maker of porn films, but after Joe Reilly did some research, he saw the company was legit. Richard had seen Lawton on *The Daily Show* and wanted to develop a reality TV show around him.

Lawton flew to California to meet Wortman and his team, including John Johnston from *A Current Affair with Maury Povich*. Johnston recruited cameraman Billy Cassara, who works for *60 Minutes, 20/20*, and whose father-in-law was Don Hewitt from *60 Minutes*.

They made a sizzle reel for the show, which is called *Lawton's Law*. Lawton was getting more calls to do TV and radio, each an opportunity to spread the word of the Reality Check Program.

In early 2010 Lawton was honored by the Brevard County Commission for his work with at-risk teens. Commissioner Andy Anderson called him to say he had heard about his work from his constituents, and he wanted to honor him with a resolution on local TV. For the one and only time, Lawton wore a tie to the meeting.

The resolution reads:

BOARD OF COUNTY COMMISSIONERS
Resolution

WHEREAS, since his release from the United States Federal Prison System, **LAWRENCE LAWTON** has created the **REALITY CHECK PROGRAM** and had dedicated his life to the mission of helping teens and young adults make the right choices; and

WHEREAS, the **REALITY CHECK PROGRAM** helps teens and young adults with serious issues that lead to criminal prosecution and subsequent incarceration; specifically, the **REALITY CHECK PROGRAM** addresses the issues of drugs, gangs, behavior problems, crime, attitudes, and violence; and

WHEREAS, the **REALITY CHECK PROGRAM** is divided in four sessions; session one covers choices and decisions; session two focuses on what prison is really like; session three informs **REALITY CHECK PROGRAM** participants on certain crimes, the penalties, and what they will lose after conviction of those crimes; and finally, the preventative session specifically addresses the smart decisions involving avoiding and dissolving bad associations; and

WHEREAS, the **REALITY CHECK PROGRAM** has developed a DVD that is currently being used by Law Enforcement Officers (LEOs) and other community organizations to educate troubled youth and parents prior to the juveniles being arrested and convicted of serious criminal activity; and

WHEREAS, currently, the **REALITY CHECK PROGRAM** is working with over 600 youth and over 600 young adults annually, many of whom are placed in the **REALITY CHECK PROGRAM** as a pre-trial diversion; and

WHEREAS, the **REALITY CHECK PROGRAM** has formed the Reality Check Foundation as a nonprofit organization dedicated to being proactive with teens and young adults before they are arrested.

NOW, THEREFORE, BE IT RESOLVED THAT THE BOARD OF COUNTY COMMISSIONERS OF BREVARD COUNTY, FLORIDA, does hereby unanimously recognize

LAWRENCE LAWTON, PRESIDENT
of REALITY CHECK PROGRAM

for his untiring work with the youth and adult population of Brevard County.

DONE, ORDERED AND ADOPTED, in regular session, this 15th day of December, A.D., 2009.

ATTEST:

MARY BOLIN, CHAIRMAN
BOARD OF COUNTY COMMISSIONERS
BREVARD COUNTY, FLORIDA

Around that time Lawton also was asked to host a weekly show on a local Brevard County radio station. The catch was that Lawton and Reilly would have to finance the show, money they could recoup by selling ads to sponsors. They decided to give it a try, and in the past couple of years have been able to attract some very prestigious guests including Congressman Bill Posey, Sheriff Jack Parker, Judge David Silverman, Department of Justice Director Dennis Greenhouse, actor Lane Garrison from the show *Prison Break*, and various mayors, ex-cons, teens, and parents.

The radio show has given Lawton exposure and clout in and around Brevard County. As a result of the show he has been asked to speak and tell his story of survival and how he helps at-risk kids to many social and business groups in the area.

One meeting Lawton was invited to attend was a forum at the Brevard County Commissioner's chamber concerning crime and how to make neighborhoods safer. Among those scheduled to speak were Norman Wolfinger, the state attorney for Brevard and Seminole counties, various sheriffs, and Lawton.

Lawton was surprised to discover that as far as he could see, the purpose of the meeting was to embarrass state attorney Wolfinger. While Wolfinger was speaking, Police Chief Tony Bollinger of Titusville got up and called him a liar. At the same time a number of the other police chiefs walked out.

"The meeting was a witch hunt," said Lawton, "and I was very uncomfortable."

Lawton ended up speaking for a few minutes on finding solutions to the crime problem, and when he left he was feeling really upset over what he saw. Lawton didn't agree with everything the state attorney did, but he knew one thing: Norm Wolfinger cared about kids.

As far as Lawton was concerned, this was no time for politics. He decided he was going to do what he thought was right and not worry about the fallout.

He called Wolfinger on the phone to express his support, and Wolfinger asked him to come by the next day. Lawton talked about the compassion Wolfinger had for kids whenever he saw him in action, and at the same time noted what he considered to be the unprofessionalism of Police Chief Bollinger.

Grateful for his support and impressed by Lawton's work, Wolfinger authorized his attorneys to make the at-risk kids who come before them watch the Reality Check DVD. He ordered that the program be placed on every plea form and pre-trial diversion program. As many as a hundred offenders a month go through Lawton's program.

Wolfinger wrote to Lawton on his letterhead, "Watching your tape for the second time, I can see why you influence these young adults to consider making good choices – you're real and your stories were lived."

Lawton and another police chief, who he doesn't wish to identify, also didn't see eye to eye about much. Their biggest disagreement was over how public funds should be spent to protect the community. Lawton expressed his belief in community policing, while the chief said he preferred the use of technology. Lawton saw that the chief also didn't think much of his program.

One time Lawton bristled when the chief told him, "Some of your kids are no good and will never be saved."

"You're wrong about that, chief," said Lawton.

"Not all law enforcement officials are like that," said Lawton. "What I've learned from my travels and dealing with the public is that there is good and bad in all people. It's no different from when I was in prison. I'm sure I've lost business because of my passion and willingness to tell the truth as I see it, but I'm not going to give up what I believe in just for the sake of business or to please some police chief or school official.

"The more people I come across, the more I believe that what I am doing is right. I often say, 'Who among us is an angel? Who of us hasn't made mistakes? What's sad is that some people get a badge of authority and lose the compassion they need to do a good job. Like some of those prison guards I ran up against, they lost the human side of their soul, and that's sad."

This fact hit home with a vengeance when in August of 2010 Lawton's nephew Brendan, my sister's son who helped him set up his computer program, was found dead face down in a river in upstate New York. Lawton was sure he was murdered.

"Brendan was just like me, a risk taker and very smart," said Lawton. "He was at a party in upstate New York, and he ended up dead in the river. There was no blunt trauma to his body and no drugs in his system, and no one seems to know how he died, but someone at that party knows more than what they're saying. I was told he had an argument with another one of the kids there, and he didn't come home. There was an exhaustive search with helicopters and search teams, and three days later his body was found.

"I was devastated. He was my second nephew to die violently. Ten years ago while I was in prison, my brother's son, David, was shot in the head at point blank range. David used to live with me in the summers before I went to prison. He would play with my son when he came to visit me. These terribly sad situations helped form the structure of the adult Reality Check Program.

"I tell kids about Brendan and David. I tell them, 'This is the life you're going to lead.' David was into drugs, into bad shit in Philadelphia. Brendan made bad choices as well.

"Helping young people just like Brendan and David drives me. Their legacies are saving lives every day. As I said, there is no magic number that says you're an adult and ready for the world. Times have changed, and young adults, not just teenagers, need guidance."

*

Lawton met with Judge David Silverman who wanted to see whether his program could help adults as well as juveniles.

"Why shouldn't it?" Lawton said. "After all, just because you're 22 year olds doesn't make you an adult. A lot of 22 year olds make dumb choices."

Larry had first met Judge Silverman on a golf course during a charity golf outing. In the foursome was Satellite Beach Police Chief Lionel Cote. Chief Cote was a believer in Lawton's program and introduced Larry to the judge. Larry and the Judge were paired together, and after they spent four hours together on a golf course, Judge Silverman saw first-hand how strongly Lawton felt about his program.

Judge Silverman was a ten-year veteran on the bench, primarily dealing with misdemeanor criminal cases. He had been a prosecutor and before that had been a public defender dealing with capital cases. He was impressed with Larry's knowledge of the law and his passion for helping kids.

Lawton gave Judge Silverman a copy of the Reality Check Program DVD. The judge promised to watch it and get back to him. In his chambers Judge Silverman watched the DVD alongside his 19-year-old college intern.

The intern said that watching Larry on the DVD was like watching the Exorcist.

"You'll never forget it," he said.

Lawton didn't know it but Judge Silverman, ordinarily a cautious man, was sick and tired of ordering young people to eight hours of anger management and then seeing them again in his court room six months later. Jails were crowded with these people, and he was looking for an alternative. These weren't murderers, rapists, or seriously violent offenders. These were wild kids involved with underage drinking, getting caught with under 20 grams of marijuana, multiple driving tickets, and petty theft. The judge decided that the

Reality Check Program just might be what these young people needed to keep them from repeating the bad choices that were getting them in trouble.

Judge Silverman started sentencing people to the Reality Check Program, and the results were astonishing. When the judge asked those who went through the program what they thought of it, resoundingly, they all came back with, "This is the best program I've ever been to, judge." And to Judge Silverman's surprise, most never returned to his courtroom.

Lawton also got a call from Administrative Judge Judy Adkins, who asked to see him. She said, "I'd like to host a meeting in my chambers, and I'm going to invite all the judges."

Judge Adkins had seen that the plea form included a reference to the Reality Check Program, and she wanted to learn more about it. In attendance was Chief Judge Preston Silvernail along with ten other Brevard circuit and county court judges.

When Lawton walked in, he asked Judge Atkins, "Where do you want me to sit?"

"Sit at my desk," she said. Just three years after getting out of prison, there was ex-con Larry Lawton was sitting in a judge's chair with all the judges sitting around looking up at him and listening to what he had to say.

Joe Reilly whispered to him, "What a photo this would be!"

*

Early on Lawton knew his program was effective, because after six months he did a quick quantitative analysis involving thirty offenders who went through his program. He found that 70 percent of them never got in trouble again – an excellent result. After eighteen months an independent quantitative analysis was done by an outside agency, the Brevard Community College honors involvement class did a more comprehensive study. They questioned over a hundred families, asking them four questions.

A: Has your son been arrested since attending the Reality Check Program?

B: Has his attitude improved?

C: Has your son's grades improved?

D: Has his attendance at school improved?

The numbers were off the charts. A full ninety percent never got in trouble with the law again. School grades improved by forty-three percent, school attendance rose by thirty-one percent, and their attitudes improved by a resounding seventy percent.

The Reality Check Program is a life changer, and there's no other program like it.

CHAPTER 17

Spreading the Word

Near the start of 2009 Larry Lawton received a phone call from Robin Lemonidis, a well-respected criminal defense attorney in Brevard County. Six months earlier, as Larry was starting his program, he was outside Judge Reinmann's courtroom waiting for the deputies to open the courtroom doors after the noon lunch break when he heard a family having an argument.

The family was arguing about their 16-year-old son who was in trouble with the law. The father, a burly man of Italian descent, was getting loud. Larry could see his temper flaring.

Larry saw this slight, red-headed woman, perhaps five foot one and 110 pounds, in between the husband and wife, trying to calm the situation with no luck. Larry got up, looked at the father, and in a commanding voice said, "Calm down, buddy. Can I talk to you?"

The man, confused, looked at Larry while he explained his past and what he did for a living.

The little red-headed woman turned out to be Lemonidis, who asked for his card. The 16-year-old boy was Robin's client. With the situation diffused, Robin asked Larry more about what he did, and Larry explained in more detail. A business relationship was born.

Lemonidis began sending more and more of her clients to Lawton's pre-trial diversion program and using the positive results to help her clients get less time in jail and more rehabilitation.

Robin was getting some unwanted phone calls from a man she once prosecuted twenty years earlier. The man was out of prison, and Robin was getting nervous. Larry and Robin set up a meeting with the man at the courthouse.

Larry showed up early, and as Larry predicted, so did the man.

"I had no description of the guy, except he was black and around 45," said Lawton. "I can spot an ex-con from a mile away, and I wanted to speak to the guy before Robin showed up. It turned out the man thought he was wrongly convicted and wanted Robin to write a letter saying things to that effect."

Larry told him, "She can't write a letter. It won't help you. And you can't have contact with Miss Lemonidis, or you'll go back to prison." The man saw that Larry knew what he was talking about, got the hint, and when Robin arrived, Larry said, "Robin, I explained to him why you can't get involved in his case, and he understands." And that was the end of it.

A convict speaking to a convict is more effective than if cops showed up with guns blazing. That is how people get killed. How you speak to people is a key. Larry has a gift.

After Robin saw how effective Larry was with ex-cons, she said, "Larry, I have a case I want you to look at. I have a young man in the Brevard County detention center up in Sharpes, Florida, and he's facing at least two years in the big house. If he goes there, he'll never make it. Can you help?"

Lawton wasn't sure exactly what he could do, but he agreed to go see the young man. Lawton knew the commander at the jail and called up to see if he would be allowed in. He then set up a meeting with the young inmate. Visitors to the county jail could only talk to inmates via a phone and a television monitor.

Lawton picked up his phone, and when the image of the inmate popped up on the monitor, he was shocked to see that before him was a kid no older than twenty.

"What are you in for?" Lawton asked.

"Drugs and robbery," said the boy.

Lawton began by telling him what prison was really like.

"This is county jail," Lawton said. "Prison is far worse than this."

Lawton told the boy how during his eleven years in prison he had lost his wife and children and the time with them he could never get back. How he had felt helpless when he learned his grandmother had died and the gut wrenching feeling when his nephew was killed. The stories went on and on.

When the boy started crying, Lawton was pleased to see that the kid had a heart.

For an hour Lawton told the boy about the horrors he had experienced in prison. When it was time for Lawton to get up and leave, the boy had tears in his eyes.

"Thank you," he said, "and whatever happens, you helped me a lot."

Lawton called Lemonidis the next day and told her about

his visit. She asked if he would come to Judge Jim Earp's courtroom on the fourth floor of the Brevard County court house in Viera, Florida, and be an expert witness at his sentencing. She wanted Lawton to tell the judge what life in prison was like compared to life in a county jail. She was hoping to get the judge to keep him out of the state prison system.

On the day of the hearing, Lawton couldn't help but think about how his own life had changed. Once he had stood in front of a judge to face sentencing. On this day he was testifying on behalf of a young man who himself stood to go to prison.

The boy's parents spoke first. When his mother pleaded for leniency and began to cry, Judge Earp, a fair man who had seen his share of these cases, said to her, "Where were you when he was doing these things? You're crying now, but you should have done more beforehand."

Lawton thought to himself, *What's the judge going to say to me?*

Lawton was called to the podium. He stood beside Lemonidis, who started to tell the judge who Lawton was in order to qualify him as an expert.

"I've heard of him," said Judge Earp. "He's qualified."

Lemonidis asked Lawton to discuss the difference between the county jail, where the boy currently resided, and the state prisons.

"The real difference," said Lawton, "is that in a county jail the inmates come and go, and they really never get a chance to organize like in a state facility. In a state facility there are more gangs, more drugs, more violence, and in general more disorder than in a county jail. County jails may not have the programs some state facilities have, but if you want to keep a person away from gangs and drugs, a county jail is always better – not perfect, but better."

Lawton stepped back. The young defendant was then asked to speak. He expressed his sorrow over what he did and told the judge he had changed, that he had learned from his mistakes.

Judge Earp looked at the boy, and then looked at Lawton, and he said, "Son, because of that man right there, I am going to sentence you to eight months in the county jail and give you time served for the time you've already spent in jail. And when you get out, you will attend the Reality Check Program. I hope you learned your lesson."

At the end of the hearing Judge Earp asked Lawton to approach the bench.

"I would like to go to lunch with you," he said. "I want to know more about your program, prisons, and what really goes on in there."

Lawton would be called on as an expert witness in future cases. Lawton had found another way to make a difference in people's lives.

*

The Reality Check Program was gaining more recognition and acceptance and a business decision was made to change the company name to Lawton 911. The words Reality Check were hard to copyright, and changing the name would make it easier for people to remember Larry when he appeared on TV. It is still referred to as the Reality Check Program as well as Lawton 911.

In January of 2010 Lawton was invited to Congress by U.S. Congressman Bill Posey from Florida. The year before Congressmen Posey had been a guest on Larry's radio show. Impressed by what he had heard, he invited Larry to come to Washington to spread the word about what he was doing.

When Lawton arrived in his office, Congressman Posey announced to the dozen or so staffers and guests, "I'm glad to see Larry in Washington spreading the message about the good work he does. You can't put a price on stopping a child from falling into an adult life of crime."

President Obama was scheduled to make his state of the union speech, and the halls of Congress were packed with visitors. George Cecala, the communications spokesman from Congressman Posey's office, escorted Lawton to see a half-dozen other Congressmen including Tom Rooney, Louie Gohmert, Jason Chaffetz, Don Lungren, and Debbie Wasserman-Shultz. While walking the halls of Congress Lawton couldn't help but be overwhelmed by the feeling that so much history had taken place there.

While in Washington Larry also stopped into the offices of the Department of Justice to meet with Dennis Greenhouse, the director of the Community Capacity Development Office.

"Dennis, a career government employee, sees things in a different way," said Lawton. "He looks for solutions, not a paycheck."

Greenhouse told Lawton a story about when he was attempting to help inmates in the Delaware state prison system when he was the comptroller of Delaware. There was an issue of how best to spend state funds on inmates. Greenhouse, a compassionate man, preferred to spend the money on counseling rather than punishment. During his stay Greenhouse introduced Lawton to Sam Beamon, who ran the Florida operation for the CCDO. Lawton had another opportunity to spread the word about the Reality Check Program.

*

While visiting Washington Larry was staying in the Capitol Hill suites up the street from the Cannon Capitol office building. During a break between meetings, he returned to his hotel room. There was a knock on the door.

Larry opened the door. Standing in front of him were two tall men in dark suits with dark sunglasses.

"Are you Lawrence Lawton?" he was asked. They showed their badges. They were from the Secret Service.

Wow, thought Lawton, *right out of central casting.*

"May I have your identification, please," he was asked. Meanwhile, the second secret service agent looked into the suite while the first one checked his ID.

For Larry, who had with him his probation papers from his probation officer in Cocoa, Florida, it was a reminder that no matter how much good he may be doing, he was still an ex-con.

The agents never asked for the papers. They thanked him and left. Lawton figured that because the President was coming to Congress, secret service agents were checking everyone in the vicinity.

"I'm sure my ex-con status raised a flag and they wanted to check me out," said Lawton. "It kind of freaked me out knowing Big Brother was everywhere and knew everything."

*

In March of 2010 Lawton attended the Sheriff's Association convention in Destin, Florida, and among those in attendance he had a chance to meet Jeff Kottkamp, Lieutenant Governor of Florida. Kottkamp had created the Children and Youth Cabinet, whose stated mission was for "all children in Florida to grow up safe, healthy, educated and prepared to meet their full potential.' Lawton and Kottkamp spoke for a few minutes, and Lawton could see that the lieutenant governor had a genuine interest in helping young people.

Lawton invited Kottkamp to be a guest on his radio show, and they became friends. Lawton visited him in his home county in Fort Myers, Florida, and Kottkamp introduced Lawton to judges, the public defender, and the state attorney from Fort Myers' Twentieth Judicial District.

While he was attending the Sheriff's Association convention, Lawton was invited by Randy Wecker, the host of the *Healing Today Show* which airs on the Christian Television Network to come on the show as a guest. The CTN has studios in California and in Punta Gorda, Florida, across the state about five hours from Lawton's home in Melbourne. Lawton agreed to drive there and tape a show.

Lawton brought with him his file of graphics, media material, and DVDs to hand out to the cast and crew. Joe Reilly suggested that during the taping of the show Lawton make sure to take his jacket off to reveal his cut-off red tee shirt and his tattoos.

"That will be your signature move," said Reilly, and when Lawton did that, hosts Randy and Rhonda Wecker just about fell out of their chairs. Lawton was their guest for the entire half hour. He found the Weckers to be good people.

"I have been very lucky with all the TV I've done," said Lawton.

*

All the while Lawton was learning more and more about marketing. He was doing all his own emails, newsletter articles, and research for his TV appearances. A workaholic, he routinely works fifteen to sixteen hours a day. It's not unusual to get an email from Lawton at 1 a.m. and then at 7:30 in the morning. People ask him, "Do you ever sleep?" He only laughs.

*

One of the shows Lawton was emailing was *The Huckabee Show* on Fox. One morning in June of 2010 Larry got a call from the producer of the show asking him to come on and talk about redemption. Other guests on the show were Maury Davis, a pastor who thirty years before brutally killed a man and was imprisoned, and the comedian Tommy Chong, who had done nine months in prison for selling drug paraphernalia.

Lawton was flown to New York and housed right in the heart of Times Square. He brought with him his sister and her family so they could meet Mike Huckabee.

While Lawton waited in the green room to go on, Tommy Chong began complaining about having to do jail time for selling bongs.

"Tommy, stop bitching," Lawton said, "I did more time in the hole than you did in prison." Chong began laughing.

Governor Huckabee announced on the show that he was giving everyone in the audience a copy of the Reality Check Program DVD. The exposure Larry and his program got from coming on the show was enormous. The show was aired in August of 2010, and even before the show concluded the phones at the Reality Check offices rang off the hook, and the website was flooded with hits. Larry received two hundred orders for DVDs in minutes.

After the show Lawton asked Huckabee, the former governor of Arkansas, if he was going to run for the Presidency in 2012. Huckabee said he had lost his bid for the Republican nomination in 2008 after he pardoned a group of inmates in Arkansas, only to see one of them commit a murder.

"That showed me a lot," said Lawton. "Whether you like his politics or not, you have to respect a man who sticks by his beliefs."

"Larry," Gov. Huckabee said, "I did that against party advice, but I did the right thing, and I would do it again."

*

In August of 2010 Lawton was presented an award from a local Melbourne bank called the Hometown Hero award. He had been a Rotarian for about a year, and he was proud of the good things the organization did. Lawton was honored to have gotten the award, but when he returned to his office he was thinking, *I got an award for something I love to do. I need to create an award that recognizes people who give back to their community outside their profession.*

Lawton and Joe Reilly began the Reality Check Foundation whose purpose it was to provide DVDs to those families who couldn't afford them. They also instituted the Community Champion Award, which recognizes young adults between the ages of 20 and 45 who give back to their community outside their profession, like a firefighter who donates his time on weekends to help people with disabilities or a police officer who helps the elderly, or a city employee who goes around and helps single Moms fix up their homes.

The Reality Check Foundation also runs an annual golf outing, which is unlike any other. The foundation invites judges, states attorneys, sheriffs, and other community leaders and matches them up to play nine holes of golf with at-risk teenagers from the inner city.

"It's really a two-fold event," said Lawton. "It shows the kids that adults in powerful positions aren't out to get them, and it also shows the powerful people that these kids are human and not all are bad.

"When can an inner city kid golf with a judge? The only time they see a judge is when the judge is sentencing him. When do they see a state attorney, except when he is prosecuting him? When does he see a cop, except when the cop is trying to arrest him? We have all these people come together for a day of fun, food, gifts, and mentoring. It's an amazing event, the only one of its kind."

As Lawton tells the teens and young adults, "Don't get mad at the guy who arrests you. Get mad at yourself for not thinking and not making the right choice. Understand that it's your actions that brought the law down on you. Yes, there are bad cops and bad officials, but for the most part, if you do right, you won't have the cops coming down and arresting you."

*

Lawton's initial program design hasn't changed much, but he has perfected the program by changing stories, bringing in guest speakers, and adding more humor and video clips. Larry also invites judges, law enforcement officials, prosecutors, and public defenders to his program. What Lawton always asks is for them to come as a regular person. Most of the youngsters who attend Larry's program are street smart and can pick out a *suit* (a person in an official capacity). Police officers are asked to wear civilian clothes, to leave the uniform at home. Prosecutors are asked to dress more casually than they do in court.

As a matter of principle Larry won't bend to pressure to change his program, no matter who asked him to. Back in 2009 Larry was at a function and he asked Sheriff Jack Parker if he would use the DVD as a law enforcement tool.

"The DVD is perfect for law enforcement to give out to the community," said Lawton. "It breaks down the *us against them* mentality a lot of people in the public and in law enforcement have. I hate that. The police and general public have to come together and be partners against crime and illegal activity. Somewhere along the line it became a battle. Look, I don't want a murderer or rapist living next to my mom or me. We need cops, but cops also have to know they are part of the community and they work for the citizens of that community. Both parties need to be better at being friends."

Sheriff Parker called Lawton aside and said, "Larry, some chiefs and law enforcement people think your DVD is a slam on cops and guards. I have three hundred plus corrections officers working for me and I have to protect them. Would you change some things in the DVD?"

Lawton asked Sheriff Parker if he had watched the DVD. He was honest and said no. Lawton said, "Jack, watch the DVD and you tell me if I am against guards." Sheriff Parker watched the part in the DVD where Lawton said that some guards had saved his life. He also saw where Lawton talk about the abuse he suffered at the hands of bad guards.

Sheriff Parker, a man of his word, watched the DVD and gave Lawton a call.

He said, "Larry, you are correct. The DVD is good, and there isn't anything in there that is wrong."

Said Lawton, "Sheriff Parker ordered five hundred DVD's to put in his patrol cars to give out to kids making bad choices and doing things that weren't serious. Sheriff Parker is a man who wants to help. He can be hard on one hand and very compassionate on another. That is the sign of a good law enforcement officer.

"Slowly but surely law enforcement officials are coming around. The old guard is moving on, and their old ways are leaving with them. I am the first person in the world who understands the need for law and order, but law enforcement agencies need the communities help. It is a proven fact that community policing is a successful, cost effective way to reduce crime."

Through a friend, Rockledge City Manager Jim McKnight, Rockledge Police Chief Ron Kruger got to know Lawton. The three met to discuss ways that Rockledge can help the young people in their city. There's a lot of crime in Cocoa, a city just north of Rockledge, and they were hoping to find a way to keep it from crossing the city line into Rockledge. After the meeting, Chief Kruger asked Larry if he could talk to him privately.

He said, "Larry, I know you and I know your heart. You're a good man with good intensions, but sometimes when you write an article about a specific chief or city you are hurting the rank and file police officers of that city."

Lawton explained to Chief Kruger that he never intended to be in battle with law enforcement.

"We all need to work together to save our young people," he said. "I can reach a young person easier than a cop, and the cops have to understand that. A lot of teenagers and young adults have had bad experiences with law enforcement. I am not siding with either side. I am trying to find a solution to make these young people respect cops and do the right thing."

Lawton once offered $5,000 worth of free DVD's to a city Police Athletic League, and his offer was refused for no good reason except that the chief of police, who had a lot of pull with PAL, and he didn't see eye to eye.

"I don't want the same bullshit to keep going on," said Lawton. "When people don't point out problems, they keep happening. Just like in the Norm Wolfinger, Tony Bollinger incident. That kind of stuff has to stop.

"If teens and young adults see me working with law enforcement, that gives the cops instant credibility. The teens say, 'Wow, if an ex-con like Larry who isn't a rat is working with the cops, the cops must be good guys.' I am not a supporter of ratting, and the young people know that. I am not talking about a dangerous situation. If two kids are selling weed, and one tells on the other to save his own neck that is wrong.

"I understand how ratting works. I'm not talking about a civilian calling the cops or anything like that. I was at a conference at the government center, and I said to the audience, 'Ninety percent of all rats commit another crime. Are you okay with letting a drug dealer off knowing he is going to sell drugs again? If that guy who you let off sells bad drugs to a young person and that person dies, are you okay with that? I know I wouldn't be okay with that.

"Yes, to get a murderer off the streets, I understand that totally. But I am talking about a system that has gotten lazy. Informants have become part of the system, and in most situations I am not a believer in the system. If a person wants to tell for the right reason, he should still be held accountable for what he did. Do we need to be putting these people in prison for life and ungodly amounts of time? No. Criminals have figured out how to play the system, and that's why our system is broken.

*

Larry's continued rise in the public eye came during the Casey Anthony case, a high-profile murder case centered in Orlando, Florida. Because of Larry's vast knowledge of prisons and the code of federal regulations, Larry was asked to be an expert on Fox news, Orlando. Casey Anthony beat the case and since she was going to be released, Larry was asked what would happen to her when she left confinement. Who better to answer that question than Larry?

Larry's straightforward approach and his ease on TV helped make him a local celebrity and has helped him grow the Reality Check Program and Lawton 911.

CHAPTER 18

The Reality Check Program

What makes the Reality Check Program so successful is the way it's presented and how the participants view me. The high success rate shows that we are getting through to young people. That is all I care about. Here's how it works.

The Program consists of four parts;
1. My Life.
2. What Prison Is Really Like.
3. What Will You Lose?
4. Avoiding and Dissolving Bad Associations.

Part One: My Life

The difference between the Reality Check Program and say some other program by a cop or counselor is that it is coming from someone who has been there. Young people for the most part aren't book learners, They are watch-and-do learners. If a cop gets up and starts talking about prison, a teenager or young adult will be saying inside, *What does this guy know? He's never been to jail.* They can't say that with me.

Another important factor is that when I was being prosecuted for robbery I didn't rat on my accomplices. Whether a kid says it or not, he doesn't want to be known as a rat. I have been through so much and survived and young people see that. I always say a kid can spot bullshit a mile away, and they know I'm telling the truth and that I truly want to help them. Deep down they want to change and make better choices. The thing is, we don't know what will trigger them to finally start to *get it*. I often tell parents, "Don't give up. People do change. Look at me, I did." It's all about hope and respect.

When I first enter a room I'm usually wearing a sports jacket and jeans. (That's my work outfit.) I never yell at a person or look down on him. Who am I? I'm no better or worse than anyone else. I bring the program down to their level, and that is another reason it works. The delivery is the most important part. A professor friend of mine who himself gives speeches asked me if I ever took speaking lessons. I haven't. He said, "People pay thousands of dollars to learn the things you do naturally." -- like raising my hands in a disarming way when I speak on a stage. I just do it, and I do it from the heart. It's all about passion.

When I developed the program I kept thinking to myself, *What would I want to hear?* Telling my life story brings the human side into the equation. The kids in the program see they're just like me. I tell the good and the bad. I open my heart to a past that hurts me deeply when I talk about it. I also talk about my glory days of being a gangster. It's all about opening the mind, and once the mind is open, you can teach good things and bring true and lasting change.

The reason *Scared Straight* doesn't work is that if you scream and yell at someone, he or she will shut down, whether it's a child or an adult. Once a person is thinking about nothing except getting out of the situation, he will never trust you enough to learn from you. He might act like he's listening to make you happy, but once he gets away from the situation he'll tend to block out the good message that was given. People who have been to my program come up to me years later and say, 'Mr. Lawton, I will never forget that story you told about hiding a knife up your ass,' or 'I will never forget about your losing your grandmother.' It's amazing what I hear and very rewarding at the same time.

Telling the truth about myself opens up a person to wanting to learn. That's the key. If a person makes the choice to change himself, he has a better chance of success. When does a person want to change? That's the million-dollar question. But hitting bottom seems to be one of the keys to wanting to change.

Everybody has a bottom. How far down that bottom is is different in every person. A person who almost kills someone driving his car after having a few drinks might be home shaking and realize that his life just passed in front of his eyes, and for him that's his bottom. He will never drink and drive again. Another person might spend a night in the county jail and realize this isn't for him. A third person might go to prison and still not get it. Like I said, everyone is different.

When I went to prison I still didn't get it. It took me going to the "hole" and experiencing things no human should have to experience to find my bottom. Being brutalized by the guards, having friends kill themselves, watching guys get stabbed, or hearing the blood-curdling sounds of a guy getting raped was what it took for me to change.

Change comes from within. What I do is show a person that if he doesn't change, he will learn the hard way. Like I did. It breaks my heart when I see people who make the choices that will land them in prison, and they still think it's a joke.

The horror stories I experienced, all true stories, were terrible to endure, but the worst part of prison life was the loneliness. To me nothing is sadder than watching men who shuffle to the mail call table and *never* get a letter. Everyone on the outside has forgotten about them. That was sad and heartbreaking to see. It's a fact of prison life, but most people don't understand that until it's too late.

After my introduction, one of the lines I use when I walk into a room is, "Can you hide a knife up your ass? I did." It's a total shock. Sometimes I get chuckles, and I know that's a nervous chuckle. I then begin to tell how I had to hide a knife up my ass to save my life.

"Can you do it?" I ask them.

I explain how I took half a toothbrush holder and put the shank in there and then taped the open end with masking tape. I say, "Then I inserted the holder in my rectum past my sphincter."

I give them all the details of how I had to get through three metal detectors, and how every time you go through a metal detector the alarm sounds. The guards pull you out and you have to strip down until you're naked. They tell you to lift your nuts and then turn around and grab your ass and spread your ass cheeks. Of course, the knife is way up your ass, so they can't see it. They don't know if you have metal screws in your knee or a bullet in you and they tell you to dress and move on.

I tell them, "Once you get to the yard you find a corner and squat down and pull the toothbrush holder out of your rectum and you extract the knife and put it in a wooden handle you've hidden on the yard."

The kids ask me, "Why don't you just hide the knife on the yard." The reason is because the guards are smart, and while we're locked in our cells the guards will run metal detectors all over the yard and find your metal shank you've hidden along the walkway or under the dirt on the softball field.

I tell them, "A metal detector won't find a wooden handle, so you're good. Once you have your knife attached to a handle you can defend yourself. That knife saved my life. I was on the yard and a guy I had an earlier argument with wanted to stab me. I had my knife and because I had a knife I held off the guy long enough for the guard in the tower to sound the alarm and draw down with a rifle and announce for everyone to get down.'

I emphasize to them that life in prison is all about survival. I say, "You will do what you have to do to survive."

Young people need to know that prison is not a vacation or a rite of passage on the way to being some big-shot criminal.

Part Two: What Prison is REALLY Like

The second part of my program is the truth about prison. I begin by having the class read an article about what happened to me in Edgefield prison. It's an eye-opener. I then read a strong letter from a friend of mine in a federal penitentiary who is doing a life sentence. I had him write to the kids on what prison is like and how you can get trapped in a system that's broken. In the letter the man describes how his best friend told on him, and he was convicted for conspiracy to sell drugs. No actual act occurred, but he went to trial and got a life sentence. It's a raw letter, and I read it verbatim. You can hear a pin drop when I'm reading the letter.

I then go to the PowerPoint and go over all the aspects of prison life including death, rape, drugs, gangs, fighting, and work. It's hard to know when discussing one of those grim topics hits home. When I was speaking at Lehman High School in the Bronx to 700 kids, it seemed like the topic drugs really hit home. When I talk to upper-middle class kids, the topic that makes them squirm is work. Yes, work. For them money is often no object, and they are shocked when I tell them how in prison I was making $5.25 cents a month. Yes, a month. They seem to think that isn't possible. It is. I used to buy twenty-one Ramen noodle soups that cost a quarter each. I explain how I went from being a millionaire jewel robber to buying cheap soup to stay full. I explain how you crush up the Ramen noodles and eat them raw and then drink water so the noodles expand in your stomach and you aren't hungry.

I talk about the dangers of prison life, how I never slept past 6 a.m. when the guards cracked the doors. The guards, called Turnkeys, open the doors one by one manually with a key at 6 a.m. If you're smart, you will be up and ready to go when the doors are cracked. I once saw a guy sleep in, when three other guys he must have had a beef with went into his cell and stabbed him.

With regards to showers: I tell them if there's tension in the air, you never go to the shower alone. I don't mean you go into the shower together. I mean you and your buddy go to the shower with boots on. One guy goes in and starts showering. If he sees a threat coming he will knock on the wall, and the guy in the shower gets his boots on and gets his shank ready.

I told them how I once watched a newbie go to the shower, get stabbed, fall, and cover the drain cover. His blood was running down the tier.

In Atlanta I saw a guy get stabbed for cutting in the chow line. It was a real wake up call. *You get stabbed for cutting in line? Jesus.*

I go on to explain how all these prison TV shows don't show the whole truth. Yes, they show some horror stories and crazy people. What they won't show is what happens when the camera's off. They don't show a guard who's had a bad day with his wife, come in and take it out on a guy who is handcuffed and defenseless. I'm not knocking all guards or even suggesting that the majority are bad. What I am saying is they're human beings, and human beings do stupid things. Just because a guy has a uniform doesn't mean he's right. It doesn't mean he's a great guy. You read about cops abusing people all the time. To me what's sad is that you *never* read about a guard abusing an inmate. Do you really believe no abuses by guards are taking place? Of course they are. That's because the abuse is pushed under the rug. *Who cares? It's only an inmate.*

A country is judged on how it treats its elderly, infirmed, and incarcerated. Sadly, in this country we are failing on a lot of those fronts. It can be changed; we only have to *want* to change it.

*

Here's a stat that will shock you. One out of ten juvenile inmates is sexually abused by guards. Read this report by the U.S. Bureau of Justice Statistics:

Shocking Report Reveals Epidemic of Sexual Abuse in Juvenile Prisons.

A new report says more than one out of every 10 child prisoners in state custody are molested or raped. February 17, 2010. And nearly all of the time it's by the guards!!! Top of Form

An unprecedented report released last month by the U.S. Bureau of Justice Statistics (BJS) has revealed some disturbing statistics about sexual abuse in U.S. juvenile detention facilities. Twelve percent of youth held in such facilities say that they have been sexually abused over the course of one year. Or, to put it another way, more than 1 in 10 of young people under state supervision are molested and/or raped. Nearly all of these incidents involve a staff member (about 85 percent), while the rest involve another incarcerated youth.

According to the study, male prisoners were more likely than females to report sexual activity with facility staff, but less likely than females to report forced sexual activity with other youth. Surprisingly, a whopping 95 percent of all youth reporting staff sexual misconduct said they had been victimized by female staff members. In the most troubling facilities, between 20 and 30 percent of incarcerated youth reported abuse.

These stunning figures have come to light thanks to a provision within the National Prison Rape Elimination Act (PREA) of 2003, which included a mandate to produce such a study. Officially dubbed the National Survey of Youth in Custody (NSYC), the report limited its data to incidents occurring in the previous 12 months, or since the youth's admission to the facility if he or she had been in custody for fewer than 12 months. While nearly 93,000 people are held in a juvenile detention center on any given day in the U.S., the survey does not represent those held for a short time, those held in small facilities, or young people who are held in adult facilities. This survey includes responses from nearly 200 juvenile facilities, with an estimated total of 10,000 interviews with youth.

Jamie Fellner, senior counsel with Human Rights Watch, said that having a comprehensive report like this one is crucial to grasping a horrific problem.

"(The high rate of abuse) is symptomatic of a detention system that does not serve the rehabilitative purpose for which it is designed," said Fellner. "States put the youth there, and (the youth) don't come with any political or social clout. So who pays attention to them? No one but their families, if that." Fellner added that the reported rates of sexual abuse are much higher in juvenile facilities than adult prisons, which she attributed to the fact that kids are less likely to be able defend themselves.

A notoriously difficult problem to gauge, the NSYC struggles against the tendency of some youth to not report abuse they've *experienced, even when they are promised anonymity. At the same time, some youth make false or inflated claims, or may not have a clear understanding of what is being asked of them. Fellner said it's her hunch that even the high reported numbers undercount the actual rate of abuse. "If one in three kids are being abused at one facility, why in the world would they go to officials of the facility that's abusing them, that hasn't helped them, to report it?" Fellner asked.*

But David, who teaches at a Michigan detention facility -- and who asked that his real name not be used in this article -- said that he was surprised at the high rate of abuse revealed by the NSYC. "I know there's a lot of individual sexual activity between youth, but most of it is what you'd probably call consensual, unless you want to get into age stuff," David said.

He added that he is, however, familiar with one youth "grooming" another -- that is, latching onto them and setting them up for a sexual encounter. David has also noticed that "some female staff that really like to flirt with the boys," a phenomenon that he described as "really pathetic."

"If I had to go with my gut feeling about how often (abuse) happens, I'd say it's way less (than the report indicates)," David said. "You do have to wonder how kids define sexual activity when asked about it."

The BJS survey, which collected responses using a touch-screen laptop and audio feed in a private setting, used different questionnaires for youth of different ages. Ninety-eight percent of the interviews were conducted in English; 2 percent were in Spanish.

The surveys for older youth read:

By sexual contact, we mean sexual intercourse, oral sex, anal sex or any other touching or rubbing of someone else's private parts in a sexual way. By private parts, we mean any part of the body that would be covered by a bathing suit. ...

... Sexual contacts can happen to boys as well as girls. People who try to have sexual contact with young people are not always strangers but can be someone they know well like a youth, a staff member, teacher, counselor, or minister. People who try to have sexual contact with young people aren't always men or boys -- they can also be women or girls. And sometimes people try to make young people have sexual contact even if the young person doesn't want to do it.

Among the questions in the same survey were:

-- Have you rubbed another person's penis with your hand or has someone rubbed your penis with their hand?

-- Have you rubbed another person's vagina with your hand?

-- Have you had any other kind of sexual contact with someone at this facility? ... What kind of sexual contact was that?

While it isn't strictly physical, and not clearly measured by the NSYC, David notes that staff at the detention facility he works at has a tendency to make graphic comments and gay jokes around the incarcerated youth.

"When around kids, a lot of (staff) say really crude things, a lot of stuff that really pushes the line, and there's not a lot of consequences that I've seen," he said.

Martin, who teaches at the same detention facility as David and also asked that his name not be used, echoed the notion of sexually aggressive language creating a hostile environment.

"There's a lot of talk, a lot of the word 'faggot,'" Martin said. "In our place, we have a lot of very disgusting jokes told by staff to the kids."

Martin added that in his 16 years of employment with this facility, he only heard of one complaint between about sex between a staff member and a youth, who was 16 years old. There was a trial, and the staff was found not guilty.

In another story from Martin, one youth was released from the facility when he turned 21; a short time later, he married a staff member, a female teacher.

"It was legal, technically, but it begs the question if they messed around before he got out," Martin said.

He added that the uneven dynamic between the two is troubling.

"A locked-up person can never be consensual with a worker, who has power over them," Martin said.

It is a crime for staff to have sex with inmates in all 50 states, but such cases are rarely pursued in criminal court, according to The New York Times Book Review.

Whether this first effort to collect comprehensive data on the persistence of sexual abuse of youth undercounts or overcounts the reality, Martin makes the matter plain: "One incident is too many."

The dizzying numbers collected by the NSYC are poised to galvanize a comprehensive response that makes facilities safer. So what, exactly, is to be done?

If Fellner had it her way, much fewer kids would be put into *detention centers in the first place.*

"There should be a tighter screen on who gets removed from their community," she said, adding that most of the incarcerated youth are nonviolent offenders. In fact, only 34 percent of youth in detention are confined for violent crimes (a number that doesn't count those charged as adults and serving time in prison).

In addition, Fellner would like to see zero tolerance for staff misconduct, as well as other common-sense practices outlined in the PREA report on sexual abuse in U.S. prisons and detention centers. The report outlines practical standards, including screening inmates for their vulnerability to abuse; hiring practices; medical and mental health services; and external audits.

The recommended standards, established by eight commissioners over five years of extensive research, was submitted to Attorney General Eric Holder last June. Holder has until June 23, 2010 to issue a final version of the national standards.

U.S District Judge Reggie B. Walton, the commission chair, addressed how a broader culture change must happen alongside facility improvements if people -- both adults and youth -- can depend upon being physically safe when they are incarcerated.

"... (T)here is an attitude of indifference on the part of a lot of people who feel that just because somebody has committed a crime and they're incarcerated that it's appropriate for them to be abused while they're in detention," said Walton at the press conference that issued the proposed standards.

Fellner, who served on the PREA commission, said that an attitude change among those in charge of detention facilities is crucial.

"People connected to juvenile facilities need to understand that detention isn't intended to be just punitive, but rehabilitative," she said.

It is a notion that calls back to the mission put forth by the first juvenile court in the world, created in Chicago in 1899 by Jane Addams and Hull House, which was intended to act in the best interests of the children before them, serving as "a kind and just parent."

"It's not a question of we don't know what to do (about abuse of youth)," Fellner said. «It›s a question of political will.»

*

The judicial system and prison system are broken, and complaining rarely gets you anywhere. Instead I have devoted my life to trying to keep kids and young adults out of prison. As I said earlier, prisons are needed. I don't want a murderer or rapist living next to me. But as a society we incarcerate way too many non-violent drug offenders. That is sad because those people need treatment, not an education on how to be a better criminal.

When I explain what prison is really like, I let them know that there are *more* drugs in prison than on the streets. They look at me like I'm crazy. It's the truth. On a cell block with one hundred guys, there might be three or four drug dealers selling pot, cocaine, heroin, acid, etc. In a typical neighborhood on the streets you might have to drive a few miles to get your drugs. In prison you walk down two cells and can usually get whatever you want.

Teens and young adults need to hear the truth. Hell,

everyone needs to hear the truth. I'll say it again: the system is broke and needs some serious fixing.

Continuing in Part Two, What Prison is REALLY Like, I tell those in the program the truth about abuses, rotten food, and the mayhem that goes on in the prisons when the cameras are off. Let's face it, if the camera crews for TV shows tried to show the whole truth, do you think the Federal Bureau of Prison would let them in? Do you think any state prison facility would let a camera crew in uncensored? Of course not! Do you think they'd show the guy with no legs who was in a cell across from me and how they let him defecate on himself and how they didn't feed him? The guards had to go in there with masks over their faces. This is the stuff that happens in Third World countries – it shouldn't be happening in American. Some people will say, "Well, they deserve it." I just laugh. Imagine if that was one of your family members. This statement is the truest of all: **but for the grace of God, go I.**

Part Three: What Will You Lose

Part three of the Reality Check Program hits the kids and adults in the heart. I explain what I lost in a way that strikes home. It's in this part of the program that I see some kids and adults cry. I lay my soul on the line every time I do the program, and I show pictures of my own kids at a young age. I lost them, and I want kids and adults to see what they will lose. I missed the best years of my son Larry Jr.'s and daughter Ashley's lives. That's hard to swallow. I caused it and I have to accept complete responsibility for it. It's not about anything monetarily. That's all bullshit, and they see it here in this part.

One day in late 2008 I was sitting in my small, upstairs office when I get a call from Karolena Declercq, a woman who had heard about me through another person I helped. She said she was in the area and wanted a few minutes of my time.

"Sure," I said, "Come on up. I'll be here for a few more hours."

She must have been real close, because within ten minutes she was knocking on my door.

Karolena was a woman in her early forties, and she began to tell me the story about her son getting shot in the head in Cocoa, Florida. What a sad story. Karolena went on to say that after many years of struggling with the death of her son, she had heard about what I do, and would I like to use the pictures and story in my program?

Ms. Declercq is a strong Christian woman who is an RN and runs assisted living facilities. She had been carrying around the pictures of her son's death for years. Karolena felt God had directed her to me. She handed me the pictures, and I was shocked. Her son had been shot in the head and was left a bloody corpse sitting in his car.

I have seen a lot of death in my life, but to see these pictures was an eye-opener even for me. My first thought was, *Kids need to see these pictures.* My next thought was, *At what age do I show these pictures?*

I decided they were inappropriate for teens, so I held onto the pictures for a long time until I developed the adult program. There would be no reason I shouldn't show the pictures to adults heading in the wrong direction fast. They need a wake-up call, and this was it. I worked on a delivery of the message for the program.

The story and pictures are so powerful I decided to show the pictures to older teenagers. We get permission slips from parents for the juveniles to attend the program. All the parents *want* me to show the pictures.

When I talk about making bad choices that result in your losing your life, I start with a picture of a little kid as he's growing up. He's a cute kid and then he grows up into a good-looking young man. I'm light hearted and then I say, "Does he look like me?" Some say yes and others say no, and they're wondering. Then, BAM!! I show a picture of Karolena's son on a morgue table. The gasps are audible and the shock is visible. Some people turn away. The next pictures are of him with a bullet hole in his head and the blood on the car seat.

I then go on to tell the story of this young man who was 20 years old when he was needlessly murdered. He was hanging around the wrong crowd. His friends were gang members involved in serious crime. The police investigation concluded that he committed suicide, but I don't believe it and neither does a private detective hired by Karolena. Her son was left-handed and he shoots himself with his right hand and there are no powder burns? It just doesn't add up.

Some parents laugh when I say I use some tough language and tell some tough stories. They tell me that their kids know more about sex and use language that would make a sailor blush. How I explain it to parents is, "If the worst thing your teenager hears is the word *fuck,* we're doing okay. I don't advocate foul language, but when I use it correctly, it can gain acceptance and a realization that I am not a regular teacher."

Teens and adults need to hear reality, and they need to hear it with no sugarcoating. I am direct, and my approach is to acknowledge that they are smarter than we give them credit for. Let's not insult them by holding back. I may come into a room wearing a sports jacket, but when I take it off, I reveal my tattoos. I tell them, "Listen, I am not your mom, dad, teacher, counselor, or a cop. I am an ex-con who has been to a place you never want to go. I am no Harvard professor reading from a book. I am a man who survived the worst of the worst."

As I said, they need to hear the truth with no sugarcoating.

During Part Three of the program the teens and adults hear about all the things that matter in life. I've already gained their trust, and they're listening. They are relating to me, and you can see them looking into their soul. When they see pictures of my young son and daughter when I went to prison, that's a wake-up call. My son turned seven a few days before my arrest and my daughter was fifteen months old. It's hard, really hard, to look at those pictures.

I'll never be able to get that time back with my kids, but if I can save another kid from going to prison, I feel that in some way this is what God had planned for me. My dad was diagnosed with Alzheimer's just before I got out of prison in 2007 and I missed more than ten good years of his life. When I speak to the class I convey that in a strong and passionate way. What will you lose? In short, EVERYTHING!

Part Four: Avoiding and Dissolving Bad Associations

Part four is the most important part of the Reality Check Program. I begin this part by having the class open the folder I gave them at the beginning of the program with information about prison, letters, articles and self-help information. I ask them one question and one question only and I ask them to write it on the inside front cover of the folder. The question is; **What is the most important thing in your life?** I repeat that four or more times. **What is the most important thing in your life? What is the most important thing in your life?** I then ask them to close their folders when they are done. When the last person closes his folder, I begin.

I usually talk for between ten to fifteen minutes. I could make it longer, but it isn't necessary. We talk about ways to get out of situations and ways to not get caught up in what their so-called friends are doing. I explain that it is *their* choice, and when they get caught, not to cry about it. I tell them, "You made the choice to get in the car with the drugs. Don't blame mom. Nobody put a gun to your head and said, 'Get in the car.'"

I talk about friendships and who a real friend is. I tell them, "If you're on probation, and your friend is offering you marijuana, that person isn't your friend. That person is just someone you know, an acquaintance, someone to be avoided. If a person doesn't care if you get in trouble, he isn't your friend."

I say, "A friend would tell you, 'What are you doing that for? You'll get in trouble.' That is a *true* friend."

I talk to them about family. I say, "Your family has no ulterior motives. They only want the best for you. That's who will be writing you if you're arrested and in prison. That's who'll try and bail you out and get you the help you need. It's all about family." (And I'm not talking about a family member who enables a child. Sadly, that happens a lot.)

I then tell them "Think before you act. Don't get in the car when you know someone has drugs or a gun."

I emphasize **CHOICES, CHOICES, CHOICES**. We all make them and it is the choices we make that will affect the rest of our lives.

When you think about it, it seems pretty simple. All I'm doing is showing them what they have, and what they will lose. But they're hearing it from a man who was once a high-flying millionaire who had it all: *horses, a boat, houses, jewelry, money*.

I had it all, and lost it all, and in the end what was important to me had nothing to do with money, possessions, or things. It was all about God, family and doing right. It's that easy.

I tell them, "I don't blame the cops, the FBI, the judge, or the prosecutor. I blame myself for losing my children, my grandmother, and the time that we can never get back."

Yes, of course it's wrong to be tortured, abused, and treated like an animal while I was in prison, but ultimately, it was *my* choices that lead me to the life I lived.

I also show them hope, let them know they can change. I tell them, "I don't care what you did last year, last month, last week, or yesterday. I don't care if you smoked a joint before you came in this room. You *can* change. I did it, and I am no better or worse than anyone in this room. I am no smarter or dumber. I am a man who lost the most important things in his life and I also understand the consequences of my actions."

I tell them, "If someone had showed me all this when I was your age, I would have thought twice before I got into the life I did. It was my choice to become a criminal and nobody else's. I made the choices that landed me in prison."

I then have everyone open their folders and write the answer to the question, **What is the most important thing in your life?** We go around the room, and I ask everyone to read what they wrote. Almost all write *my family, my mom, my children, God, my education.* They never write things like *money, a big house, a fancy car,* etc. This shows me they have a heart and truly understand the message I was giving them. They were listening, and after two and a half hours they realize what's truly important in their lives. That is powerful.

One time I did an experiment in which I asked that same question at the start of the class. The answers included: *be the boss at my job, be a millionaire, be a celebrity,* etc. What that showed me was that after hearing all my horror stories and seeing what I lost, they didn't want to lose the things that were important to them. That my message could reach such a large percentage of the kids to me was amazing.

I tell them, "Before you go out tonight, open your folder and look at what YOU wrote. If you're willing to lose the most important things in your life, go rob, go smoke dope, hang with a gang, and go be a criminal. Nobody can stop you because you're willing to lose the most important thing in your life. And as sure as the sun rises every morning, you will get caught and lose the most important thing in your life."

*

There is no final exam. There is no pass or fail grade given for the program. But in my eyes the test of whether they pass or fail is their answers to that one question: **"What's the most important thing in your life?"**

It's my reward and it makes me feel so good.

Sometimes at the end of the program I will show *The Daily Show* clip of me yelling at the Harvard and MIT students. The clip puts everyone in a good mood, and they see me as a totally different character. They see a person who's funny and can laugh at himself. The class loves that. When I start giving out the certificates of completion needed for the courts or community service, I ask each of them what they have learned. Most say, "I didn't know the prison system was like that," or "I don't want to lose my family or kids." That shows me they "got it."

My greatest joy is to have people come up to me and say that when they enrolled in the program they thought it was going to be some guy yelling at them, but they were wrong and they're going to change, and this was the best program they ever attended.

I leave a program totally exhausted because I put my heart and soul into every program I do. It truly is a passion and that's why I made the Reality Check Parenting Program which is being introduced as I write this. The Reality Check Parenting Program was born out of all the questions and requests for help. Speaking with thousands of parents, teens, and young adults makes me understand the issues and solutions. My straight-forward approach is used in that program as well.

The best part of the Reality Check Program is: IT WORKS!!!

CHAPTER 19

It Works

The most rewarding part of the Reality Check Program is seeing how well it works. Getting results is what it's all about.

Take Kyle, a typical 16-year-old kid who took part in the program. He had long hair, baggy jeans, and he walked in with this *I Don't Give a Fuck* attitude. He sat through the first part of my talk, and during one of the breaks outside the building where I was talking I asked him if he would like to come on my radio show as a guest. I like having kids come on the show as well as politicians, law enforcement personnel, and judges. The kids make the best guests because they tell it like it is, and they don't have an agenda. While I was talking to him, I was very matter of fact and didn't try to lecture him. I saw that he was an interesting young kid. I told him I would interview him even if he ended up in jail. He looked at me funny, and without another word we went back into the building.

After he completed the class, I could see he was a changed kid. I could see it in the way he walked and presented himself to me. His eyes were different. They were no longer hard. It's like the pissed-offedness had gone. He hung on every word I said. He wasn't just trying to get through it. He called me Mr. Lawton.

"Please call me, Larry," I told him.

I never know when I get through to a kid, and I never know when the information will sink in. A lot of adults give up on a kid like Kyle, but I never will.

He waited around until everyone else had left, and he started to tell me about the things he was into. He wasn't into serious drugs. He was smoking weed. He was car hopping, when you look for unlocked cars and steal the contents. He was shoplifting and hanging with the wrong crowd. He was headed for jail for sure.

Later that evening I was still working like I normally do when I received this email:

thanks larry
From: "Kyle ▮▮▮▮▮▮▮▮▮▮▮▮▮"
To: Larry@realitycheckprogram.org
Saturday, July 11, 2009 11:34 PM

Hey Larry, i was in your program today july 11th, Dude your shit was straight up and it really made me open up my eyes and realize i cant fuck up. And that radio thing im down man give me a place date and time and im there i wanna tell kids how much good your program can do for them. im not gonna lie this morning when i woke up i was expecting some dumb ass guy to be telling me how what a stupid fuck i was for stealing. but no you understood im not a bad person i just made a bad choice. i want to thank you for what you have done. ive put your name and website all over my myspace. ive told a few of my trouble making friends that i recomend goin to your program and that i would go with them because i liked the shit you had to say. if there is any way i can help you out man let me know. you helped me because without hearing you today i probly would still be goin and pullin licks and stealin shit. but after your course ive changed. you are a good man Larry.
sincerely,
      Kyle ▮▮▮▮

Its emails like Kyle's that keep me smiling from the inside out.

I also hear back from community leaders and people who work with the youth. I encourage them to come to my program and maybe learn something they can bring back to the community to help the kids. I met Yvonne Minus at a community center when I was asked to speak at a local function. Her passion and dedication to saving the kids was infectious. Yvonne works with the Melbourne police community relations board, and after seeing me at a local event asked if I would come to the community center to speak to a group of her kids.

Yvonne deals with inner city kids in a pro-active way and understands that getting to them *before* they make a choice that will land them in prison or worse is the answer. Helping people and communities like Yvonne is what I am here to do. She wrote:

I just want to say thank you for such a dynamic job you and the Reality Check program are doing to help save our youth locally as well as across America.

I am so grateful for your heartfelt dedication and love of reaching our youth and getting them to think first before they make that choice, which may be a wrong one.

I truly believe you are a Godsend to our youth of tomorrow. Keep up the great work for they indeed are our future.

May God Bless You
Yvonne Minus, President
Melbourne Police Community Relations Council

*

Another important figure in south Florida when it comes to helping at risk kids is Karen Locke, the COO at Crosswinds Youth Services. Karen is a leader in the field of child behavior. Karen invited me to attend a seminar in Miami, and the whole trip there and back we talked about saving kids. Karen, who's a visionary, sees the benefit of what I do. She was the one who told me I would be wasting my talents if I didn't continue in this field. She also made me realize that wherever I decided to live, it really doesn't matter, whether a rich neighborhood or poor, troubled kids are everywhere.

It was at one of Karen's programs that I met Michelle, who was 16. She was a girl who grew up in a rough neighborhood and who was running the streets when I met her.

After I finished my class, Michelle came up to me with tears in her eyes. She talked about how much the class affected her. I hugged her, told her to stay strong and to make one good choice each day.

I received this email from Michelle:

hey   Sunday, July 12, 2009 1:46 PM
From: "michelle
To: larryfl2007@yahoo.com
Cc:

hey larry how are you doing its me michelle thank you for helping me turn my life around and relizeing everything in this world can be different u just have to change it yourself well my jpo is currently turminating my probation a year early because i done everything i was suppose to and never got in trouble so thats good and now im currently pregnant 6 months as of today and i find out what its going to be tomarrow ...im just so glad im out here and stayed outa trouble so i can be here with my baby... thanks again all to you.

A lot of people would say she is pregnant; that she is still making bad choices. I don't look at it that way. She has stayed out of jail, and that's what's most important.

*

Class knows no boundaries when it comes to at-risk kids. One of the girls who came to my program was Janaisha, who was 13 and came from a solid upper middle class family. Her dad works for a beverage company, and her mom is a paralegal. They want nothing but the best for their daughter.

Janaisha stood about 5 foot 3 and had a smile that could melt the hardest of men. It took all of my inner strength not to cry when seeing the bad choices this little girl was making. She had fights in school, once stole her brother's camera, was disrespectful to her parents, and let her grades drop from A's and B's to C's and D's. She had all the signs of ending up in reform school or worse.

Her parents came to me asking for help. I was in the process of filming the pilot for my reality TV show, and asked them if they didn't mind including her in the show.

After my crew placed a hidden camera in her room, I surprised her one day. I went into her room and tossed it. I did a prison shake-down. I searched for drugs and any other evidence to show her slide toward serious trouble.

I then took her down to the jail in the Rockledge police department. During the thirty-minute ride I talked to her about what was going to happen if her slide got any worse. Even with a camera and crew present, she was overwhelmed and totally forgot they were there. I talked quietly, didn't yell, and she began to cry. I don't have to yell and scream to make a kid understand the consequences of their actions.

When I arrived at the police station, the police put her in handcuffs, and after they put her cuffed in the back of a squad car, we took her to a crack house. I rode in the back of the police car with her.

"This is where you are heading," I told her.

Janaisha did change for a little while, and then she began to slide back to her old habits. This is typical with some teens. With some it takes time for the message to sink in. I see her parents at various functions, from my parenting program to the grocery store. It's now two years later, and Janaisha is doing great. The lessons are deep and sink in a various times.

There's no magic pill to cure a kid from making bad choices.

It's a process, and it takes time. What really makes me happy is to see the relief on the part of the parents when a child finally turns the corner and is headed in the right direction. The following is a letter sent to me by Janaisha's parents.

> *Larry & John...*
> *Jonathan and I just wanted to thank you both and all the guys for the weekend. It really meant a lot to us what you guys did For Janaisha. We were also glad to be a part of Reality Check.*
> *Larry, you are doing some great stuff. I am so glad God put you in my direction. You all were just wonderful and very helpful.*
> *Janaisha said she'll never complain about doing the dishes every Again. What was really neat was that over Mother's Day dinner with my parents, she shared her experience. My parents were impressed.*
> *John, it was really cool that you had Claudia call Janaisha. Thank You so much for that. She is still talking about it. We are just so impressed with Reality Check. Larry, if you ever need me to speak to parents about the program, let me know. You guys are the best.*
> *My husband was really impressed by the crew and how the guys really just showed they cared about Janaisha. Thank you for watching out for her and protecting her. Larry, please give my gratitude to Broken Barrel and the Rockledge PD for all their help.*
> *We really thank God for you guys!*
> *Lots of love and much gratitude!*
> *Cynthia & Jonathan Scott*

*

I met Robert Likos through a friend who said he and his family needed my services. First, I met the dad and mom. The dad said that Robert had just turned 18, and he had stolen a gun from his gun locker and took it for a joy ride. Robert was defiant, they said. He didn't think before he acted. I told them he definitely needed to see where he was headed before he did something to take him there.

Since Robert was 18, I had to handle his case a little differently. At 18, he's an adult, and basically he can tell me to fuck off and not bother to listen to what I have to say. I decided my approach would be to build a relationship with him.

We went out several times, and I proceeded to show him what prison life was really like. Through the course of our conversations I found Robert to have a good heart, and I could see that deep down he cared for his family. He truly loved his dad, mom, and sister, and that to me was a major positive. He showed that he could be reached.

About four months after seeing Robert I received this email from his dad:

Hi Larry,
Thanks for the call...He just told his Aunt that is visiting that your course was the best thing he ever did. He told her that he didn't want to go to prison...
Happy New Year!! Tks again!! Robert
PS Robert respects you very much, your name comes up allot...

It is emails like this that keep me pumped and ready to tackle the problems all parents face.

*

As I said before, it's not only teens who are headed for trouble. Some people in their mid-20s don't mature and see the consequences of their actions. I met Ashlee, a 23-year-old young lady who was arrested for possession of drugs. As part of her pre-trial diversion program, she enrolled in my program. After class she and I spoke about the things that go on inside prisons, things the public has no idea about.

Ashlee could have been sentenced for months or even years, but the judge saw how contrite she was and only sentenced her to a month in the Brevard County jail.

After she got out, she sent me this email. I could see she had learned her lesson and wouldn't end up in jail again.

> From: Ashlee
> Sent: Thursday, July 23, 2009 8:17 PM
> To: larry@realitycheckprogram.org
> Subject:
>
> hey whats up. thank you again for a great program, i cant help but make the right choices now. prison freaks me out now for sure. i cant believe what you had to go threw. i wnated to tell you a story from when i was in jail. this poor girl had ben throwing up for 36 hrs str8. well she made sick calls because she also had pains in her side. well the nurse told her to lay down and shes not a dr. so she cant give her anything for the painh or upset stomach. well a day later she was screaming bloody murder. she was in so much pain she couldnt walk. she was on the floor puking and passedout. well it took five female guards to get her down stairs but it took like three minutes for them to get there. well she was gone for like a month. she came back and said she had gall stones and it looked like a glove with marbles and one was the size of a golf ball. they didnt even notify her mom or anything. we all new it was a gall stone, or her pancrease. so the nurse felt like shit. so that was my story pretty bad huh? well i got to go for now keep in touch. thank you so much again. loved the site. and class.

I am fortunate to know the commander of the jail and the sheriff who runs it. They are caring individuals and very professional. I showed the commander the email, and she looked into the situation and got back to me. In my heart of hearts I felt the jail did everything, not only by the book, but by what's right.

*

My frustration is that even though the Reality Check Program has had a proven record second to none, certain school board members and administrators refuse to use it because they don't care as much for kids who don't score high on the S.A.T. or who aren't top athletes. I've had school board members come on my radio show and tell me they won't use the program because of some bullshit regulation that forbids ex-cons from coming on campus.

To me that's putting your head in the sand. They aren't helping the community they say they want to help. Wouldn't it be better for them to show their students that a person can make a mistake, turn around, and rebuild his life? Why not use the nationally recognized Reality Check Program video?

Every one of us has skeletons in his or her closet. I say that to every class I teach and to every group I address. It doesn't matter whether it's Congress, school boards, or sheriffs. We're all human, and we all make mistakes. It's just a matter of whether you got caught or not.

I was chatting with a group of judges and police chiefs, and each one of them said they could well have ended up where I did. They just didn't get caught. When a person tells me they have never broken the law, I ask them whether they have ever been speeding. They all say yes. I then say, 'If you got in an accident and killed someone, you could have gone to jail for vehicular homicide.' They all look at me, and I can see them thinking.

Which is what I want them to do.

After an independent quantitative analysis for helping teens was taken of the Reality Check Program, the success rate was shown to be 70 percent of the kids had better attitudes, 43 percent had better school grades, 31 percent had better school attendance and 90 percent didn't get arrested again, people came up to me and said, "Aren't you proud of the results? You must be ecstatic."

My answer is always, "The results are great, and I'm very proud of them, but what makes me even more proud and happy is the successes I don't know about. How many kids watched the video or listened to me speak and then didn't get in a car when they knew there were drugs in there? Or didn't hang with the kid they knew had a gun on him? Having taken my program, how many kids made the right choices with regards to school, friends, and family? I will never know the numbers, but I am sure there are some kids and alive and free today because of what I do, and that is what makes me the proudest.

The Reality Check Program.

It works.

THE REALITY CHECK PROGRAM

www.Lawton911.com

What some officials are saying about the Reality Check Program DVD:

Jeff Kottkamp, Lieutenant Governor of Florida - *"Larry Lawton's 'Reality Check' program is not only impactful---it has the potential to be life changing. Children that watch the program will learn some very valuable life lessons."*

Norm Wolfinger, Brevard & Seminole County State Attorney: *"Watching your tape for the 2nd time, I can see why you influence these young adults to consider making good choices – your real and your stories were lived."*

Judge David Silverman: *"The Reality Check Program is designed to impart hope to each participant ... Coming from an ex-con who reinvented himself, it is a message that resonates with force and clarity for many teens and young adults and that can have a profound effect on their self image, their conduct and their future."*

Lieutenant Ray Dixon, Fort Mill South Carolina Police Department: *"We offer this video to everyone, to those who are at risk and to those who have already made a mistake and could face a slippery slope if they aren't reached in time.*

Those who view it aren't just doing medial work, they are learning something, and what I've found is that this program is one of the best, most proactive tools in the country."

What people are saying about the Reality Check Program DVD:

Bob Peterson, Denver Colorado – *Thanks Reality Check, this DVD program gave my son back to us. It is helping him to make good choices. He is at risk as all teenagers are, now he thinks before he acts – he doesn't want to ruin his life because of a stupid mistake.*

Bill Cassara, New York - *"In 30 years of working in television news programs (60-minutes, 20/20) I would count Larry Lawton's "Reality Check" DVD as one of the most important videos for teens and young adults. It's tough talk from a man who knows first-hand about how easy it is to make poor choices. Larry Lawton's Reality Check Program is making a difference"*

Jackie Thomas, Iowa City, Iowa - *I am a mother, grandmother and para-educator in the Iowa City Public School System. I have been a Montessori pre-school teacher for 7 years and have worked with children for 25 years. I believe the Reality Check Program DVD by Larry Lawton is wonderful. It definitely describes the consequences of what can happen when a person gets on the wrong path. It is real and eye-opening. Both teenagers and adults would definitely benefit from watching this DVD. I highly recommend it!*

Buzzy Martin; a Californian, musician, child advocate and author of "Don't Shoot! I'm the Guitar Man" - *I have spent the last seventeen years working with and teach incarcerated at-risk youth in juvenile halls and share Mr. Lawton's wish that those at-risk youth of adult criminality get an accurate picture of what may lay ahead in prison life. After watching Mr. Lawton's DVD "The Reality Check Program" I would highly recommend this amazing most powerful story to all juvenile halls and probation camps for at-risk youth to hear this incredible experience. My friend Larry walks the walk and talks the talk. He has a message that everyone should hear. This* man's personal story of survival in Prison and the transformation to what he is now is a must see.

Matt Crystal (Father) - *"Hi Larry - just wanted to let you know that Kyle really got a lot out of your program today. He was full of stories. He's a very proud kid, so he's not the type to say "gee Dad, thanks getting this DVD for me." But I think it was a wakeup call for him because he has been making some VERY bad choices. Thanks so much for all you do Larry. It's obvious that you have a passion for helping young people make better choices and realize the potential that each and every one of them have to lead happy, healthy, and successful lives and make choices that will help them grow and thrive. You're truly one in a million. Thanks again!"*

Pam D - *Your Reality Check DVD is very is a real eye opener. My husband and I watched it, first. But I broke down in the middle and couldn't finish. Our son and my husband then watched it together. It had quite an effect on our 19 yr. old son. Thank you for letting God use you in this way to help our teens and young adults.*

Gary Bacon, Father - *This is a GREAT program. My son has done a 180 degree turn around. I highly recommend the DVD.*

Sam Zurich, Professional Bowler and Father - *"Every bowling center has a youth program, but this DVD is the best tool I have ever seen to help kids stay on the straight and narrow, on target and out of the gutter"*

Rockledge Police Chief, John Shockey: *"The DVD's have proven to be a wise and valuable investment in the youth of our community. I highly recommend the Reality Check DVD to any law enforcement agency."*

Cai Griffiths, College Student - *"Even if just a few of Larry's hard-earned lessons hit home, or at least encourage a little independent thought, it's worth the watch."*

Faith Wheeler, Mother - *"I first heard about Larry Lawton and Reality*

Check Program when my son was getting into a little trouble last year. I did some research and when I found out what it was about I figured it couldn't hurt. I got a copy of the DVD and Zac and I watched it together. I was a little taken at first from some of the things I heard on the DVD and wasn't sure I wanted Zac to hear them. The next day I came home to find Zac watching the DVD again. Then a couple days' later he was watching it a third time with his cousin. I started to talk to Zac more about it and I understood that what he got out of it was different than what I got out of it. I'm an adult and already know the difference between right and wrong and he is just learning so therefore he really learned something from it. I can honestly say it was money worth spending; it has been a year since Zac got in trouble and 9 months since he watched the DVD. I recommend this DVD to every teenager even if they haven't got in trouble I will make them think about making bad choices. Kudos to Reality Check, thank you for caring."

John Stafford, College Student - *"The Reality Check Program describes what prison life is really like and how you have the ability to make the right choice in life. Lawrence Lawton paints a very vivid picture of the reality you will face because of a bad choice. He lost his freedom and served eleven years in jail. Mr. Lawton had to watch his children grow up from behind bars. He cares about you and gives you an honest and straight forward plan for staying out of jail. He doesn't want you to have to go through any sort thing similar to the hell that he faced every day. You will think twice before making a wrong decision that could land you in the slammer."*

Tracy DeGraaf, Mother of 5 Boys – Monee, IL - *"Larry Lawton's DVD, The Reality Check Program, should be required viewing for every parent and adolescent in America! Whether you think your kids would never stray down the wrong path, or if they are already on the slippery slope leading to trouble, this DVD is for YOU! I encourage all parents to purchase the program and watch it with the young people in your life. You'll be glad you did!"*

Perry Seibert, All Movie Guide ~ Reality Check Program DVD - *This documentary features ex-convict Lawrence Lawton explaining his harrowing time behind bars, and educating viewers on how they can make the right* choices so they don't follow in his footsteps. Aimed primarily at teens, Lawton's forceful stories detail how making the right decisions early in life can lead to a much happier existence.

School Library Journal, February 1, 2010
The Reality Check Program DVD

Gr 7 Up—*Lawrence Lawton admits to making many bad choices in his life, some of which led him to spend 11 years in prison for racketeering and other crimes. He lost his family and was denied many freedoms taken for granted by most of us. From the perspective of someone who has "been there," he developed this program as part of a broader series of services (realitycheckprogram.org) which aim to help teenagers and young adults avoid a similar fate. In clear and sometimes explicit language, he shares exactly what occurs in prisons on a daily basis as well as the long-term consequences of an arrest record and incarceration. His emphasis throughout is on good decision making, especially in the choice of friends. It's not as if young people haven't heard these warnings before, but this time they come from a person who speaks from first-hand experience. The program, which offers a chapter selection option, employs prison photographs which might be unsettling to viewers, but that's exactly the reaction desired. Lawton, who is now a paralegal, stresses that young people can easily lose many of their prime years in a hostile, threatening, and sometimes deadly environment and then return to an unforgiving society. The presentation sometimes seems preachy and canned, which may turn off some of those he is trying to reach, but getting through to even one potential inmate makes it all worthwhile. The film can be used in a variety of individual, school, and community settings. A careful preview is warranted before purchase, but school support staff members may welcome this title.—Dwain Thomas, formerly of Lake Park High School, Roselle, IL*

GANGSTER REDEMPTION

Below you will see a few actual surveys from teens and young adults who attended the Reality Check Program class. Larry reads every survey.

Reality Check Program Survey Form

Name: Pedro   Date: June 4, 2011

Age: 16

What session did you like best and why?
Seeing what you lose.

Did this program help you see things in a different way? Explain:
Yes. I realized that everything, even the bad, isn't worth losing because of a bad choice.

Moving forward, do you think this program will help you to make good choices?
Yes: ✓   No:____   Maybe:____   Not Sure:____

Can you comment on this?
I'm definately not ever using drugs, going to jail, or being influenced by fake friends.

Would you recommend this program to a friend and why?
Yes. It can help them get right so they don't go to prison or die.

What did you think of the instructor and why?
He's real as fuck and doesn't give a shit what people think.

How can we improve the program?
I don't know, I liked it.

LARRY LAWTON

Reality Check Program Survey Form

Name: Scott ████████   Date: 3-5-11

Age: 14

What session did you like best and why?
I liked all of the sessions.

Did this program help you see things in a different way? Explain:
Yes, because it helped me see what my life would be like if I comitted crimes and did drugs.

Moving forward, do you think this program will help you to make good choices?
Yes: ✓   No: ____   Maybe: ____   Not Sure: ____

Can you comment on this?
I think it will make me think twice about everything I do.

Would you recommend this program to a friend and why?
Yes, because I think some of my friends could really use this program.

What did you think of the instructor and why?
I think he was good and he was real about everything.

How can we improve the program?
I dont really know about much that you can improve in the program.

GANGSTER REDEMPTION

Reality Check Program Survey Form

Name: Ray

Date: 8-6-11

Age: 17

What session did you like best and why?
The 3rd session because it makes me see what I can really loose.

Did this program help you see things in a different way? Explain:
Yes it changes the way other people make jail sound like and what it really is.

Moving forward, do you think this program will help you to make good choices?
Yes: ✓   No:____   Maybe:____   Not Sure:____

Can you comment on this?
Its a good class.

Would you recommend this program to a friend and why?
Yes because the path that they are going in is a kind of life that could end them in prison.

What did you think of the instructor and why?
He is an awsome guy who really know how to talk to teen who are going threw what he went.

How can we improve the program?
Just keep doing what he is doing.

LARRY LAWTON

Reality Check Program Survey Form

Name: Erica   Date: 5/7/11
Age: 21

What session did you like best and why?

"The choices you make"

Did this program help you see things in a different way? Explain:

yes very much. I realized and captured that I need to look at my life a little closer and realize how important my freedom is to me.

Moving forward, do you think this program will help you to make good choices?

Yes: X   No: ___   Maybe: ___   Not Sure: ___

Can you comment on this?

I feel that it was really a "reality check" for me.

Would you recommend this program to a friend and why?

yes I would because I do know a few people that are also making bad choices that this class would definatly help.

What did you think of the instructor and why?

very inteligent on things that can happen to you.

How can we improve the program?

expand more classes?

AFTERWORD:

Larry Lawton

Larry Lawton – *A teen expert with one of the highest success rates with changing teen behavior. An independent quantitative analysis of the Reality Check Program by Brevard Community College shows a 70% positive change in kid's attitudes, 90% not re-arrested, 31% improved school attendance and 43% improved grades. Mr. Lawton deals with thousands of teens and young adults and is a certified paralegal and an expert on the C.F.R. (Code of Federal Regulations – Regulations the Attorney General sets for Federal Agencies – Like the Bureau of Prisons) Larry founded the Reality Check Program in 2008 and it is used by Judges, Law Enforcement, State's Attorney's, and numerous other organizations. Mr. Lawton is frequently used as an expert witness on issues dealing with teen behavior, juvenile crime, sentencing, prison regulations and reentry issues. Supporters of the Reality Check Program are Congressmen, Department of Justice, numerous Judges, Sheriffs, FDLE, Jail Commanders, School Board Officials, and parents all over the country. A TV show is in the works that deals with kids being shown the "Real Deal". Mr. Lawton was the expert on the Casey Anthony case, has appeared on the Huckabee show on FOX News, Making a Difference on CBS Orlando, The Healing Today show on CTN, The 700 Club with Pat Robertson, The Daily Show with Jon Stewart (humor piece) and many many other shows. As a motivational speaker and program facilitator Larry brings some of the most entertaining and inspirational stories and messages*

LARRY LAWTON

to audiences all over the country. To contact Larry for a private consultation to help your loved one, expert witnessing, motivational speaking , keynote speaking, or to get more information on what Lawton911 does. Visit www.lawton911.com *or email Larry at* larry@lawton911.com.

BIOGRAPHY OF PETER GOLENBOCK

 Peter Golenbock, one of the nation's best-known sports authors, was born on July 19, 1946 in New York City. He grew up in Stamford, Connecticut, and in 1963 graduated St. Luke's School in New Canaan, Connecticut. He graduated Dartmouth College in 1967 and the New York University School of Law in 1970.

Golenbock was hired to work as an editor for Prentice-Hall in the summer of 1972. After six weeks of writing about President Nixon's wage and price controls, during one lunchtime he rashly knocked on the door of Nick D'Incecco, the head of the Prentice-Hall trade book division. He told D'Incecco he wanted to write a history of the Casey Stengel Yankees. D'Incecco liked the idea and incredibly gave him a contract, almost on the spot.

Dynasty: The New York Yankees 1949-64, the definitive history of the Casey Stengel-Ralph Houk-Yogi Berra era of Yankee greatness, a period of fourteen pennants in sixteen years, became an instant best-seller.

Since 1975, Golenbock has written some of sports' most important books, including seven New York Times best sellers. Some of his best-known books include The Bronx Zoo, which he wrote in 1979 with New York Yankee pitcher Sparky Lyle; BUMS: An Oral History of the Brooklyn Dodgers (1984), Personal Fouls (1988), a look at corruption in college basketball; American Zoom (1993), a history of NASCAR; and Wild, High and Tight (1994) his lurid biography of Yankee manager Billy Martin, and Idiot (2005), with Boston Red Sox star outfielder Johnny Damon. (2008) Golenbock collaborated with movie idol Tony Curtis to write American Prince, another best seller. (2009) George a book about the owner of the New York Yankees. In 2010 Peter teamed up with with Larry Lawton to write the most exciting and emotional book of his career; Gangster Redemption, to be published in 2012. Peter truly believes this will be his 8th bestseller.

Golenbock was a radio sports talk show host in 1980 on station WOR in New York City. He was the color broadcaster for the St. Petersburg Pelicans of *the Senior Professional Baseball League in 1989-90 and has been a frequent guest on many of the top television and radio talk shows including Biography on A&E, the Fifty Greatest Athletes and the Dynasties on ESPN, Good Morning America, Larry King Live, and Up Close with Roy Firestone.*

Golenbock lives in St. Petersburg, Florida, with Wendy Grassi, their cat Chauncey, and their basset hound, Fred.

ACKNOWLEDGMENTS:

This book is not about me and what I do. The book was a way for me to express myself and explain to the world what goes on behind bars in the United States prison system. In 2005, while in prison, I explained in some specific detail the horrors of prison and compared the prison I was in to Abu Ghraib, the prison in Iraq where United States soldiers abused civilians. You can Google Larry Lawton and Abu Ghraib and read the full article. I am all for our soldiers and one of the most patriotic men you will ever meet, but where do you think the soldiers who abused those people in Iraq learned how to abuse people? From being guards in the United States prison system! People ask me all the time if I am hateful towards corrections officers. Absolutely not, in-fact some saved my life. I have no bitterness at all. There is good and bad in all people.

I have to acknowledge and thank a lot of people. I am sure I will miss some. You know who you are and because of all of you, this book came about. To Peter Golenbock, my co-writer for spending countless hours talking with me; getting things out of me and rewriting my words to make them all fall into place. He is a professional who understood my personality and respected me throughout the whole process. He didn't try to change the tone of the book; he made it a book. To Joe Reilly, my business partner, for keeping me focused. To Uncle Louie and Phyllis Constantino, who are like my second parents. To Joe Fraumeni, for his support, solid business advice, and guidance throughout this whole process and to this day. To Judge Silverman and his wife Michelle for reviewing the book and telling me things straight: the good, bad and ugly. To my cousin Carol Kalet, for reviewing and helping edit the book. To my good friends Billy Cassara, a cameraman for 60 Minutes and his wife Lisa Hewitt Cassara, who reviewed my work and who keep me encouraged to this day. To John Johnston from Cheri Sundae Productions, who has a sense of humor only a New Yorker could understand, but believes in me and helps me with industry advice and guidance. To Dennis and Glenda Broderick, friends from my childhood, for always being there for me. To Tommy Boehm, a friend through thick and thin. To Jackie Thomas, my big supporter in Iowa. To Justin Wasson, for help in reviewing my work and for your strong moral character. To Mike Smith from TD bank, for believing in me from day one. To Steve Lander, an attorney and close friend who I have known for years -- we helped each other out with advice, money and support -- without Steve's support this book wouldn't have been accomplished. To Ron Nance, my protector in prison. To John Stewart and the staff of The Daily Show, who believed in me, even after a long trip to Montana that didn't pan-out. That comedy appearance jump-started my media career. To Mike Huckabee, who gave me the opportunity to tell the world my story from a serious point of view. To Dory Nissen and Pat Robertson, for showing my story in a compassionate way and understanding redemption. To Randy Wecker & Rhonda Bible-Wecker from The Healing Today Show for believing in me and giving me support. To State Attorney Norm Wolfinger and Public Defender J.R. Russo of the 18th Judicial Circuit, men who care about teens and believe people can change. To Dominic Calabro, the CEO of Florida Tax Watch, who never judged me and would call with advice and encouragement just at the right time. To former Florida Lt. Governor Jeff Kottkamp, who cares deeply for young people, believes in me and what I do so much, he traveled all over the state with me to spread the word. To all my nephews and nieces and cousins. To George and Ann Watson, who never judged me and love me for who I am. To my cousin and rock, Cheryl Geoffrion, who I know is always there for me and will be there for me forever. I love you. I hope to have inner-peace like you someday. To my brother David, sisters Lynne, Debbie, and Donna, who keep me grounded when I ramble on about everything. To my Mom, who is the family matriarch. Mom encourages me and is my #1 fan. To Helen Moss, my other mother. To my children Larry Jr. and Ashley -- I am so proud of you. I love you both so much and missing your early lives is a hole in my heart that will never heal. To both my ex-wives Roselyn and Missy, who are still true friends and put up with me during my worst times. To my long time girlfriend Theresa Nunez, who had to put up with me during this whole process. She walked around quietly while I was on the phone and computer for hundreds of hours and she comforted me when I had some emotional moments after Peter got things out of me. Your silent support will never be underestimated. To my Dad, who passed away while doing this book. He was, and is, my father, mentor and best friend. He never liked what I did, but he never judged me, and always knew I had a big heart. Dad was always *there for me. As he told me, hate the sin, love the sinner.*

To the following men behind bars who wrote letters, called me, and supported me during our time in prison and still do to this day: Paul Tallini, Nick Vasiliades, Jon Goetz, Daniel Poe, Elvis and to all the men behind bars who are experiencing the horrors that prison really is. Torture, abuse, etc. Sadly, it is going on as I write this.

And most importantly, to God who has protected me and guided me on the course I am on today.

A lot has happened since Larry Lawton completed Gangster Redemption in 2012.

On August 16, 2013, Larry Lawton became the only ex-con in the United States to be sworn-in as an Honorary Police Officer.

On November 21, 2013, Larry became the only ex-con to be recognized on the Floor of the United States Congress for helping young people and police agencies.

Larry is currently working on his YouTube channel to tell his story, entertain his fans and bring awareness to a broken prison system.

The following people weren't mentioned in the acknowledgments on the previous page, but have helped me in ways they don't even know. Without their support I would never have been able to be the person I am today and accomplish what I have. Peter Meluso, Darien Attridge, John and Laura Bomalaski, Frank and Chris Filiberto, Ray and Julie Burke and the whole lunch gang at Matt's Casbah. It's cigar time!

Below is a QR code with a link directly to our YouTube channel. Share with friends and family and help us spread the word.

Lawrence "Larry" Lawton appears regularly on national TV and Radio as an expert on teen issues, crime, schools, prisons and community policing.

Larry brings the most entertaining, inspirational, motivational and informative stories to audiences throughout the United States and around the world.

Larry Lawton is available for presentations, keynote addresses, and motivational speaking. Larry has a unique way of speaking to both youth and adult audiences.

To bring Larry to your business, school, law enforcement agency or organization, email: info@RealityCheckProgram.com or call 844-922-4800.